Elements of Accounting and Finance

Module 3: Finance

Lent Term — Lectures 3-7

Third Edition

A Pearson Custom Publication

Elements of Accounting and Finance

Module 3: Finance
Lent Term — Lectures 3-7

Third Edition

Compiled from:

Financial Economics
Second Edition
by Ziv Bodie, Robert C. Merton and David L. Cleeton

PEARSON
Custom Publishing

Pearson Education Limited
Edinburgh Gate
Harlow
Essex CM20 2JE

And associated companies throughout the world

Visit us on the World Wide Web at:
www.pearsoned.co.uk

First published 2006

This Custom Book Edition © 2009 Published by Pearson Education Limited

Compiled from:

Financial Economics
Second Edition
by Ziv Bodie, Robert C. Merton and David L. Cleeton
ISBN 978 0 13 185615 8

ISBN 978 1 84776 440 9

Printed and bound in Great Britain by Hobbs the Printers Limited, Totton, Hants.

Contents

The following is taken from
Financial Economics
Second Edition
by Ziv Bodie, Robert C. Merton and David L. Cleeton

PART I FINANCE AND THE FINANCIAL SYSTEM

CHAPTER 1

Financial Economics

OBJECTIVES

- Define finance.
- Explain why finance is worth studying.
- Introduce two of the main players in the world of finance—households and firms—and the kinds of financial decisions they make. The other main players, financial intermediaries and government, are introduced in chapter 2.

CONTENTS

- You have started to save for the future and all of your savings are in a bank account. Should you invest in mutual funds? What kind of mutual funds?
- You have decided to get a car. Should you buy it or lease it?
- You worked as a waiter during your college years and are thinking about starting your own restaurant when you graduate. Is it worth doing? How much money do you need to start? Where can you get the money?
- You are advising the chief financial officer (CFO) of a major computer manufacturer whether to expand into the telecommunications business. It is expected to cost $3 billion over the next few years to enter the business, and the expected benefits are increased profits of $1 billion per year thereafter. What do you recommend?
- You are part of a team working at the World Bank analyzing an application for a loan to a small country in Latin America to finance a major hydroelectric project. How do you decide what to recommend?

These are all examples of financial decisions. This book will provide you with a way of addressing these and similar questions by exploring the basic principles of finance. In this chapter we define finance and consider why it is worth studying; then we introduce the main players in the world of finance—households and firms—and the kinds of financial decisions they make.

1.1 Defining Finance

Finance is the study of how people allocate scarce resources *over time.* Two features that distinguish financial decisions from other resource allocation decisions are that the costs and benefits of financial decisions are (1) spread out over time and (2) usually not known with certainty in advance by either the decision makers or anybody else. In deciding whether to start your own restaurant, for example, you must weigh the *costs* (such as the investment in fixing up the place and buying the stoves, tables, chairs, little paper umbrellas for exotic drinks, and other equipment you need) against the uncertain *benefits* (your future profits) that you expect to reap over several years.

In implementing their decisions people make use of the **financial system,** defined as *the set of markets and other institutions used for financial contracting and the exchange of assets and risks.* The financial system includes the markets for stocks, bonds, and other financial instruments; financial intermediaries (such as banks and insurance companies); financial service firms (such as financial advisory firms); and the regulatory bodies that govern all of these institutions. The study of how the financial system evolves over time is an important part of the subject matter of finance.

Finance theory consists of a set of concepts that help you to organize your thinking about how to allocate resources over time and a set of quantitative models to help you evaluate alternatives, make decisions, and implement them. The same basic concepts and quantitative models apply at all levels of decision making, from your decision to lease a car or to start a business, to the decision of the CFO of a major corporation to enter the telecommunications business, to the decision of the World Bank about which development projects to finance.

A basic tenet of finance is that the ultimate function of the system is to satisfy people's *consumption preferences,* including all the basic necessities of life, such as food, clothing, and shelter. Economic organizations such as firms and governments exist in order to facilitate the achievement of that ultimate function.

1.2 Why Study Finance?

There are at least five good reasons to study finance:

- to manage your personal resources.
- to deal with the world of business.
- to pursue interesting and rewarding career opportunities.
- to make informed public choices as a citizen.
- to expand your mind.

Let us elaborate on each of these reasons one at a time.

First, knowing some finance helps you to manage your own resources. Can you get along without knowing anything about finance? Perhaps. But if you are completely ignorant, then you are at the mercy of others. Remember the old adage: "A fool and his money are soon parted."

In some cases you will seek the help of experts. There are many finance professionals and financial service firms that provide financial advice—bankers, stockbrokers, insurance brokers, and firms selling mutual funds and other financial products and services. Often the advice is "free" if you are a potential customer. But how do you evaluate the advice you are given? The study of finance provides a conceptual framework for doing so.

A second reason to study finance is that a basic understanding of finance is essential in the business world. Even if you do not intend to specialize in finance, you must have a sufficient understanding of the concepts, techniques, and terminology employed by finance specialists to communicate with them and to recognize the limits of what they can do for you.

Box 1.1 Job Opportunities in Financial Engineering

At the prestigious Ecole Polytechnique in Paris, mathematics professor Nicole El Karoui continues to lead the way in teaching the modeling of derivatives to future quantitative analysts. Professor El Karoui has been instrumental in providing knowledge on derivatives through classes in financial mathematics. Her students are highly sought after by the world's top investment banks for their understanding of these increasingly important financial instruments.

Derivatives—financial contracts that derive their values from the performance of an underlying asset—were once used primarily as a hedge for banks against market risk. In the past, investment banks made most of their profits from underwriting and trading stocks and bonds in addition to providing financial advice. Presently, around 30% of their stock-related revenue comes from derivatives. Professor El Karoui's classes teach the necessary skill for students to become competitive in working in the service-sector firms driven by much of the demand caused by this change in investment structure.

El Karoui first became interested in modeling derivatives during a six-month sabbatical she spent working at a consumer credit bank. She noticed that employees in the derivatives department experienced problems similar to those facing students of stochastic calculus—the study of the impact of random variation over time. When she returned to teaching she implemented a postgraduate mathematical finance program, meeting the growing demand for understanding of derivatives among banks. Professor El Karoui's students are eagerly sought after by recruiters for their technical skills, which enable them to understand the underlying behavior of derivatives. These core quantitative skills have come to constitute an integral part of the work of investment bankers.

Source: "Why Students of Prof. El Karoui Are in Demand," *Wall Street Journal,* March 9, 2006.

Box 1.2 Debt Finance in Higher Education, University Bonds

Universities across the country are realizing the financing potential of issuing debt in order to raise money for operations and investment. For many years colleges have entrusted financial planners to manage their endowment funds, and now several wealthier schools have shown an increased eagerness to raise money by issuing bonds. In 2006, an estimated $33 billion was raised in the initial issue market for higher-education debt, and this figure is expected to rise rapidly in the future.

Public and not-for-profit private institutions can issue tax-free debt—due to their nonprofit status—and invest this money in high-yield markets. This strategy has been shown to be extremely profitable, aided by the fact that public and not-for-profit private universities are also exempt from taxes on the investment earnings produced. In turn, universities can use these expanded resources to help build new facilities, such as stadiums, athletic facilities, and theaters—all in high demand by incoming students. It is likely that as students continue to expect top-notch facilities in their universities, schools will continue to finance a significant portion of their operations by issuing more bonds.

Source: "An Education in Finance," *The Economist,* May 18, 2006.

Third, you may be interested in a career in finance. There are varied and potentially rewarding career opportunities in the field of finance and many possible paths you can follow as a finance professional. Most finance professionals are employed in the financial services sector of the economy—such as banking, insurance, or investment management. However, many others work as financial managers in nonfinancial firms or in government. Some even pursue academic careers.

Households, businesses, and government agencies often seek the advice of financial consultants. Moreover, a background in finance provides a good foundation for a career in general management. Many of the chief executives of major corporations around the world started in finance.

Fourth, to make informed public choices as a citizen, you should have a basic understanding of how the financial system works. The financial system is an important part of the infrastructure of any market-oriented society. Indeed, a sound set of financial institutions is believed by many to be an essential element in economic growth and development. As citizens we sometimes must make political choices that affect the functioning of the financial system. For example, do you want to vote for a political candidate who favors abolishing government deposit insurance or one who would impose strict controls on stock-market trading?

Fifth, finance can be a fascinating field of study on purely intellectual grounds. It expands your understanding of how the real world works. The scientific study of finance has a long history. Adam Smith's *The Wealth of Nations,* published in 1776, is widely regarded as the beginning of the science of economics. Finance theorists today are generally economists specializing in financial economics. Indeed, in 1990 and again in 1997, the Nobel Prize in economics was awarded to scholars for their scientific contributions in the field of finance (see Box 1.3).

1.3 Financial Decisions of Households

Most households are families. Families come in many forms and sizes. At one extreme is the *extended family,* which consists of several generations living together under one roof and sharing their economic resources. At the other extreme is the single person living

Box 1.3 Nobel Prize in Economics for Work in Finance

In 1990 the Nobel Prize in economics was awarded to three scholars—Harry Markowitz, Merton Miller, and William Sharpe—for scientific contributions that have had a powerful impact on both the theory and practice of finance. Let us briefly explain their contributions.

Harry Markowitz is the father of modern portfolio theory, the scientific study of how to trade off risk and reward in choosing among risky investments. In his seminal article, "Portfolio Selection," which appeared in the *Journal of Finance* in 1952, he developed a mathematical model showing how investors could achieve the lowest possible risk for any given target rate of return. The Markowitz model has been incorporated into basic finance theory and is widely used by practicing investment managers.

William Sharpe took Markowitz's results as his starting point and developed their implications for asset prices. By adding the assumption that at all times asset prices will adjust to equate demand and supply for each risky asset, he showed that a very specific structure must exist among the expected rates of return on risky assets ("Capital Asset Prices: A Theory of Market Equilibrium under Conditions of Risk," *Journal of Finance,* 1964). The structure suggested by Sharpe's theory is widely used today as the basis for making risk adjustments in many areas of finance theory and practice.

Merton Miller has contributed mainly to the theory of corporate finance. He and Franco Modigliani (an earlier recipient of the Nobel Prize in economics) addressed the dividend and borrowing policies of firms in a series of articles, starting with "The Cost of Capital, Corporation Finance, and the Theory of Investment," which appeared in the *American Economic Review* in 1958. Their fundamental contribution was to focus the attention of theorists and practitioners of finance on how corporate dividend and financing policies affect the total value of a firm. The M&M (Modigliani-Miller) propositions developed in their joint papers are among the basic building blocks of modern corporate finance.

Again in 1997 the Nobel Prize in economics was awarded to financial economists. The laureates were Robert C. Merton (one of the authors of this textbook) and Myron Scholes. The prize committee also mentioned a third scholar, Fischer Black, whose untimely death in 1995 at age 57 made him ineligible to share the prize. These three men discovered a mathematical formula for the pricing of options and other derivative securities that has had an enormous impact on both the theory and practice of finance. It is generally known as the Black-Scholes option pricing formula.

alone, whom most people wouldn't think of as a "family." In finance, however, all are classified as households.

Households face four basic types of financial decisions:

- *Consumption and saving decisions:* How much of their current wealth should they spend on consumption and how much of their current income should they save for the future?
- *Investment decisions:* How should they invest the money they have saved?
- *Financing decisions:* When and how should households use other people's money to implement their consumption and investment plans?
- *Risk-management decisions:* How and on what terms should households seek to reduce the financial uncertainties they face or when should they increase their risks?

As a result of saving part of their income for use in the future, people accumulate a pool of wealth, which can be held in any number of different forms. One form is bank accounts, another might be a piece of real estate or a share in a business venture. All of these are **assets.** *An asset is anything that has economic value.*

When people choose how to hold their pool of accumulated savings, it is called *personal investing* or **asset allocation.** In addition to investing in their own homes, people will often choose to invest in financial assets, such as stocks or bonds.

Box 1.4 New Trends in the Market for College Loans

Private student loans have become a growing, lucrative segment of consumer finance. Their profitability is derived from the relatively high interest rates they carry and the continually increasing demand generated by a growing number of students financing college tuition. Unlike federal loans, private loans can earn revenue by charging market rates in addition to up-front fees. These fees, which make private loans so rewarding for investors, can constitute 6% to 7% of the total amount of the loan. Furthermore, tuition increases around the country, combining with a growing number of baby boomers' children attending colleges, are the main factors that underlie a strong demand for student loans. Not only do college costs continue to rise, but federal aid in the form of grants and loans has remaining stagnant—and in many cases actually declined. The gap between the higher price of an education and the ability of families to pay is widening; private student loans have come to fill this gap.

Private loans, packaged by lenders such as Sallie Mae, have recently exploded in popularity, currently capturing 22% of the volume of federal student loans, up from 5% in 1994–1995. They are being praised as the fastest-growing and most profitable segment of consumer finance, with a total of $13.8 billion in student loans in the 2004–2005 school year—with the expectation of a further doubling within the following three years. As the number of college students continues to increase along with their tuitions, the private student loan industry is expected to maintain its strong record of growth.

Source: "Thanks to the Banks," *The Economist,* February 16, 2006.

When people borrow, they incur a **liability,** which is just another word for debt. A household's wealth or **net worth** is measured by the value of its assets minus its liabilities. Say you own a house worth $100,000 and have a $20,000 bank account. You also owe $80,000 to the bank on your home mortgage loan (a liability) and have a $5,000 credit card debt outstanding. Your net worth is $35,000: your total assets ($120,000) minus your total liabilities ($85,000). Ultimately, all of society's resources belong to households because they own the firms (either directly or through their ownership of shares of stock, pension plans, or life insurance policies) and pay the taxes spent by governments.

Finance theory treats people's consumption preferences as given. Although preferences may change over time, how and why they change is not addressed by the theory.[1] People's behavior is explained as an attempt to satisfy those preferences. The behavior of firms and governments is viewed from the perspective of how it affects the welfare of people.

Quick Check 1-1

What are the four basic types of financial decisions households have to make? Give an example of each.

1.4 Financial Decisions of Firms

By definition, business firms—or simply firms—are entities whose primary function is to produce goods and services. Like households, firms come in many different shapes and sizes. At the one extreme are small workshops, retail outlets, and restaurants owned by a

[1]Elements of a theory that are not explained by the theory itself are called ***exogenous.*** In contrast, those elements that are explained by the theory are called ***endogenous.*** In finance, people's preferences are exogenous to the theory, but the objectives of firms are endogenous.

single individual or family. At the other extreme are giant corporations, such as Mitsubishi or General Motors, with a workforce of hundreds of thousands of people and an even greater number of owners. The branch of finance dealing with financial decisions of firms is called *business finance* or *corporate finance.*

In order to produce goods and services, all firms—small and large—need *capital.* The buildings, machinery, and other intermediate inputs used in the production process are called *physical capital.* The stocks, bonds, and loans used to finance the acquisition of the physical capital are called *financial capital.*

The first decision any firm must make is what businesses it wants to be in. This is called *strategic planning.* Because strategic planning involves the evaluation of costs and benefits spread out over time, it is largely a financial decision-making process.

Often a firm will have a core business defined by its main product line, and it may branch out into related lines of business. For example, a firm that produces computer hardware may also choose to produce the software. It may also choose to service computers.

A firm's strategic goals may change over time, sometimes quite dramatically. Some corporations enter into businesses that are seemingly unrelated to each other. They may even abandon their original core business altogether so that the company's name ceases to have any connection with its current business.

For example, ITT Corporation started out as a telephone company in 1920. Its name stood for International Telephone and Telegraph. In the 1970s ITT became a large multinational conglomerate, operating a diverse set of businesses including insurance, munitions, hotels, bakeries, automobile rentals, mining, forest products, and gardening products in addition to telecommunications. During the 1980s, ITT shed many of its businesses and focused on operating hotels and casinos. By 1996 it had abandoned its original core business of producing telephone equipment and telecommunication services.

Once a firm's managers have decided what businesses they are in, they must prepare a plan for acquiring factories, machinery, research laboratories, showrooms, warehouses, and other such long-lived assets and for training the personnel who will operate them all. This is the *capital budgeting process.*

The basic unit of analysis in capital budgeting is an *investment project.* The process of capital budgeting consists of identifying ideas for new investment projects, evaluating them, deciding which ones to undertake, and then implementing them.

Once a firm has decided what projects it wants to undertake, it must figure out how to finance them. Unlike capital budgeting decisions, the unit of analysis in *capital structure* decisions is *not* the individual investment project but the firm as a whole. The starting point in making capital structure decisions is determining a feasible financing plan for the firm. Once a feasible financing plan has been achieved, the issue of the optimal financing mix can be addressed.

Firms can issue a wide range of financial instruments and claims. Some are standardized securities that can be traded in organized markets, such as common stock, preferred stock, bonds, and convertible securities. Others are nonmarketable claims, such as bank loans, employee stock options, leases, and pension liabilities.

A corporation's capital structure determines who gets what share of its future cash flows. For example, bonds promise fixed cash payments, whereas stocks pay the residual value left over after all other claimants have been paid. Capital structure also partially determines who gets to control the company. In general, shareholders have control through their right to elect the board of directors. But often bonds and other loans include contractual provisions, called *covenants,* restricting the activities of management. These covenant restrictions give the creditors some control over the company's affairs.

Working capital management is extremely important to the success of a firm. The best long-term plans can go away if the firm's management does not attend to the day-to-day financial affairs of the business. Even in a growing, successful firm, cash flows in and out may not match up exactly in time. Managers must worry about collecting from customers, paying bills as they come due, and generally managing the firm's cash flow to ensure that operating cash-flow deficits are financed and that cash-flow surpluses are efficiently invested to earn a good return.

The choices that a firm makes in all areas of financial decision making—investment, financing, and working capital management—depend on its technology and on the specific regulatory, tax, and competitive environment in which it operates. The policy choices are also highly interdependent.

Quick Check 1-2

What are the basic types of financial decisions firms have to make? Give an example of each.

1.5 Forms of Business Organization

There are three basic types of organizational form for a firm: a sole proprietorship, a partnership, and a corporation. A **sole proprietorship** is a firm owned by an individual or a family, in which the assets and liabilities of the firm are the personal assets and liabilities of the proprietor. A sole proprietor has *unlimited liability* for the debts and other liabilities of the firm. This means that if the firm cannot pay its debts, the proprietor's other personal assets can be seized to satisfy the demands of the firm's creditors.

Many firms start out as sole proprietorships and then change their organizational form as they become established and expand. But frequently a business such as a restaurant, a real estate agency, or a small workshop will remain a sole proprietorship throughout its existence.

A **partnership** is a firm with two or more owners, called the partners, who share the equity in the business. A partnership agreement usually stipulates how decisions are to be made and how profits and losses are to be shared. Unless otherwise specified, all partners have unlimited liability as in the sole proprietorship.

However, it is possible to limit the liability for some partners called *limited partners.* At least one of the partners, called the general partner, has unlimited liability for the debts of the firm. Limited partners typically do not make the day-to-day business decisions of the partnership; the general partner does.

Unlike a sole proprietorship or a partnership, a **corporation** is a firm that is a legal entity distinct from its owners. Corporations can own property, borrow, and enter into contracts. They can sue and be sued. They are usually taxed according to rules that differ from the rules that apply to the other forms of business organization.

The charter of a corporation sets down the rules that govern it. Shareholders are entitled to a share of any distributions from the corporation (e.g., cash dividends) in proportion to the number of shares they own. The shareholders elect a *board of directors,* which in turn selects managers to run the business. Usually there is one vote per share, but sometimes there are different classes of stocks with different voting rights.

An advantage of the corporate form is that ownership shares can usually be transferred without disrupting the business. Another advantage is *limited liability,* which means that if the corporation fails to pay its debts, the creditors can seize the assets of the corporation but have no recourse to the personal assets of the shareholders. In that sense a corporation serves the same function as a general partner in a partnership, and its shareholders are like limited partners.

Box 1.5 How to Identify That a Firm Is a Corporation

In the United States, corporations are identified by the letters *Inc.* after their name. It stands for the English word *incorporated.* In France the letters are *SA* (Societé Anonime); in Italy *SpA* (Societa per Azioni); in the Netherlands *NV* (Naamloze Vennootschap); and in Sweden *AB* (Aktiebolag).

In Germany, public corporations are called Aktiengesellschaften, identifiable by the letters *AG* after the company name, whereas private corporations are Gesellschaften mit beschränkter Haftung, denoted by *GmbH.* The parallel designations in the United Kingdom are *PLC* for public limited company, and *LTD* for private corporations.

The earliest known corporations were formed in Amsterdam and in London in the 1600s and were called *joint stock companies* in English. That term has fallen into disuse.

Around the world, large firms are almost always organized as corporations, although ownership of the corporation may be restricted to a single person or family. In the United States, corporations with broadly dispersed ownership are called *public corporations;* those with concentrated ownership are called *private corporations.*

Laws governing the corporate form of organization differ in their details from country to country, and even within a country they may differ from one jurisdiction to another. In the United States, for example, laws governing corporations are created and administered at the state level (see Box 1.5).

Quick Check 1-3

A corporation owned by a single person is not a sole proprietorship. Why?

1.6 Separation of Ownership and Management

In sole proprietorships and even in many partnerships the owners and the active managers of the business are the same people. But in many firms, especially the large ones, the owners do not themselves manage the business. Instead they delegate that responsibility to professional managers, who may not own any shares in the business. There are at least five reasons for the owners of a firm to turn over the running of the business to others to manage.

First, professional managers may be found who have a superior ability to run the business. This may be because the professional managers have better technological knowledge, more experience, or a more suitable personality to run the business. In a structure in which the owner is also the manager, the owner must have both the talents of a manager and the financial resources necessary to carry out production. In the separated structure, no such coincidence is required.

For example, consider the entertainment industry. The people most qualified to manage a film studio or a television network may not have the financial resources to own the business, and the people with the wealth to own such a business may have no ability to manage it. Therefore, it makes sense for the managerially competent people to produce and distribute the movies and for the wealthy people to simply provide the capital.

Second, to achieve the efficient scale of a business the resources of many households may have to be pooled. For example, the cost of producing a single movie is in the millions of dollars for a low-budget film, and the average feature-length movie costs many millions of dollars to produce. The need to pool resources to achieve an efficient scale of production calls for a structure with many owners, not all of whom can be actively involved in managing the business.

Third, in an uncertain economic environment, owners will want to diversify their risks across many firms. To diversify optimally requires the investor to hold a portfolio of assets, in which each security is but a small part. Such efficient diversification is difficult to achieve without separation of ownership and management.

For example, suppose an investor thinks that firms in the entertainment industry will do well over the next few years and would like to buy a diversified stake in that industry. If the investor had to also manage the firms she invests in, there is no way she could diversify across many firms. The corporate form is especially well suited to facilitating diversification by investor-owners because it allows them to own a relatively small share of each firm.

Fourth, the separated structure allows for savings in the costs of information gathering. Managers can gather the most accurate information available about the firm's production technology, the costs of its inputs, and the demand for its products. The owners of the firm need to know relatively little about the technology of the firm, the intensity at which it is being operated, and the demand for the firm's products.

Again, consider the entertainment industry. The information needed to successfully manage the production and distribution of a movie is substantial. Although information about top actors and directors who might be hired to star in a movie is readily available at low cost, this is not so with respect to other resource inputs to movie production and distribution. Establishing information networks of agents and jobbers is costly and is most efficiently handled by having movie executives specialize in doing it.

Fifth, there is the "learning curve" or "going concern" effect, which favors the separated structure. Suppose the owner wants to sell all or part of his technology either now or at a later date. If the owner must also be the manager, the new owners have to learn the business from the former owner in order to manage it efficiently. However, if the owner does *not* have to be the manager, then when the business is sold, the manager continues in place and works for the new owners. When a company issues shares to the public for the first time, the original owner-managers often continue to manage the business even if they no longer own any shares in the business.

The corporate form is especially well suited to the separation of owners and managers because it allows relatively frequent changes in owners by share transfer without affecting the operations of the firm. Millions of shares in corporations around the world change hands and rarely is there any effect on the management or operations of the business.

Quick Check 1-4

What are the main reasons for having a separation of management and ownership of firms? How does the corporate form of organization facilitate this separation?

Offsetting all the reasons in favor of a separation of ownership and management, the separated structure creates the potential for a *conflict of interest* between the owners and the managers. Because the owners of a corporation have only incomplete information about whether the managers are serving their interests effectively, managers may neglect their obligations to the shareholders. In extreme cases, managers may even act *contrary* to the interests of their shareholders. Adam Smith, the father of classical economics, summed it up as follows:

> The directors of such [joint-stock] companies, however, being the managers rather of other people's money than of their own, it cannot well be expected, that they should

> watch over it with the same anxious vigilance with which the partners in a private copartnery frequently watch over their own. Like the stewards of a rich man, they are apt to consider attention to small matters as not for their master's honour, and very easily give themselves a dispensation from having it. Negligence and profusion, therefore, must always prevail, more or less, in the management of the affairs of such a company.[2]

In those business environments in which the potential for conflicts of interest between owners and managers can be resolved at a reasonable cost, we would expect to find that the owners of business firms will not be the managers. And we would expect that the ownership of firms is dispersed among many individuals. Furthermore, we would expect to observe that, over time, the changes in the composition of the ownership would be far more common than the changes in the composition of the management.

1.7 The Goal of Management

Because the managers of corporations are hired by the shareholders (through the board of directors), the managers' primary commitment is to make decisions that are in the best interests of the shareholders. This is not the exclusive goal of management. Like everyone else in society, corporate managers must obey the law. They are also expected to respect ethical norms and to promote desirable social goals when it is possible to do so at a reasonable cost to shareholders.[3]

However, even if we restrict the goal of corporate management exclusively to serving the best interests of the shareholders, it is not obvious how managers can achieve this goal. In principle, managers could review each decision with the owners including the production choices, cost of obtaining capital, and so on and ask them which combination they prefer. But, in that case, the owners would have to have the same knowledge and spend essentially the same amount of time as they would if they were managing the business themselves. There would, therefore, be little point in hiring managers to run the business.

Moreover, although this procedure might be feasible when there are a few owners of the firm, it becomes completely impractical as the number of shareholders becomes large. Indeed, for a large multinational corporation, the number of shareholders can exceed a million, and they may reside in many different countries. Hence, it is essential to find a goal or rule to guide managers of the firm without having to "poll" the owners about most decisions.

To be effective, such a rule should not require the managers to know the risk preferences or opinions of the shareholders because such data are virtually impossible to obtain. And even if the data were available at one point in time, they change over time. Indeed, because shares of stock change hands every day, the owners of the corporation change every day. Thus, to be feasible, the right rule should be independent of who the owners are.

If a feasible rule for the managers to follow were found that would lead them to make the same investment and financing decisions that each of the individual owners would have made had they made the decisions themselves, then such a rule would clearly be the right one. To *maximize the wealth of current stockholders* is just such a rule.[4] Let us explain why.

For example, suppose you are the manager of a corporation trying to decide between two alternative investments. The choice is between a very risky investment project and

---

[2]Adam Smith, *The Wealth of Nations* (Chicago: University of Chicago Press, 1977).

[3]We assume that the goal of maximizing shareholder wealth does not necessarily conflict with other desirable social goals.

[4]This rule, like any all-encompassing dictum, is not always correct. It needs to be qualified in several respects. First, it assumes well-functioning and competitive capital markets. It also assumes that managers do not make decisions that are illegal or unethical.

a very safe one. Some shareholders might want to avoid taking these risks, and others might be pessimistic about the future of the investment. Still other shareholders might be risk lovers or might be optimistic about the outcome of the investment. How then can management make a decision in the best interests of all shareholders?

Suppose that undertaking the risky project would increase the market value of the firm's shares more than would the safe project. Even if some shareholders ultimately want to invest their money in safer assets, it would not be in their best interests for you as the firm's manager to choose the safer project.

This is because in well-functioning capital markets shareholders can adjust the riskiness of their personal portfolios by selling some of the shares in the firm you manage and investing the proceeds in safe assets. By your accepting the riskier project, even these risk-averse shareholders will wind up better off. They will have extra dollars today, which they can invest or consume as they see fit.

Thus, we see that individual owners would want managers to choose the investment project that maximizes the market value of their shares. The only risks relevant to the decision by managers are those of the project that affect the market value of the firm's shares.

The shareholder-wealth-maximization rule depends on the firm's production technology, market interest rates, market risk premiums, and security prices. It leads managers to make the same investment decisions that each of the individual owners would have made had they made the decisions themselves. At the same time, it does not depend upon the *risk aversion* or *wealth* of the owners, and so it can be made without any specific information about the owners. Thus, the shareholder-wealth-maximization rule is the "right" rule for managers to follow in running the firm. They can follow it without polling the owners each time a decision arises.

Scholars and other commentators on corporate behavior sometimes assert that the goal of managers is to maximize the firm's *profits.* Under certain specialized conditions, profit maximization and maximizing shareholder wealth lead to the same decisions. But in general there are two fundamental ambiguities with the profit-maximization criterion:

- If the production process requires many periods, then which period's profit is to be maximized?
- If either future revenues or expenses are uncertain, then what is the meaning of "maximize profits" when profits are described by a probability distribution?

Let us illustrate each of these problems with the profit-maximization criterion. First, the problem of many periods.

Suppose the firm faces a choice between two projects, both of which require an initial outlay of \$1 million but last for a different number of years. Project A will return \$1.05 million one year from now and then is over. Its profit is, therefore, \$50,000 (\$1.05 million–\$1 million). Project B will last for two years, return nothing in the first year, and then \$1.1 million two years from now. How do you apply a profit-maximization criterion in this case?

Now let us illustrate the difficulty of using a profit maximization criterion in an uncertain environment. Suppose you are the manager of a firm trying to choose between two investment projects, both of which require an initial outlay of \$1 million and produce all of their returns one period from now. As in the previous example, project A will pay \$1.05 million with certainty. We can, therefore, say unambiguously that the profit on project A is \$50,000 (\$1.05 million–\$1 million).

Project C has an uncertain return. It will either pay \$1.2 million or \$0.9 million, each with probability 0.5. Thus, project C will either produce a profit of \$200,000 or a loss of \$100,000. What does it mean in this context to say "choose the project that maximizes the firm's profits"?

Unlike profits, it is clear that the current market value of the firm's shareholders' equity is still well defined (e.g., the future cash flows of the IBM corporation are uncertain, but there is a current price for its stock that is not uncertain). Hence, unlike the profit-maximization rule, the shareholder-wealth-maximization rule causes no ambiguities when future cash flows of the firm are uncertain.

Quick Check 1-5

Why is the shareholder-wealth-maximization rule a better one for corporate managers to follow than the profit-maximization rule?

Of course, management still has the difficult task of estimating the impact of its decision on the value of the firm's shares. Thus, in our preceding illustrations, in order to choose between projects A and B, or between A and C, management would have to determine which of them is likely to increase the value of the firm the most. This is not easy, but the criterion for making the decision is unambiguous.

Thus, the goal of management is to make decisions so as to maximize the firm's value to its shareholders. The main challenge in implementing this criterion is to obtain information about the likely impact of its decisions on the firm's value. Management's task is made much easier when it can observe market prices of its own and other firms' shares.

Indeed, in the absence of such market price information, it is difficult to see how they can implement this criterion at all. Although it is reasonable to assume that good managers will have as much information about their firm's production technology as anyone, such *internal* (to the firm) information is not sufficient to make effective decisions. In the absence of a stock market, managers would require *external* (to the firm) information that is costly if not impossible to obtain: namely, the wealth, preferences, and other investment opportunities of the owners.

Thus, the existence of a stock market allows the manager to substitute one set of external information that is relatively easy to obtain—namely, stock prices—for another set that is virtually impossible to obtain—information about the shareholders' wealth, preferences, and other investment opportunities. The existence of a well-functioning stock market, therefore, facilitates the efficient separation of the ownership and management of firms.

Note that in one respect the corporation's own senior managers and outside stock analysts who follow the corporation face a common task. Both groups are concerned with answering the question: How will the actions taken by management affect the market price of the firm's shares? The big difference is that the managers are the ones who actually make the decisions and have responsibility for implementing them.

One place to look for a statement of the goals of a corporation's top managers is the annual report to shareholders. Often the opening letter from the company's chief executive officer states what management's financial goals are and the general strategic plan for achieving them (see Box 1.6).

Quick Check 1-6

How does the existence of a well-functioning stock market facilitate the separation of ownership and management of firms?

Box 1.6 Corporate Financial Goals and the Annual Report

Here is an excerpt from Honeywell Corporation's 1994 annual report to shareholders. Honeywell's chairman and chief executive officer, Michael R. Bonsignore, writes in his letter to the shareholders:

> Profitable growth. Delighted customers. Worldwide leadership in control. This is the vision for Honeywell that I and Honeywell people around the world have set for ourselves. It embodies what we want to be. It underpins how we set our goals. And it defines how we will fulfill the purpose of the company—which is to create value for our shareholders. . . .
>
> The company is now poised to achieve our primary financial objective: first-quartile total shareholder returns among our peers. We define total shareholder returns as share price appreciation plus dividends reinvested in the stock.
>
> Our management team is steadfast in achieving this objective. It is a key goal in our long-range incentive system. Our short-term executive compensation program rewards economic value added. We have constructed an integrated financial plan that sets aggressive targets in each driver of shareholder value: sales growth, operating margins, working capital, capital expenditures, and taxes.

1.8 Market Discipline: Takeovers

What forces are there to compel managers to act in the best interests of the shareholders? The shareholders could fire the managers by voting them out. But because a major benefit of the separated structure is that the owners can remain relatively uninformed about the operations of the firm, it is not apparent how these owners could know whether their firm is being mismanaged.

The value of voting rights as a means of enforcement is further cast into doubt if ownership of the firm is widely dispersed. If that is the situation, then the holdings of any single owner are likely to be so small that he or she would not incur the expense to become informed and to convey this information to other owners.[5] Thus, voting rights alone can do little to solve this dilemma.

The existence of a competitive stock market offers another important mechanism for aligning the incentives of managers with those of shareholders. It is called the *takeover.*

To see how the threat of a takeover can compel managers to act in the best interests of shareholders, suppose some entity, call it the takeover bidder, has identified a significantly mismanaged firm (i.e., one whose management has chosen an investment plan that leads to a market value that is significantly less than the maximum value that could be achieved from the firm's resources). If the bidder successfully buys enough shares of the undervalued firm to gain control, it replaces the managers with ones who will operate it optimally.

Having announced the change in the firm's investment plans, the bidder now sells the shares of the firm at the new market price for an immediate profit. Note that the bidder did not have to add any tangible resources to the firm to achieve this profit. Hence, the only expenses incurred are the cost of identifying a mismanaged firm and the cost of acquiring the firm's shares.

Although the cost of identifying a mismanaged firm will vary, it can be quite low if the takeover bidder happens to be a supplier, customer, or competitor of the firm because much of the information required may have been gathered for other purposes already. For this

[5]This is called the "paradox" of voting. The paradox is that when there are many voters, none of whose individual vote would appreciably affect the final outcome, it does not pay any individual voter to incur the costs of becoming informed and exercising the right to vote.

reason, the takeover mechanism can work even if resources are not spent for the explicit reason of identifying mismanaged firms.

However, if significant mismanagement of firms were widespread, then it would pay to spend resources in search of such firms in much the same way that resources are spent on research of new physical investment projects. There are indeed firms that specialize in making hostile (to the management) takeovers. Therefore, the threat of a takeover is credible and the subsequent replacement of management provides a strong incentive for current managers (acting in their self-interest) to act in the interests of the firm's current shareholders by maximizing market value.

Indeed, even in the absence of any explicit instructions from the shareholders or knowledge of the theory for good management, one might expect managers to move in the direction of value maximization as a matter of self-preservation. Moreover, it should be noted that it does not matter whether the source of the mismanagement is incompetence or the pursuit of different objectives, the takeover mechanism serves equally well to correct either one.

The effectiveness of the takeover mechanism can be reduced by government policies. For example, in an attempt to prevent the formation of monopolies in various product markets, the U.S. Department of Justice will take legal action under the antitrust laws to prevent mergers or acquisitions that might reduce competition. Because it is more likely that a supplier, customer, or competitor will be the takeover bidder who identifies the mismanaged firm, this public policy will tend to reduce the threat of takeover.

Quick Check 1-7

How does the threat of a takeover serve as a mechanism to deal with the conflict of interest between owners and managers of a corporation?

1.9 The Role of the Finance Specialist in a Corporation

Virtually all decisions made in a corporation are at least partially financial because they involve making trade-offs between costs and benefits that are spread over time. Therefore, in large corporations virtually all managers from the chief executive at the top down to managers of individual production units, marketing units, research labs, or other departments make use of the services of finance specialists.

The Financial Executives Institute, a voluntary organization of corporate executives who specialize in finance, offers a broad definition of a financial executive as anyone who has authority for one of the functions listed in Table 1.1.

The organization of the finance function and its relation to other departments vary from company to company, but Figure 1.1 shows a typical organization chart in a large corporation.

At the top is the firm's chief executive officer (CEO) who often is also the president. The chief financial officer (CFO) is a senior vice president with responsibility for all the financial functions in the firm and reports directly to the CEO. The firm also has senior vice presidents in charge of marketing and operations. In large firms, there is sometimes a chief operating officer (COO), who takes responsibility for implementing the CEO's strategy for the firm.

The CFO has three departments reporting to him or her: financial planning, treasury, and control, each headed by a vice president. The vice president for financial planning has responsibility for analyzing major capital expenditures such as proposals to enter new lines

TABLE 1.1 Financial Functions in a Corporation

1. PLANNING

Establishment, coordination, and administration, as an integral part of management, of an adequate plan for the control of operations. Such a plan, to the extent required in the business, would provide the following:

a. Long- and short-range financial and corporate planning
b. Budgeting for capital expenditures and/or operations
c. Sales forecasting
d. Performance evaluation
e. Pricing policies
f. Economic appraisal
g. Analysis of acquisitions and divestments

2. PROVISION OF CAPITAL

Establishment and execution of programs for the provision of the capital required by the business.

3. ADMINISTRATION OF FUNDS

a. Management of cash
b. Maintenance of banking arrangements
c. Receipt, custody, and disbursement of the company's monies and securities
d. Credit and collection management
e. Management of pension funds
f. Management of investments
g. Custodial responsibilities

4. ACCOUNTING AND CONTROL

a. Establishment of accounting policies
b. Development and reporting of accounting data
c. Cost standards
d. Internal auditing
e. Systems and procedures (accounting)
f. Government reporting
g. Report and interpretation of results of operations to management
h. Comparison of performance with operating plans and standards

5. PROTECTION OF ASSETS

a. Provision of insurance coverage as required
b. Assure protection of business assets and loss prevention through internal control and internal auditing
c. Real estate management

6. TAX ADMINISTRATION

a. Establishment and administration of tax policies and procedures
b. Relations with taxing agencies
c. Preparation of tax reports
d. Tax planning

TABLE 1.1 **Continued**

7. INVESTOR RELATIONS
   a. Establishment and maintenance of liaison with the investment community
   b. Establishment and maintenance of communications with company stockholders
   c. Counseling with analysts—public financial information

8. EVALUATION AND CONSULTING

   Consultation with and advice to other corporate executives on company policy, operations, objectives, and the effectiveness thereof

9. MANAGEMENT INFORMATION SYSTEMS
   a. Development and use of electronic data processing facilities
   b. Development and use of management information systems
   c. Development and use of systems and procedures

Source: Financial Executives Institute.

FIGURE 1.1

Organization Chart for ZYX Corporation

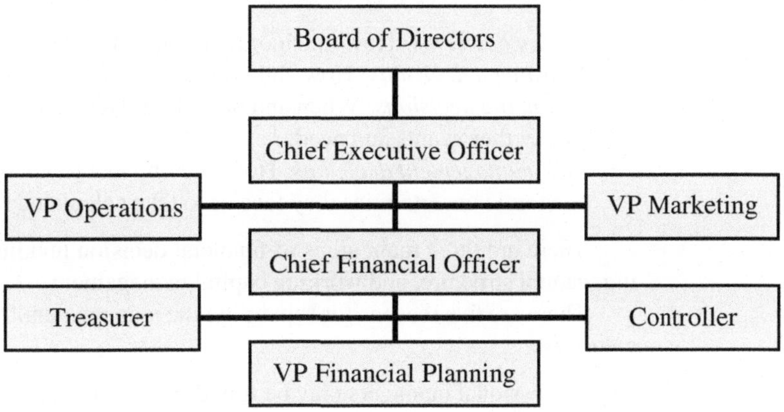

of business or to exit existing businesses. This includes analyzing proposed mergers, acquisitions, and spin-offs.

The treasurer has responsibility for managing the financing activities of the firm and for working capital management. The treasurer's job includes managing relations with the external investor community, managing the firm's exposure to currency and interest rate risks, and managing the tax department.

The controller oversees the accounting and auditing activities of the firm. This includes preparation of internal reports comparing planned and actual costs, revenues, and profits from the corporation's various business units. It also includes preparation of financial statements for use by shareholders, creditors, and regulatory authorities.

Summary

Finance is the study of how to allocate scarce resources over time. The two features that distinguish finance are that the costs and benefits of financial decisions are spread out over time and are usually not known with certainty in advance by either the decision maker or anybody else.

A basic tenet of finance is that the ultimate function of the system is to satisfy people's *consumption preferences.* Economic organizations such as firms and governments exist in order to facilitate the achievement of that ultimate function. Many financial decisions can be made strictly on the basis of improving the trade-offs available to people without knowledge of their consumption preferences.

There are at least five good reasons to study finance:

- To manage your personal resources.
- To deal with the world of business.
- To pursue interesting and rewarding career opportunities.
- To make informed public choices as a citizen.
- To expand your mind.

The players in finance theory are households, business firms, financial intermediaries, and governments. Households occupy a special place in the theory because the ultimate function of the system is to satisfy the preferences of people, and the theory treats those preferences as given. Finance theory explains household behavior as an attempt to satisfy those preferences. The behavior of firms is viewed from the perspective of how it affects the welfare of households.

Households face four basic types of financial decisions:

- *Saving decisions:* How much of their current income should they save for the future?
- *Investment decisions:* How should they invest the money they have saved?
- *Financing decisions:* When and how should they use other people's money to satisfy their wants and needs?
- *Risk-management decisions:* How and on what terms should they seek to reduce the economic uncertainties they face or to take calculated risks?

There are three main areas of financial decision making in a business: capital budgeting, capital structure, and working capital management.

There are five reasons for separating the management from the ownership of a business enterprise:

- Professional managers may be found who have a superior ability to run the business.
- To achieve the efficient scale of a business the resources of many households may have to be pooled.
- In an uncertain economic environment, owners will want to diversify their risks across many firms. Such efficient diversification is difficult to achieve without separation of ownership and management.
- To achieve savings in the costs of gathering information.
- The "learning curve" or "going concern" effect: When the owner is also the manager, the new owner has to learn the business from the former owner in order to manage it efficiently. If the owner is not the manager, then when the business is sold, the manager continues in place and works for the new owner.

The corporate form is especially well suited to the separation of ownership and management of firms because it allows relatively frequent changes in owners by share transfer without affecting the operations of the firm.

The primary goal of corporate management is to maximize shareholder wealth. It leads managers to make the same investment decisions that each of the individual owners would have made had they made the decisions themselves.

A competitive stock market imposes a strong discipline on managers to take actions to maximize the market value of the firm's shares.

Key Terms

- finance 2
- financial system 2
- assets 5
- asset allocation 5
- liability 6
- net worth 6
- sole proprietorship 8
- partnership 8
- corporation 8

Answers to Quick Check Questions

Quick Check 1-1 What are the four basic types of financial decisions households have to make? Give an example of each.

Answer:

- Consumption/saving decisions, such as how much to save for a child's education or for retirement.
- Investment decisions, such as how much to invest in stocks or bonds.
- Financing decisions, such as what type of loan to take to finance the purchase of a home or a car.
- Risk-management decisions, such as whether to buy disability insurance.

Quick Check 1-2 What are the basic types of financial decisions firms have to make? Give an example of each.

Answer:

- Capital budgeting decisions, such as whether to build a plant to produce a new product.
- Financing decisions, such as how much debt and how much equity it should have in its capital structure.
- Working capital decisions, such as whether it should extend credit to customers or demand cash on delivery.

Quick Check 1-3 A corporation owned by a single person is not a sole proprietorship. Why?

Answer: In a corporation the liability of the single shareholder would be limited to the assets of the corporation.

Quick Check 1-4 What are the main reasons for having a separation of management and ownership of firms? How does the corporate form of organization facilitate this separation?

Answer: Five reasons:

- Professional managers may be found who have a superior ability to run the business.
- To achieve the efficient scale of a business the resources of many households may have to be pooled.
- In an uncertain economic environment, owners will want to diversify their risks across many firms. Such efficient diversification is difficult to achieve without separation of ownership and management.
- To achieve savings in the costs of gathering information.
- The "learning curve" or "going concern" effect: When the owner is also the manager, the new owner has to learn the business from the former owner in order to manage it efficiently. If the owner is not the manager, then when the business is sold, the manager continues in place and works for the new owner.

The corporate form is especially well suited to the separation of ownership and management of firms because it allows relatively frequent changes in owners by share transfer without affecting the operations of the firm.

Quick Check 1-5 Why is the shareholder-wealth-maximization rule a better one for corporate managers to follow than the profit-maximization rule?

Answer: There are two fundamental ambiguities with the profit-maximization criterion:

- If the production process requires many periods, then which period's profit is to be maximized?
- If either future revenues or expenses are uncertain, then what is the meaning of "maximize profits" when profits are described by a probability distribution?

Quick Check 1-6 How does the existence of a well-functioning stock market facilitate the separation of ownership and management of firms?

Answer: In the absence of a stock market, managers would require information that is costly if not impossible to obtain: namely, the wealth, preferences, and other investment opportunities of the owners.

Quick Check 1-7 How does the threat of a takeover serve as a mechanism to deal with the conflict of interest between owners and managers of a corporation?

Answer: Managers know that if they fail to maximize the market value of the firm's shares, the firm will be vulnerable to a takeover in which managers might lose their jobs.

Sources of Information

On the Internet you can complement your understanding of the core structures of financial markets and corporations with the following links:

Survey on Corporate Social Responsibility, ***The Economist,*** January 20, 2005,
http://www.economist.com/surveys/displayStory.cfm?Story_ID=3574392

Financial Market Trends, Organization for Economic Cooperation and Development
http://www.oecd.org/document/36/0,2340,en_2649_201185_1962020_1_1_1_1,00.html

Quarterly Review, Bank for International Settlements
http://www.bis.org/publ/quarterly.htm

EDGAR Database, U.S. Securities and Exchange Commission
http://www.sec.gov/edaux/searches.htm

Questions and Problems

Defining Finance

1. What are your main goals in life? How does finance play a part in achieving those goals? What are the major tradeoffs you face?

Financial Decisions of Households

2. What is your net worth? What have you included among your assets and your liabilities? Would you list the value of your potential lifetime earning power as an asset or liability? How does it compare in value to other assets you have listed?

3. How are the financial decisions faced by a single person living alone different from those faced by the head of a household with responsibility for several children of school age? Are the tradeoffs they have to make different, or will they evaluate the tradeoffs differently?
4. Family A and Family B both consist of a father, mother, and two children of school age. In Family A both spouses have jobs outside the home and earn a combined income of $100,000 per year. In Family B, only one spouse works outside the home and earns $100,000 per year. How do the financial circumstances and decisions faced by the two families differ?
5. Suppose we define financial independence as the ability to engage in the four basic household financial decisions without resort to the use of relatives' resources when making financing decisions. At what age should children be expected to become financially independent?
6. You are thinking of buying a car. Analyze the decision by addressing the following issues:
   a. Are there other ways to satisfy your transportation requirements besides buying a car? Make a list of all the alternatives and write down the pros and cons.
   b. What are the different ways you can finance the purchase of a car?
   c. Obtain information from at least three different providers of automobile financing on the terms they offer.
   d. What criteria should you use in making your decision?
7. Match each of the following examples with one of the four categories of basic types of household financial decisions.
   - At the Safeway paying with your debit card rather than taking the time to write a check
   - Deciding to take the proceeds from your winning lottery ticket and use it to pay for an extended vacation on the Italian Riviera
   - Following Hillary's advice and selling your Microsoft shares to invest in pork belly futures
   - Helping your 15-years-old son learn to drive by putting him behind the wheel on the back road into town
   - Taking up the offer from the pool supply company to pay off your new hot tub with a 15-month loan with zero payments for the first three months

Forms of Business Organization

8. You are thinking of starting your own business, but have no money.
   a. Think of a business that you could start without having to borrow any money.
   b. Now think of a business that you would want to start if you could borrow any amount of money at the going market interest rate.
   c. What are the risks you would face in this business?
   d. Where can you get financing for your new business?
9. Choose an organization that is not a firm, such as a club or church group, and list the most important financial decisions it has to make. What are the key tradeoffs the organization faces? What role do preferences play in choosing among alternatives? Interview the financial manager of the organization and check to see whether he or she agrees with you.

Market Discipline: Takeovers

10. *Challenge Question:* While there are clear advantages to the separation of management from ownership of business enterprises, there is also a fundamental disadvantage in that it may be costly to align the goals of management with those of the owners. Suggest at

least two methods, other than the takeover market, by which the conflict can be reduced, albeit at some cost.

11. *Challenge Question:* Consider a poorly run local coffee shop with its prime location featuring a steady stream of potential clients passing by on their way to and from campus. How does the longtime disgruntled, sloppy, and inefficient owner-manager of Cup-a-Joe survive and avoid disciplining from the takeover market?

The Role of the Finance Specialist in a Corporation

12. Which of the following tasks undertaken within a corporate office are likely to fall under the supervision of the treasurer? The controller?
    - Arranging to extend a line of credit from a bank
    - Arranging with an investment bank for a foreign exchange transaction
    - Producing a detailed analysis of the cost structure of the company's alternative product lines
    - Taking cash payments for company sales and purchasing U.S. Treasury Bills
    - Filing quarterly statements with the Securities and Exchange Commission

CHAPTER 2

Financial Markets and Institutions

OBJECTIVES

- To provide a conceptual framework for understanding how the financial system works and how it changes over time.
- To understand the meaning and determinants of rates of return on different classes of assets.

CONTENTS

Chapter 1 set down the main purpose of this book, which is to help you make better financial decisions. Such decisions are always made within the context of a financial system that both constrains and enables the decision maker. Effective financial decisions thus require an understanding of that system.

Suppose, for example, that you want to further your education, buy a house, or start a new business. Where can you get the funds to do it? The answers to these questions depend very much on where you are located. The roles played by families, governments, and private sector institutions (such as banks and securities markets) in financing economic activities vary considerably among countries. What's more, these roles change over time.

This chapter provides a conceptual framework for understanding how the financial system works and how it changes over time. It starts with an overview of the central role played by financial markets and intermediaries in facilitating the flow of funds, the transfer of risk, and several other basic financial functions. The chapter provides a broad overview of the current structure of financial markets and institutions around the world, and it shows that the way the basic financial functions are performed changes over time and differs across borders. Finally, the chapter provides a brief overview of how interest rates and rates of return on risky assets are determined and reviews the history of these rates.

2.1 What Is the Financial System?

The financial system encompasses the markets, intermediaries, service firms, and other institutions used to carry out the financial decisions of households, business firms, and governments. Sometimes a market for a particular financial instrument has a specific geographic location such as the New York Stock Exchange or the Osaka Options and Futures Exchange, which are institutions housed in buildings in New York City and in Osaka, Japan, respectively. Often, however, the market has no one specific location. Such is the case for the **over-the-counter markets**—or off-exchange markets—in stocks, bonds, and currencies, which are essentially global computer and telecommunications networks linking securities dealers and their customers.

Financial intermediaries are defined as firms whose primary business is to provide financial services and products. They include banks, investment companies, and insurance companies. Their products include checking accounts, commercial loans, mortgages, mutual funds, and a wide range of insurance contracts.

Today's financial system is global in scope. Financial markets and intermediaries are linked through a vast international telecommunications network, so that the transfer of payments and the trading of securities can go on virtually around the clock. If a large corporation based in Germany wants to finance a major new investment, for instance, it will consider a range of international possibilities, including issuing stock and selling it on the New York or London stock exchanges or borrowing from a Japanese pension fund. If it chooses to borrow from the Japanese pension fund, the loan might be denominated in German marks, in Japanese yen, or even in U.S. dollars.

2.2 The Flow of Funds

The interactions among the various players in the financial system are shown in Figure 2.1, a flow-of-funds diagram. Funds flow through the financial system from entities that have a surplus of funds (the box on the left) to those that have a deficit (the box on the right).

For example, a household that is saving a portion of its current income for retirement has a surplus of funds whereas another household seeking to buy a house has a deficit.

FIGURE 2.1

The Flow of Funds

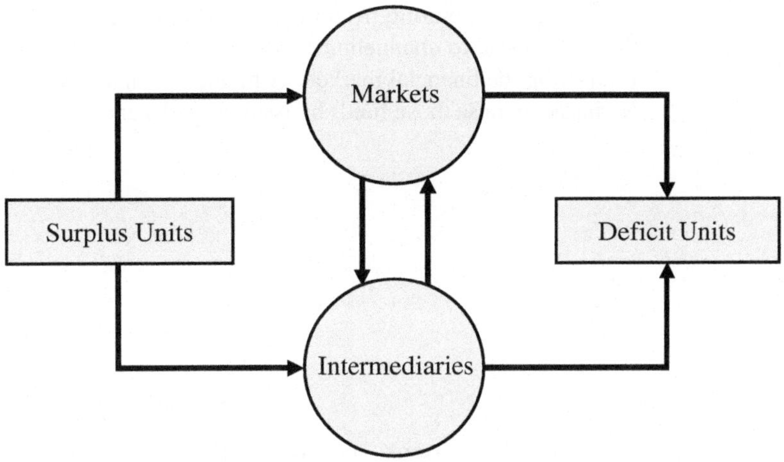

A firm with profits in excess of its need for new investment spending is a surplus unit, whereas another firm that needs to finance a major expansion is a deficit unit.[1]

Figure 2.1 shows that some funds flow from the surplus units to the deficit units through financial intermediaries such as banks (the lower route in Figure 2.1), whereas some funds flow through the financial markets without going through a financial intermediary (the upper route).

To illustrate the **flow of funds** along the upper route, a household (surplus unit) buys shares of stock from a firm (deficit unit) that issues them. In some cases—firms that have dividend reinvestment plans, for example—the household buys the shares directly from the firm issuing them without using a broker. In most cases, however, a broker or a dealer would likely be involved in this flow of funds, collecting the money from the household and transferring it to the issuing firm.

A large part of the funds flowing through the financial system, however, never flow through markets and, therefore, do not follow the upper route in Figure 2.1. Instead, as shown in the lower half of Figure 2.1, they go from the surplus units to the deficit units through financial intermediaries.

To illustrate the flow of funds through intermediaries, suppose you deposit your savings in an account at a bank, and the bank uses the funds to make a loan to a business firm. In this case, you do not own a direct claim on the borrowing firm; instead you have a deposit at the bank. The bank in turn has a claim on the borrowing firm. Your bank deposit has different risk and liquidity characteristics from the loan to the business firm, which is now an asset of the bank. Your deposit is safe and liquid (i.e., you can withdraw the full amount at any time), whereas the loan held as an asset by the bank has some default risk and may be illiquid. Thus, when funds flow from surplus units to deficit units through a bank, the risk and liquidity of the financial instruments created along the way can be substantially altered. Of course, someone has to absorb the risk of the loans—either the bank's owners or the government entity that insures the bank's deposits.

The arrow pointing from the circle labeled *intermediaries* up to the circle labeled *markets* indicates that intermediaries often channel funds into the financial markets. For example, a middle-aged couple saving for retirement (surplus unit) may invest its savings in an insurance company account (intermediary), which then invests its funds in stocks and bonds (markets). Through the insurance company, the couple indirectly provides funds to the firms (deficit units) issuing the stocks and bonds.

[1]Funds that flow among members of a family or among different units of the same firm are not usually considered part of the flows in the financial system.

The arrow pointing from the *markets* circle down to the *intermediaries* circle indicates that in addition to channeling funds *into* the financial markets, some intermediaries obtain funds *from* the financial markets. A finance company that makes loans to households might, for instance, raise those funds by issuing stocks and bonds in the markets for those securities.

Quick Check 2-1

A depositor puts $5,000 into a bank account and you take a $5,000 student loan from the bank. Trace this flow of funds in Figure 2.1.

2.3 The Functional Perspective

For a variety of reasons—including differences in size, complexity, and available technology, as well as differences in political, cultural, and historical backgrounds—financial institutions generally differ across borders. They also change over time. Even when the names of institutions are the same, the functions they perform often differ dramatically. For example, banks in the United States today are very different from what they were in 1928 or in 1958, and banks in the United States today are very different from the institutions called banks in Germany or the United Kingdom today.

In this section we try our hand at setting forth a unifying conceptual framework for understanding how and why financial institutions differ across borders and change over time. The key element in the framework is its focus on *functions* rather than on *institutions* as the conceptual "anchor." Hence, we call it the *functional perspective.* It rests on two basic premises:

- Financial functions are more stable than financial institutions—that is, functions change less over time and vary less across borders.
- Institutional form follows function—that is, innovation and competition among institutions ultimately result in greater efficiency in the performance of financial system functions.

From the most aggregated level of the single primary function of efficient resource allocation, we distinguish six basic or core functions performed by the financial system:

- To provide ways to *transfer economic resources* through time, across borders, and among industries.
- To provide ways of *managing risk.*
- To provide ways of *clearing and settling payments* to facilitate trade.
- To provide a mechanism for the *pooling of resources* and for the *subdividing* of ownership in various enterprises.
- To provide *price information* to help coordinate decentralized decision making in various sectors of the economy.
- To provide ways of *dealing with the incentive problems* created when one party to a transaction has information that the other party does not or when one party acts as an agent for another.

The rest of this chapter explains these functions of the financial system and illustrates how the performance of each has changed over time.

2.3.1 Function 1: Transferring Resources across Time and Space

A financial system provides ways to transfer economic resources through time, across geographic regions, and among industries.

Many of the funds flows shown in Figure 2.1 involve giving up something now in order to get something in the future, or vice versa. Student loans, borrowing to buy a house, saving for retirement, and investing in production facilities are all actions that shift resources from one point in time to another. The financial system facilitates such *intertemporal* (literally, "between time") transfers of resources.

Without the opportunity to take out a student loan, for example, many young people whose families do not have the means to send them to college might have to forgo a higher education. Similarly, without the ability to raise venture capital from investors, many businesses might never get started.

In addition to facilitating the shifting of resources through time, the financial system plays an important role in shifting resources from one place to another. At times the capital resources available to perform an activity are located far from where they are most efficiently employed. Households in Germany, for example, may be generating capital through saving that could be more efficiently employed in Russia. The financial system provides a variety of mechanisms for facilitating the transfer of capital resources from Germany to Russia. One way is for German citizens to invest in shares issued by firms located in Russia. Another is for German banks to make loans to those firms.

The more complex the economy, the more important is the role of the financial system in providing an efficient means for shifting resources across time and place. Thus, in today's global financial system, a complex network of markets and intermediaries makes it possible for the retirement savings of Japanese workers to be used to finance the house purchased by a young couple in the United States.

Innovation that allows scarce resources to be shifted over time or place from a use with a relatively low benefit to a use offering a higher benefit improves efficiency. For example, suppose that all families were constrained to invest their savings only within the family. In that case, Family A could earn a rate of return of 2% per year on its savings, at the same time that Family B has opportunities to earn a rate of return of 20%. Efficiency is increased by creating an investment company to collect Family A's savings and lend them to Family B.

Quick Check 2-2

Give an example of a transfer of resources over time that takes place through the financial system. Is there a more efficient way for this transfer of resources to be handled?

2.3.2 Function 2: Managing Risk

A financial system provides ways to manage risk.

Just as funds are transferred through the financial system, so are risks. For example, insurance companies are financial intermediaries that specialize in the activity of risk transfer. They collect premiums from customers who want to reduce their risks and transfer it to investors who are willing to pay the claims and bear the risk in return for some reward.

Often funds and risks are "bundled" together and transferred simultaneously through the financial system so that the flow of *funds* illustrated in Figure 2.1 can also characterize the flow of *risks*. Let us illustrate with the example of business finance and the transfer of business risk.

Suppose you want to start a business and need $100,000 to do so. You have no savings of your own, so you are a deficit unit. Let us assume that you convince a private investor (a surplus unit) to provide you with $70,000 in equity capital in return for a 75% share of the profits of the business, and you convince a bank (a financial intermediary) to lend you the other $30,000 at an interest rate of 6% per year. In Figure 2.1 this flow of $100,000 would appear as a flow of funds from others to you.

But what about the risk of business failure?

In general, it is the equity investors who absorb the risk of business failure. Thus, if your business venture goes sour, the private investor may get none of his or her $70,000 back. However, the bank may also face some risk that it will not get all of its principal and interest. For example, suppose that at the end of a year, the business has a value of only $20,000. Then the equity investors lose all of their investment of $70,000, and the bank loses $10,000 of the $30,000 it has lent to you. *Thus, lenders share some of the business risk of the firm along with the equity investors.*

Although funds and risks often come bundled together, they can be "unbundled." For example, consider the $30,000 loan from the bank to your business. Suppose the bank requires that you get other members of your family to guarantee the loan. The bank thereby transfers the risk of default from itself to your relatives. The bank is now providing you with $30,000 in funds at minimal risk to itself, and the risk of the loan has been transferred to your relatives.

As we will see, many of the financial contracts that we observe in the world of finance serve to transfer risks without transferring funds. This is the case with most insurance contracts and guarantees, and it is also the case with derivatives, such as futures, swaps, and options.

Quick Check 2-3

Give an example of a transfer of risk that takes place through the financial system.

Box 2.1 The Return of the 30-Year Treasury

There are many ways to be over $7 trillion in debt. In early 2006 that was the approximate size of the U.S. government debt, although in the second-half of the 1990's and into 2001 the debt was actually falling. During that period the federal government's budget surplus prompted the Treasury's decision to stop issuing 30-year Treasury bonds in October of 2001. The vacation didn't last long: as the government quickly returned to fiscal deficits the 30-year bond was called back into service less than 5 years later.

The maturity structure of the government's debt can have interesting implications. On the one hand, long-term bonds allow the government to lock in a particular interest rate and avoid the costs associated with reissuing debt. With interest rates at historically low levels, and long-term rates only slightly higher than short-term rates, long-term borrowing has been particularly appealing in recent years.

On the other hand, the government's motivations interact with the needs of the private sector. Government debt competes with private debt for available funds. At the same time, Treasury bonds act as a liquid, risk-free benchmark to the bond market, aiding in the pricing of private-sector issues.

Certain investors, especially pension funds, may have benefited the most from the return of the 30-year Treasury. Pension funds had been holding two-third of their assets in equities. Since their liabilities, corresponding to the benefits they are obliged to pay retirees, are more closely aligned with long-term debt, pension funds can reduce their risk exposure by reallocated their asset portfolios to the new long-term bonds. The government is expected to encourage pension funds to do exactly that. Pension plans nationwide are estimated to be insolvent by nearly half a trillion dollars, a burden that could fall on the Pension Benefit Guaranty Corporation, a federal entity that insures pensions.

The size of the public debt matters, but its structure also has important implications for bond markets and the private sector.

Source: "Long Ranger," *The Economist*, February 2, 2006.

2.3.3 Function 3: Clearing and Settling Payments

A financial system provides ways of clearing and settling payments to facilitate the exchange of goods, services, and assets.

An important function of the financial system is to provide an efficient way for people and businesses to make payments to each other when they wish to buy goods or services. Suppose you live in the United States and are planning a trip around the world. You believe that $5,000 should be enough money to cover your expenses while traveling. In what form should you take the funds? How will you pay for things?

Some hotels, youth hostels, and restaurants will accept U.S. dollars as payment, but others will not. You might be able to pay for everything with a credit card, but some places you're interested in visiting might not accept a credit card. Should you buy traveler's checks? In what currencies should they be denominated? Contemplation of your trip perhaps leads you to think how convenient it would be if every seller in every country were willing to accept the same means of payment.

Imagine instead that you are a wealthy person living in a country whose government limits your access to foreign currency and that you want to travel around the world. Inside your country you can buy whatever you want using the local currency, but outside your country, no one will accept that currency as a means of payment. A shortage of foreign exchange causes your government to prohibit its citizens from purchasing foreign currency or borrowing abroad. What can you do?

One possibility is to buy transportable goods (such as furs or jewelry) in your home country, pack them all in a suitcase, and try to use them to pay for your food and lodging abroad. In other words, you could engage in *barter,* the process of exchanging goods without using money. Needless to say, this would not be a convenient way to see the world. You would need to bring vast amounts of luggage, and instead of enjoying the sights much of your time and energy would be spent in finding a hotel or restaurant that accepts furs or jewelry in exchange for a room or a meal.

As these examples suggest, an important function of the financial system is to provide an efficient payments system, so that households and businesses do not have to waste time and resources in implementing their purchases. The replacement of gold with paper currency as a means of payment is an example of a change that increases efficiency of the payments system. Gold is a scarce resource that is used in medicine and in the production of jewelry. Paper money serves as a superior means of payment. Compared with gold, paper currency is easier to verify (harder to counterfeit) and more convenient to carry around in one's pocket. It doesn't cost as much to make and print currency as it does to mine, refine, and mint gold. The subsequent development of checks, credit cards, and electronic-funds-transfer as alternative means of payment to paper currency has further increased efficiency.

Quick Check 2-4

Would you accept an IOU from me in payment for a good or service that I buy from you? What factors will determine the answer?

2.3.4 Function 4: Pooling Resources and Subdividing Shares

A financial system provides a mechanism for the pooling of funds to undertake large-scale indivisible enterprise or for the subdividing of shares in large enterprises with many owners.

In modern economies, the minimum investment required to run a business is often beyond the means of an individual or even a large family. The financial system provides a variety of mechanisms (such as the stock market or banks) to *pool* or *aggregate* the wealth of households into larger masses of capital for use by business firms.

From the investor's perspective, the financial system provides opportunities for individual households to participate in investments that require large lump sums of money by pooling their funds and then subdividing shares in the investment. For example, suppose you want to invest in a racehorse that costs $100,000, but you only have $10,000 to invest. If there were a way of physically dividing the racehorse into ten pieces, then you could buy one piece. However, in this case the whole is surely worth more than the sum of its parts. A physical splitting of the horse will not do the trick. The financial system solves the problem of how to divide the horse without destroying it. By creating an investment pool and distributing shares to the investors, the $100,000 investment can be divided into $10,000 economic "pieces" without actually cutting up the horse. Any money the horse earns in race winnings or stud fees would, after training and upkeep expenses are taken out, be divided among all the shareholders.

As another example, consider money market funds. Suppose you want to invest in the most secure and liquid dollar-denominated asset, U.S. Treasury bills (T-bills). The minimum denomination is $10,000, and you have only $1,000 to invest. Therefore, the only way you can invest in T-bills is by pooling resources with other investors. In the 1970s, mutual funds that hold U.S. T-bills were developed to facilitate this process.

In a mutual fund, investors' money is pooled, and they are given accounts representing their proportional shares in the fund. The mutual fund frequently posts the price of a share and allows its customers to add or withdraw money at almost any time in almost any amount. Thus, if the price of a share is now $11 and you invest $1,000, the fund will credit your account with 1,000/11, or 90.91 shares. U.S. T-bill mutual funds, thus, improve the performance of Function 4 by transforming large-denomination Treasury bills into almost infinitely divisible securities.

Quick Check 2-5

Give an example of an investment that would not be undertaken if it were not possible to pool the savings of many different households.

2.3.5 Function 5: Providing Information

A financial system provides price information that helps coordinate decentralized decision making in various sectors of the economy.

Every day, newspapers, radio, and television announce stock prices and interest rates. Of the millions of people who receive these news reports, relatively few actually buy and sell securities. Many of those who do not trade securities nevertheless use the information generated from security prices to make other types of decisions. In deciding how much of their current income to save and how to invest it, households make use of information about interest rates and security prices.

An example may help to illustrate how even within families the intertemporal transfer of resources is often facilitated by knowledge of market interest rates. Suppose that you are 30 years old, just got married, and want to buy a house for $100,000. Your local bank will make you a mortgage loan for $80,000 or 80% of the purchase price of the house at an interest rate of 8% per year, but you need to pay 20% down (i.e., $20,000). Your 45-year-old sister has an account at a savings bank with $20,000 in it—just enough for your down payment. She is saving the money for her retirement, which is far in the future, and is currently earning 6% per year. If your sister is willing to lend you her retirement savings for your down payment, how do you decide what a "fair" rate of interest is? Clearly, it is useful to know current market interest rates. You already know that your sister is earning 6% per year on her savings account and that your local bank will charge you 8% per year on the mortgage loan.

Similarly, knowledge of market prices of assets can be helpful for decision making within families. For example, suppose you and your sister inherit a house or a family business, and it is to be divided equally between you. You don't want to sell it because one of you wants to live in it or continue to operate it. How much should the other sibling receive? Clearly, it would be useful to know the market prices of similar assets to settle on a reasonable price for the inheritance.

Asset prices and interest rates provide critical signals to managers of firms in their selection of investment projects and financing arrangements. Managers of firms with no anticipated need to transact in the financial markets routinely use those markets to provide information for decisions.

For example, a firm earns $10 million in profits in a good year and is faced with deciding whether to reinvest it in the business, pay it out in cash dividends to shareholders, or use it to buy back its own shares. Knowledge of its own and other firm's share prices as well as market interest rates will surely help in deciding what to do.

Whenever a new financial instrument is introduced, new possibilities for information extraction are created as a by-product. For example, the development of trading standardized option contracts on exchanges since 1973 has greatly increased the amount of quantitative information available about the riskiness of economic and financial variables. This information is particularly useful in making risk-management decisions.

Quick Check 2-6

Give an example of a financial transaction that provides important information to parties not involved in the transaction.

2.3.6 Function 6: Dealing with Incentive Problems

A financial system provides ways to deal with the incentive problems when one party to a financial transaction has information that the other party does not, or when one party is an agent that makes decisions for another.

As we discussed, financial markets and intermediaries serve several functions that facilitate the efficient allocation of resources and risks. There are, however, incentive problems that limit their ability to perform some of those functions. Incentive problems arise because parties to contracts often cannot easily monitor or control one another. Incentive problems take a variety of forms—among them, moral hazard, adverse selection, and principal-agent problems.

The **moral hazard** problem exists when having insurance against some risk causes the insured party to take greater risk or to take less care in preventing the event that gives rise to the loss. Moral hazard can lead to unwillingness on the part of insurance companies to insure against certain types of risk. For example, if a warehouse owner buys fire insurance, the existence of the insurance reduces his incentive to spend money to prevent a fire. Failure to take the same precautions makes a warehouse fire a more likely occurrence. In an extreme case, the owner may be tempted to actually start a fire in order to collect the insurance money if the coverage exceeds the market value of the warehouse. Because of this potential moral hazard, insurance companies may limit the amount they will insure or simply refuse to sell fire insurance under certain circumstances.

An example of moral hazard in the realm of contracting is what might happen if I pay you in advance for a job, and you get the same amount of money no matter how good or bad a job you do. There is less of an incentive for you to work hard than would be the case if I pay you after the job is done.

A more subtle example of the moral hazard problem arises in financing business ventures. Suppose you have an idea for a new business venture, and you need startup capital. Where can you get it? The first source you may look to is family and friends. Why? Because you trust them, and they know and trust you. You know your secret plans are safe with them. On the other side, your family believes that you will fully disclose the information you have about the business opportunity, including all of the pitfalls. Moreover, if the business does not immediately prosper and the going gets rough, they know that you will work hard to protect their interests.

What about a bank as a source for the loan? You are perhaps a little uncomfortable about discussing the details of your business plans with the bank loan officer, who is a complete stranger. She might disclose your plans to another customer, who could be a competitor. But even if you can resolve your concerns about the bank, there is the other side. The loan officer is reluctant to lend you the money you want because she knows that you have no incentive to disclose the pitfalls in your plans unless you have to. Thus, there is an imbalance or *asymmetry* in the exchange of information about the business opportunity: You know more about it than the loan officer.

Moreover, the loan officer knows that she is a stranger to you and that the bank is just an impersonal institution to you. Therefore, if the going gets rough, you will not necessarily work as hard to turn it around as you would for your family and friends. Instead, you may decide to walk away from the business and not repay your loan. The reduced incentive for you to work hard when part of the risk of the enterprise has been transferred to an entity whose welfare you do not care much about (such as a bank or an insurance company) is, thus, an example of the problem of moral hazard.

Quick Check 2-7

Give an example of how the problem of moral hazard might prevent you from getting financing for something you want to do. Can you think of a way of overcoming the problem?

Another class of problems caused by asymmetric information is **adverse selection**—those who purchase insurance against risk are more likely than the general population to be at risk. For example, consider **life annuities,** which are contracts that pay a fixed amount of money each month for as long as the purchaser lives. A firm selling such annuities cannot assume that the people who buy them will have the same expected length of life as the general population.

For example, suppose a firm sells life annuities to people retiring at age 65. There are equal numbers of three types of people in the general population: type A live for 10 years, type B for 15 years, and type C for 20 years. On average, people aged 65 live for 15 years. If the firm charges a price that reflects a 15-year life expectancy, however, it will find that the people who buy the annuities are disproportionately of types B and C. Type A people will find that your annuities are not a good deal for them and will not purchase them.

If the annuity firm knew the type of each potential customer, A, B, or C, and could charge a price that reflected the true life expectancy for that type, then there would be no adverse selection problem. But the annuity firm cannot get enough information about customers to know as much about their individual life expectancies as they themselves do. Unless the insurer can charge a price that accurately reflects each person's true life expectancy, a disproportionately large number of the annuities sold will be bought by healthy people who expect to live a long time. In our example, the average life expectancy of buyers of annuities might be 17.5 years, which is 2.5 years longer than in the general population.

Therefore, if annuity firms used life expectancies of the general population to price their annuities without adding an amount to adjust for the adverse selection problem, they would all lose money. As a result, firms in this market charge a price for annuities that is relatively unattractive to people with an average life expectancy, and the market is much smaller than it would be if there were no problem of adverse selection.

Quick Check 2-8

Suppose a bank offered to make loans to potential borrowers without checking their credit history. What would be true of the types of borrowers they would attract compared to banks that did checks of credit history? Would such a bank charge the same interest rate on loans as banks that check credit history?

Another type of incentive problem arises when critical tasks are delegated to others. For example, shareholders in a corporation delegate the running of the firm to its managers, and investors in a mutual fund delegate the authority to select the mix of their security holdings to a portfolio manager. In each case, the individual or organization responsible for the risks associated with a set of decisions gives up or delegates the decision-making authority to another individual or organization. Those who bear the risks associated with the decisions are called the *principals,* and those who assume the decision-making authority are called the *agents.*

The **principal-agent problem** is that agents may not make the same decisions that the principals would have made if the principals knew what the agents know and were making the decisions themselves. There can be a conflict of interest between agents and principals. In extreme cases, agents may even act contrary to the interests of their principals, as when a stockbroker "churns" a client's account only in order to generate commissions for himself.

A well-functioning financial system facilitates the resolution of the problems that arise from all of these incentive problems—moral hazard, adverse selection, and principal-agent—so that the other benefits of the financial system, such as pooling, risk sharing, and specialization, can be achieved. For example, **collateralization** of loans, which means giving the lender the right to seize specific business assets in the event of default, is a widely used device for reducing the incentive problems associated with lending. Collateralization reduces the costs to the lender of monitoring the behavior of the borrower. The lender need only be concerned that the market value of the assets serving as collateral is sufficient to repay the principal and interest due on the loan. Over time, advances in technology have lowered the costs of tracking and valuing certain types of business assets that can serve as collateral—such as goods in inventory—and thereby broadened the range of situations in which collateralized loan agreements are feasible to implement.

Principal-agent problems can be alleviated by using the financial system, too. If the compensation of management depends on the performance of the market value of the firm's shares, the interests of managers and shareholders can be more closely aligned. For example, consider the introduction of "equity-kickers" in loan contracts to help limit possible conflicts of interest between the shareholders and creditors of corporations. An equity-kicker is any provision of the loan contract that allows the lender to share in the benefits

Box 2.2 Does Investor Activism Improve Corporate Efficiency?

A company's managers and its shareholders don't always share the same objectives. As the owners of a company, shareholders usually hope for a high rate of growth in corporate earnings, which can translate into higher share prices and dividends. Managers, on the other hand, may seek things like a high salary, prestige, and a generous bonus. These goals can conflict: For example, money spent on executive compensation is not available to be distributed to shareholders.

Recently, influential shareholders at hedge funds and similar investment firms have taken a renewed interest in corporate management. Two of the most prominent are Kirk Kerkorian and Carl Icahn. In February of 2006, Kerkorian helped convince General Motors to cut its dividend, reduce executive compensation, and take on a new board member. Icahn, meanwhile, proposed splitting Time Warner into four separate companies.

Activist investors can play an important role in improving corporate efficiency by introducing new ideas and by forcing managers to act in shareholders' best interest. However, evidence is mixed over whether investor activism is actually effective, and some openly oppose it. Activist investors may distract a company's managers and divert resources away from better uses to address the concerns of a few powerful investors. A company's managers may, after all, be in the best position to determine how a company should be run.

Although managers often face incentives that cause them to pursue objectives other than shareholder value, it is not clear that interference by activist investors improves company performance.

Source: "Busy Bodies," *The Economist,* February 10, 2006.

accruing to shareholders. One common equity-kicker is a percentage sharing in profits while the loan is outstanding. Another is the right of the lender to convert the loan amount into a prespecified number of shares of stock.

Management is elected by the firm's shareholders. Thus, in cases in which there is a conflict of interest between shareholders and creditors, management has an incentive to take actions that benefit shareholders at the expense of the firm's creditors. The resulting moral hazard problem could prevent an otherwise mutually advantageous loan agreement from taking place. By including an equity-kicker in the loan contract, this problem can be reduced or even eliminated, leaving both the shareholders of the firm and the firm's creditors better off.

Quick Check 2-9

If you get financial planning advice from your insurance agent, how does this give rise to a principal-agent problem? Can you think of a way of overcoming the problem?

2.4 Financial Innovation and the "Invisible Hand"

Generally, financial innovations are not planned by any central authority but arise from the individual actions of entrepreneurs and firms. The fundamental economic forces behind financial innovation are essentially the same as for innovation in general. As Adam Smith observed:

> Every individual endeavors to employ his capital so that its produce may be of greatest value. He generally neither intends to promote the public interest, nor knows how much he is promoting it. He intends only his own security, only his own gain. And

> he is in this led by an **invisible hand** to promote an end which was no part of his intention. By pursuing his own interest he frequently promotes that of society more effectually than when he really intends to promote it.[2]

To illustrate, compare the situation faced by a college graduate traveling around the world 40 years ago with the one faced by a college graduate undertaking such a journey today. Back then you had the constant worry that you would run out of money in some place where no one could speak your language. If you ran out, then you had to wire home and try to arrange a wire transfer of money from a bank back home to a local bank. The process was costly and time-consuming. Prearranged lines of credit were available only to the wealthiest travelers.

But now, you can pay for almost anything you buy almost anywhere with a credit card. VISA, MasterCard, American Express, and some others are accepted virtually everywhere on the globe. To pay your hotel bill, you simply give the clerk your card, and she slips it into a machine connected to the telephone. Within seconds, she has verified that your credit is good (i.e., that the bank that issued you the card will guarantee payment), and you need only sign the receipt and be on your way to your next destination.

Moreover, you need not worry about your money being lost or stolen. If you cannot find your credit card, you can go to any bank that is connected with your card's network. The bank will help you to cancel the missing card (so no one else can use it) and to get another. The bank will often lend you money in the meantime.

Clearly, world travel has become less costly and more convenient as a result of credit cards. Their invention and dissemination has made millions of people better off and contributed to the "democratization" of finance.

But how has this happened? Let us use the example of credit cards to trace the key factors in the development of a financial innovation.

Technology is an important factor. Credit cards depend on a complex network of telephones, computers, and other more sophisticated telecommunications and information processing hardware and software. But for credit cards to become an important part of the contemporary economic scene, financial service firms looking for profit opportunities had to employ the advanced technology in offering credit card services, and households and businesses had to buy them.

It is not uncommon in the history of innovations (financial or otherwise) that the firm that pioneers a commercially successful innovative idea is not the one to profit the most from it. And so it is here with the credit card. The first firm to offer credit cards to be used by global travelers was Diners Club, which was formed just after World War II. The initial success of Diners Club led two other firms, American Express and Carte Blanche, to offer similar credit card programs.

Firms in the credit card business earn their revenues from fees paid to them by retailers on credit card purchases (usually a percentage of the purchase price) and from interest paid on loans to credit card customers (on their unpaid balances). Major costs stem from transactions processing, stolen cards, and loan defaults by cardholders.

When commercial banks first tried to enter the credit card business in the 1950s, they found that they could not compete with the established firms because bank operating costs were too high. In the late 1960s, however, advances in computer technology lowered their costs to the point at which they could compete successfully. Today the two big bank networks, VISA and MasterCard, dominate the global credit card business. Diners Club and Carte Blanche account for only a modest share of the business.

---

[2]Adam Smith, *The Wealth of Nations* (Chicago: University of Chicago Press, 1977), p. 408.

Thus, competition among the major providers of credit cards keeps their cost comparatively low. For most people traveling today, it is not only more convenient but also less expensive to use a credit card when they travel than to use traveler's checks.

This last observation leads us to another basic point about financial innovation. Analysis of consumer preferences and the forces of competition among financial service providers helps one to make predictions about future changes in the financial system. For example, in light of the advantages of credit cards as a method of making payments, what prediction would you make about the future of traveler's checks? Are traveler's checks destined for the same fate as the slide rule after the invention of the handheld calculator?

Credit cards are only one of a wide array of new financial products developed over the past 40 years that have changed the way we carry on economic activities. Collectively, these innovations have greatly improved the opportunities for people to receive efficient risk-return trade-offs in their personal investments and more effective tailoring to their individual needs over the entire life cycle, including accumulation during the work years and distribution in retirement.

2.5 Financial Markets

The basic types of financial assets are *debt, equity,* and *derivatives.* Debt instruments are issued by anyone who borrows money—firms, governments, and households. The assets traded in debt markets, therefore, include corporate bonds, government bonds, residential and commercial mortgages, and consumer loans. Debt instruments are also called **fixed-income instruments** because they promise to pay fixed sums of cash in the future.

A different classification is by the *maturity* of the claims being traded. The market for short-term debt (less than one year) is called the **money market,** and the one for long-term debt and equity securities is called the **capital market.**

Money market instruments are mostly interest-earning securities issued by governments (such as U.S. Treasury bills) and secure private sector borrowers (such as commercial paper of large corporations). Money markets are today globally integrated and liquid in which **liquidity** is defined by the relative ease, cost, and speed with which an asset can be converted into cash.

Equity is the claim of the *owners* of a firm. Equity securities issued by corporations are called *common stocks* in the United States and *shares* in the United Kingdom. They are bought and sold in the *stock market.* Each share of common stock entitles its holder to an equal share in the ownership of the firm. In typical cases each share is entitled to the same amount of profits and is entitled to one vote on matters of corporate governance. However, some corporations issue two classes of common stock, one with voting rights and the other without.

Common stock represents a **residual claim** on the assets of a corporation. The owners of common stock are entitled to any assets of the firm left over after meeting all of the firm's other financial obligations. If, for example, the firm goes out of business and all of its assets are sold, then common stockholders receive what is left, if anything, after all of the various classes of creditors are paid what they are owed.

Common stock also has the feature of **limited liability.** This means that should the firm be liquidated and the proceeds from the sale of its assets not be sufficient to pay off all the firm's debts, the creditors cannot assess the common stockholders for more money to meet this shortfall. The claims of the creditors of the corporation are limited to the assets of the firm.

Derivatives are financial instruments that derive their value from the prices of one or more other assets such as equity securities, fixed-income securities, foreign currencies, or commodities. Their principal function is to serve as tools for managing exposures to the risks associated with the underlying assets.

Among the most common types of derivatives are *options* and *forward contracts.* A **call option** is an instrument that gives its holder the right to *buy* some asset at a specified price on or before some specified expiration date. A **put option** is an instrument that gives its holder the right to *sell* some asset at a specified price on or before some specified expiration date. When an owner of an asset buys a put option on that asset, he effectively is insuring it against a decline in its price below the price specified in the put-option contract.

Forward contracts are instruments that *oblige* one party to the contract to buy, and the other party to sell, some asset at a specified price on some specified date. They permit buyers and sellers of the asset to eliminate the uncertainty about the future price at which the asset will be exchanged.

Quick Check 2-10

What are the defining features of debt, equity, and derivative securities?

2.6 Financial Market Rates

Every day we are showered with newspaper, television, radio, and on-line computer reports of financial market indicators. These include interest rates, exchange rates, and indicators of stock market performance. In this section we explain the meaning of these rates.

2.6.1 Interest Rates

An interest rate is a *promised* rate of return, and there are as many different interest rates as there are distinct kinds of borrowing and lending. For example, the interest rate that home buyers pay on the loans they take to finance their homes is called the **mortgage rate,** whereas the rate charged by banks on loans made to businesses is called the **commercial loan rate.**

The interest rate on any type of loan or fixed-income instrument depends on a number of factors, but the three most important are its **unit of account,** its **maturity,** and its **default risk.** Let us define each of these factors.

- The *unit of account* is the medium in which payments are denominated. The unit of account is usually a currency, such as dollars, francs, pounds, euros, pesos, yen, and so on. Sometimes the unit of account is a commodity such as gold or silver or some standard "basket" of goods and services. The interest rate varies depending on the unit of account.
- The *maturity* of a fixed-income instrument is the length of time until repayment of the entire amount borrowed. The interest rate on short-term instruments can be higher, lower, or equal to the interest rate on long-term instruments.
- *Default risk* is the possibility that some portion of the interest or the principal on a fixed-income instrument will not be repaid in full. The greater the default risk, the higher the interest rate the issuer must promise to investors to get them to buy it.

Let us consider how each of these three factors affects interest rates in the real world.

EFFECT OF UNIT OF ACCOUNT

A fixed-income instrument is risk free only in terms of its own unit of account, and interest rates vary depending on the unit of account. To see this, consider bonds denominated in different currencies.

Suppose the interest rate on U.K. government bonds is much higher than on Japanese government bonds of comparable maturity. Because these bonds are all free of default risk, shouldn't all investors prefer the U.K. bonds?

The answer is no because the bonds are denominated in different currencies. The U.K. government bonds are denominated in pounds, and the Japanese government bonds are denominated in yen. *Although the bonds offer a risk-free rate of return in their own currency, the rate of return in any other currency is uncertain because it depends on the rate of exchange between the currencies when payments are received in the future.*

Let us illustrate with an example. Suppose you are investing for one year, and the interest rate on a one-year Japanese government bond is 3%, and at the same time it is 9% on a one-year U.K. government bond. The **exchange rate,** which is the price of one currency in terms of the other, is currently 150 yen to the pound.

Suppose you are a Japanese investor, who wants a safe investment in terms of yen. If you buy the Japanese bond, you will earn 3% for sure. If you buy the U.K. government bond, however, your rate of return in yen depends on the yen/pound exchange rate a year from now.

Suppose you invest £100 in a U.K. bond. To do so you will have to convert 15,000 yen into pounds, so your initial investment in yen is 15,000. Because the interest rate on the U.K. bond is 9%, you will receive £109 a year from now. The value of the £109 in yen is not known now because the future yen/pound exchange rate is unknown.

Your realized yen rate of return will be:

$$\text{Yen Rate of Return} = \frac{\left(\text{£}109 \times \text{Future Yen Price of the Pound}\left(\text{¥}/\text{£}\right)\right) - \text{¥}15{,}000}{\text{¥}15{,}000}$$

Suppose the yen price of the pound falls during the year, so that the yen/pound exchange rate is 140 yen to the pound a year from now. What will the realized yen rate of return on the U.K. bond be?

Substituting into the preceding expression we get:

$$\text{Yen Rate of Return} = \frac{\left(\text{£}109 \times 140\left(\text{¥}/\text{£}\right)\right) - \text{¥}15{,}000}{\text{¥}15{,}000} = 0.017333$$

Thus, your *realized* yen rate of return will be 1.73%, which is less than the 3% risk-free yen interest rate you could have earned on one-year Japanese bonds.

Quick Check 2-11

In the previous example, what does the change in the exchange rate have to be at year's end for the Japanese investor to earn exactly 3% per year on the investment in U.K. bonds?

EFFECT OF MATURITY

To illustrate the effect of maturity on interest rates consider Figure 2.2, which shows the U.S. Treasury **yield curve** on May 26, 2006. The yield curve depicts the relation between interest rates (yields) on fixed-income instruments issued by the U.S. Treasury and the maturity of the instrument at a given moment in time. In Figure 2.2 we see that the annualized yield on two-year Treasury obligations was about 4.95% per year and increased with maturity to about 5.15% per year on 30-year obligations. Although we do not see this in Figure 2.2, the shape and the level of the yield curve change significantly over time. At times in the past, short-term rates have been higher than long-term rates, so that the yield curve has been downward sloping.

Box 2.3 An Anomaly in the Bond Market may Signal a Recession

Asset prices incorporate people's expectations about the future. That's why, when the bond market displays an unusual pattern called an inverted yield curve, market observers begin to worry about what future event this may foreshadow. Most of the time the yield on long-term debt securities (like 10-year Treasury bonds) is higher than the yield on short-term securities (like 3-month Treasuries). An inverted yield curve refers to a situation in which long-term bonds have a lower yield than their short-term cousins. All of the economic recessions of the past half-century have been preceded by an inverted yield curve. Only once in that time period has an inverted yield curve not been followed by a recession. In early 2006, with 10-year Treasuries yielding only 0.4 percentage points more than bonds maturing in three months, market analysts speculated that the yield curve could invert, with a recession likely to come next.

But what is the linkage between an inverted yield curve and an economic recession? The answer is expectations. Long-term rates are, to a large extent, just a combination of current and future short-term rates. Imagine that you needed a loan today that you would not be able to pay back for ten years. You could issue a single ten-year bond with an interest rate of 7.5%. At the end of ten years, you pay back the principal and interest on the loan. Alternatively, you could issue a 5-year bond with an interest rate of 5%, and in five years you could issue another 5-year bond at a 10% interest rate. In this example, you are indifferent between the two options; your average interest rate is 7.5% either way. But what if you expected rates on 5-year bonds to be 15% five years from now? Then you (and any other borrower) should definitely issue a 10-year bond. Of course, if everyone is issuing 10-year bonds and avoiding series of 5-year bonds, the yield on 10-year bonds will rise, and the yield on 5-year bonds will fall, until all borrowers are indifferent between the two options. Looked at a different way, if long-term rates are not in line with reasonable expectations of future short-term rates, there is an opportunity for arbitrage. Money could be made by selling 10-year bonds and using the proceeds to invest in a series of 5-year bonds. This buying and selling will inevitably result in interest rates that are the same on average, regardless of the maturities of the bonds used.

The final piece of the puzzle? The Federal Reserve. In the United States, the Fed effectively decides short-term rates. An inverted yield curve therefore indicates that the market believes the Fed will lower rates in the future. If the Fed lowers rates, there's a good chance the U.S. economy is not growing very quickly. For the Fed to lower rates significantly (enough to overcome the usually upward-sloping yield curve), the United States is likely to be experiencing a recession. Ultimately it is people's expectations about the future that determine the shape of the yield curve.

Source: "The Long and the Short of It," *The Economist*, January 5, 2006.

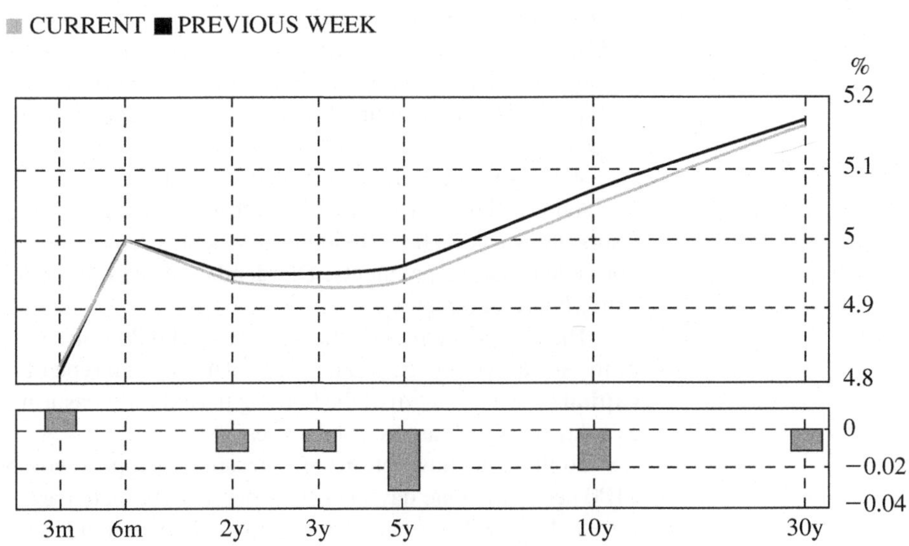

FIGURE 2.2

U.S. Treasury Yield Curve

Source: Bloomberg.com, May 26, 2006.

TABLE 2.1 **Yield Comparisons**

	Yields
Treasury 5-year	4.94
10-year	5.05
5-Year AAA Banking & Finance	5.58
10-Year AAA Banking & Finance	5.91

Source: Bloomberg.com, May 26, 2006.

Quick Check 2-12

Go on-line to Bloomberg.com and discover what the level and shape of the U.S. Treasury yield curve are. Do the same for the Japanese and German yield curves.

EFFECT OF DEFAULT RISK

The higher the default risk on fixed-income instruments, the higher the interest rate, holding all other features constant. Table 2.1 shows the interest rates on U.S.-dollar-denominated bonds for issuers with different degrees of default risk. U.S. Treasury bonds have the least default risk, followed by high-quality corporate bonds.

Consider the difference in yields—called the **yield spread**—between Treasury bonds with maturities of 10 years (10-yr)—5.05% per year and corporate bonds of high quality of the same maturity—5.91% per year. The yield spread is 0.86% per year.

Quick Check 2-13

Look on Bloomberg.com and discover what the yield spreads are between corporate bonds and U.S. Treasury bonds.

2.6.2 Rates of Return on Risky Assets

Interest rates are *promised* rates of return on fixed-income instruments that are a contractual obligation. However, many assets do not carry a promised rate of return. For example, if you invest in real estate, equity securities, or works of art, there is no promise of specified cash payments in the future. Let us now consider how to measure the rate of return on such risky assets.

When you invest in equity securities such as common stocks, the *return* comes from two sources. The first source is the cash dividends paid to the stockholder by the firm that issued the stocks. These dividend payments are not contractually required and, hence, are not called interest payments. Dividends are paid to stockholders at the discretion of the firm's board of directors.

The second source of return to the stockholder is any gain (or loss) in the market price of the stock over the period it is held. This second type of return is called a **capital gain** or **capital loss.** The length of the holding period for measuring returns on stock can be as short as a day or as long as several decades.

To illustrate how returns are measured, suppose you buy shares of stock at a price of $100 per share. One day later the price is $101 per share and you sell. Your *rate of return* for the day is 1%—a capital gain of $1 per share divided by the purchase price of $100.

Suppose you hold the stock for a year. At the end of the year, the stock pays a cash dividend of \$5 per share and the price of a share is \$105 just after the dividend is paid. The one-year rate of return, *r*, is:

$$r = \frac{\text{Ending Price of a Share} - \text{Beginning Price} + \text{Cash Dividend}}{\text{Beginning Price}}$$

In the example we have:

$$r = \frac{\$105 - \$100 + \$5}{\$100} = 0.10 \text{ or } 10\%$$

Note that we can present the *total* rate of return as the sum of the dividend income component and the price change component:

$$r = \frac{\text{Cash Dividend}}{\text{Beginning Price}} + \frac{\text{Ending Price of a Share} - \text{Beginning Price}}{\text{Beginning Price}}$$

$$r = \text{Dividend Income Component} + \text{Price Change Component}$$

$$r = 5\% + 5\% = 10\%$$

What if you decide *not* to sell your shares at the end of the year—how should we measure your rate of return?

The answer is that *you measure the rate of return exactly the same way whether or not you sell the stock.* The price appreciation of \$5 per share is as much a part of your return as is the \$5 dividend. That you choose to keep the stock rather than sell it does not alter the fact that you could convert it into \$105 of cash at the end of the year. Thus, whether you decide to realize your capital gain by selling the stock or to reinvest it (by not selling), your rate of return is 10%.[3]

Quick Check 2-14

You invest in a stock costing \$50. It pays a cash dividend during the year of \$1, and you expect its price to be \$60 at year's end. What is your expected rate of return? If the stock's price is actually \$40 at year's end, what is your realized rate of return?

2.6.3 Market Indexes and Market Indexing

It is useful for many purposes to have a measure of the overall level of stock prices. For example, people holding stocks might want an indicator of the current value of their investment, or they might want a benchmark against which to measure the performance of their own investment in stocks. Table 2.2 is a list of the stock indexes generally reported in the financial press for the stocks traded on the other major national stock exchanges around the world.

Indexing is an investment strategy that seeks to match the investment returns of a specified stock market index. Indexing is based on a simple truth: It is impossible for all stock investors in the aggregate to outperform the overall stock market. When indexing, an investment manager attempts to replicate the investment results of the target index by holding all—or in the case of very large indexes, a representative sample—of the securities in the index. There is no attempt to use "active" money management or to make "bets" on individual stocks or narrow industry sectors in an attempt to outpace the index. Thus, indexing is a passive investment strategy emphasizing broad diversification and low portfolio trading activity.

[3]This is only true of your *before-tax* rate of return. Because selling the stock can affect the income taxes you pay, your *after-tax* rate of return may be affected.

Box 2.4 A Slowing Housing Market Threatens to Become a Drag on the Economy

The housing boom that much of the world has experienced over the past several years may be coming to a close, and the consequences for GDP could be dire. Fueled by low interest rates, housing prices across the world have been increasing rapidly: between 1997 and 2005, average home prices in the United States increased 91%; in the United Kingdom, 167%; in Ireland, 212%; and in South Africa, an astounding 279%. As of early 2006, however, growth in prices had slowed considerably.

The housing boom has contributed significantly to GDP growth in the affected countries. Rising home prices can stimulate economic growth in at least two ways. First, homeowners are able to borrow against the value of their homes in the form of mortgages, home equity lines of credit, and so on. Second, increasing home prices make homeowners feel wealthier. Both of these cause consumers to spend more, and in the short run, spending can spur growth.

In the United States, diminished price growth, slowing sales of existing homes, and increasing housing inventories all point to a housing market that has peaked. Some analysts fear there may even be a housing "bubble," with prices that are up to 40% overvalued on average. If prices were to fall, the housing market's stimulating effect on GDP could be exactly reversed, leading to a period of slow growth or recession. Even if prices were to stagnate at current levels, the consequences for GDP could be severe. To prevent homeowners from losing money, housing prices have to increase to make up for transaction costs such as legal fees, real estate agents, and taxes, and foregone interest on the owner's down payment. Consumers losing money on their houses will have less to spend on other goods. A slowing housing market could seriously impede growth throughout the economy.

Source: "Soft Isn't Safe," *The Economist,* March 2, 2006.

Of course, there will always be actively managed funds that outperform index funds. It may just be luck—pure chance would say that some investment managers will provide exceptional returns and they may even have superior performance over lengthy "winning streaks." Or, it may be skill—there may be some investment managers with truly outstanding abilities who can earn superior returns over time. The problem in selecting actively managed funds is how to identify in advance those that will be consistently superior over time.

INDEXING'S COST ADVANTAGE

Since 1926, the U.S. stock market has provided investors with an average return of about 10% per year. That figure, however, is before costs. These costs come in the form of:

- The fund's expense ratio (including advisory fees, distribution charges, and operating expenses).
- Portfolio transaction costs (brokerage and other trading costs).

TABLE 2.2 **Major Stock Indexes Around the World**

Country	Indexes
United States	DJI, SP500
Japan	Nikkei, Topix
United Kingdom	FTSE-100, FTSE-ALL SHARE
Germany	DAX
France	CAC 40
Switzerland	SMI
Europe, Australia, Far East	MSCI, EAFE
China	Hang Seng

In 2005, the average general equity fund had an annual expense ratio of 1.54% (see Figure 2.3C on the following page) of investor assets. In addition, traditional mutual fund managers have high portfolio activity; the asset-weighted average fund's portfolio turnover rate was 47% (see Figure 2.3B below) in 2005. The trading costs of this portfolio turnover may be expected to subtract another 0.5% to 1% annually. Combined, fund expenses and transaction costs for the typical fund take a significant bite out of the investment-return pie. Funds charging sales commissions swallow even more of the returns.

By contrast, one of the key advantages of an index fund is its low cost. An index fund requires only minimal advisory fees, can keep operating expenses at the lowest level, and holds portfolio transaction costs to a minimum. Moreover, because index funds engage in much lower portfolio turnover than actively managed funds, there is a strong (but by no

FIGURE 2.3A

Stock Fund Operating Expense Ratios[1] (percent, 1990–2003)

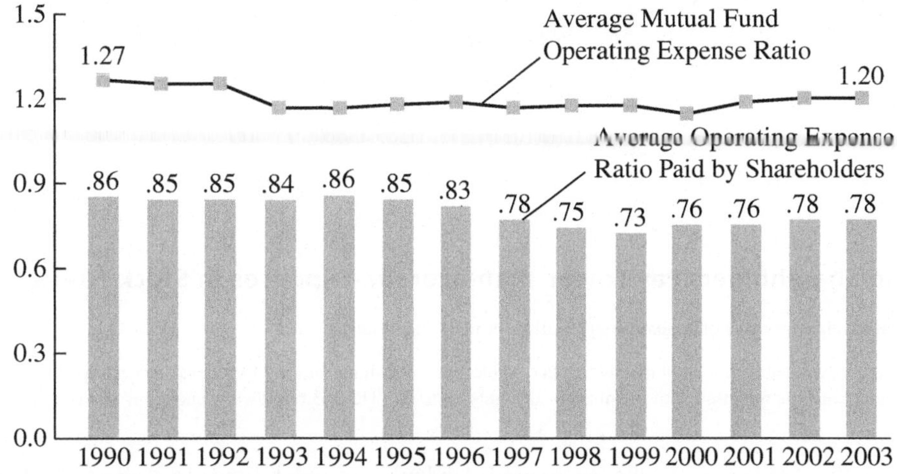

[1]Operating expense ratio is measured as the total expense ratio minus the 12b-1 fees. Download an Excel file of this data.

Sources: Investment Company Institute; Lipper; Value Line Publishing, Inc.; CDA/Wiesenberger Investment Companies Service; © CRSP University of Chicago, used with permission, all rights reserved (773.702.7467/www.crsp.com); Primary datasource & © Standard & Poor's Micropal, Inc. 1998 (617.451.1585/www.micropal.com); and Strategic Insight Mutual Fund Research and Consulting, LLC.

FIGURE 2.3B

Turnover Rate[1] Experienced by Stock Fund Investors Remains Low[2] (percent, 1971–2005)

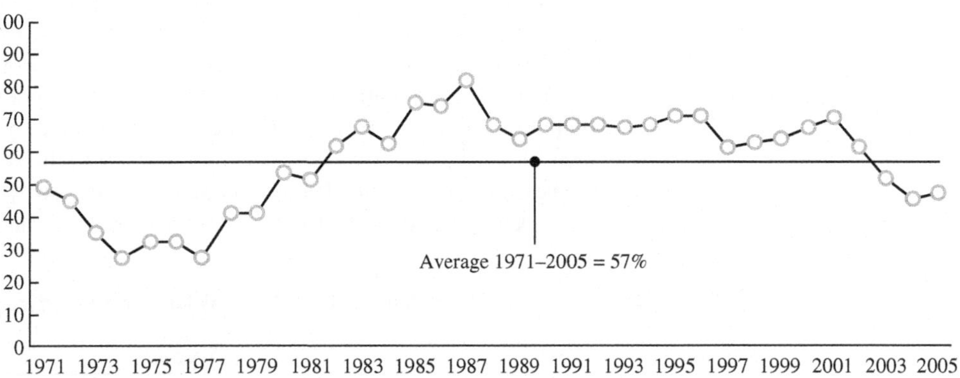

[1]asset-weighted average.
[2]excludes variable annuities.

Sources: Investment Company Institute; © CRSP University of Chicago, used with permission, all rights reserved (312.263.6400/www.crsp.com); and Strategic Insight Simfund.

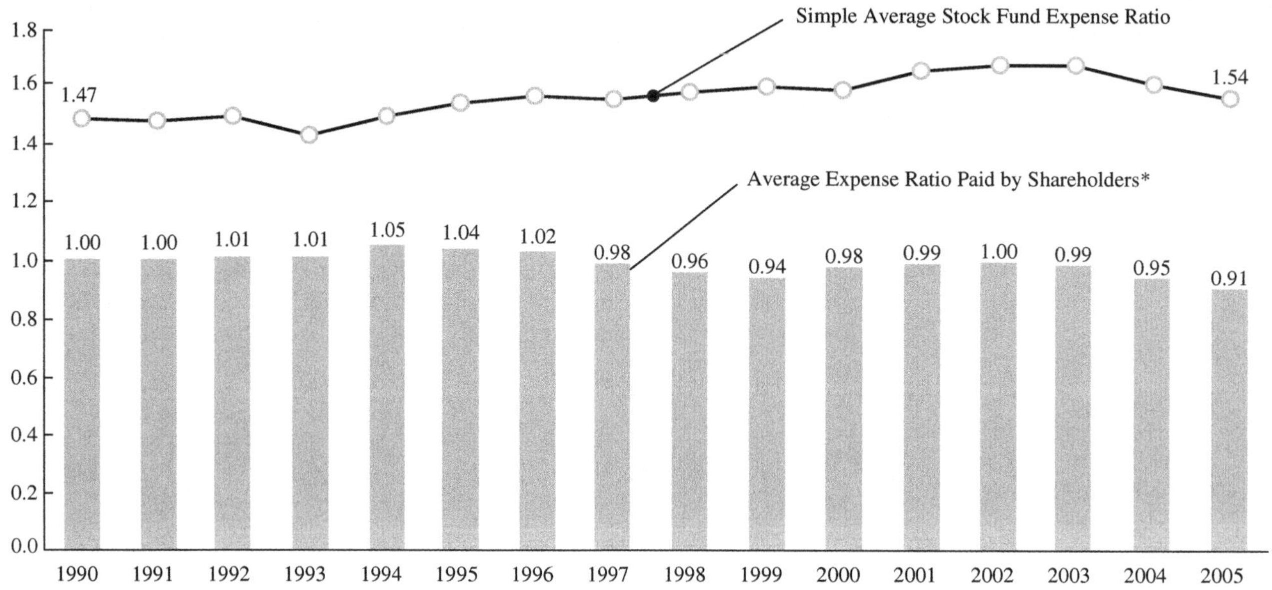

FIGURE 2.3C

Fund Shareholders Pay Lower-than-average-Expenses in Stock Funds (percent, 1990–2005)

*asset-weighted average of annual expense ratios for individual funds.

Sources: Investment Company Institute; Lipper; ValueLine Publishing, Inc.; CDA/Wiesenberger Investment Companies Service; © CRSP University of Chicago, used with permission, all rights reserved (312.263.6400/www.crsp.com); and Strategic Insight Simfund.

means assured) tendency for index funds to realize and distribute only modest—if any—capital gains to shareholders. Because these distributions are taxable for all shareholders, it is an advantage to defer their realization as long as possible.

Over time, the broad stock market indexes have outperformed the average general equity fund. Table 2.3 shows the total return (capital change plus income) of the Wilshire 5000 (a measure of the total U.S. stock market) versus equity funds.

These returns would need to be adjusted for fund expenses and portfolio transaction costs. With low expense ratios and minimal transactions costs associated with portfolio rebalancing, the index fund returns would be reduced by around 0.3% per year.

Table 2.4 shows rates of return on different asset classes around the world. Each rate of return is initially measured in its own currency unit. For example, Table 2.4 shows that stocks in the United States rose 0.8% on the S&P 500 index over the period from the end of 2005 until May 26, 2006, and in Canada they increased by about 1.3%. To compare performance across the two countries, one must convert to the same currency unit.

The Canadian stock market over the same period rose by 5.2% in dollar terms. Ignoring any cash dividends earned on stocks, this must have been associated with an increase in the value of

TABLE 2.3 **Annualized Total Return (ending May 26, 2006)**

	1-year	3-year	5-year
DJ-Wilshire 5000 Index	11.06%	15.01%	3.36%
Average U.S. Stock Funds	13.45%	15.75%	3.48%

Source: Morningstar.

TABLE 2.4 **Financial Market Indicators (May 27, 2006)**

Stock Market		% Change Since End of 2005		Interest Rates (% per year)		Currency Units (per $)	
Country	Index	Local Currency	$ Terms	Short Term 3-month	Long Term 10-year	Latest	Year Ago
Australia	All ordinaries	6.10	8.70	5.87	5.68	1.33	1.31
Britain	FTSE-100	−0.60	8.10	4.64	4.57	0.54	0.55
Canada	Toronto Composite	1.30	5.20	4.08	4.34	1.12	1.27
Denmark	OMXCB	−4.90	2.90	2.95	3.88	5.84	5.91
Japan	Nikkei 225	−1.30	3.40	0.10	1.85	113.00	108.00
Sweden	Affarsvarlden Gen	−0.70	8.30	2.12	3.71	7.29	7.29
Switzerland	Swiss Market	−1.40	6.70	1.41	2.68	1.22	1.23
U.S.	S&P 500	0.80	0.80	5.06	5.05	–	−0.79
Euro area	FTSE Euro 100	0.90	9.20	2.91	3.83	0.78	0.79

Source: *The Economist,* May 27, 2006.

the Canadian (C$) compared to the U.S. (US$) dollar. In fact, the final two columns of Table 2.4 show that over a year-long period running up to May 26, 2006, the C$ strengthened in terms of the US$: Only C$1.12 was needed to convert to a US$ as opposed to C$1.27 per US$ one year earlier. The significant increase in the C$ in early 2006 turned a small positive gain in the Canadian stock market into a significantly larger gain in terms of a US$-based rate of return.

Box 2.5 Financing a College Education

Lending to college students makes sense. A college education can be very expensive, and college students are often relatively poor. College graduates, on the other hand, have extensive opportunities to earn a good living. The problem is, you have to be a college student first in order to be a college graduate later. A student loan helps you borrow against your future earnings to pay for college now.

One of the biggest providers of college loans in the United States is Sallie Mae, which was recently bought by a conglomeration of two private equity firms and two banks for $25 billion. The deal itself is what's called a leveraged buy-out—the banks and private equity firms borrowed two-thirds of the purchase price to complete the deal.

Sallie Mae is in an unusual business because of a high level of government involvement. Because the federal government wants to encourage young people to pursue college educations, it subsidizes many student loans. The government may pay the interest on a loan while a student is still in school, offer loans at low rates, or provide a loan guarantee. A guarantee on a loan is a kind of insurance whereby the government promises to pay back the lender if a student defaults.

Sallie Mae attracted its new buyers because of its healthy cash flow and profitability. It has also made money outside of its core business by providing unsubsidized private loans, debt collection services, and funds for saving for college. However, there are considerable risks in the market for student loans. The government can alter its subsidies at any time: cutting interest rates, limiting eligibility, or guaranteeing fewer loans. New York's attorney general recently took an interest in Sallie Mae because of its alleged use of deceptive sales techniques, and the company was forced to pay a $2 million settlement. Because interest rates on government-subsidized loans are regulated, margins can be very thin. Worst of all, students often turn out to be irresponsible borrowers, amassing large debts that they are later unable to pay off.

Despite the many risks, Sallie Mae's new owners seem to agree that, overall, lending to college students makes sense.

Source: "Pay-Back Time," *The Economist,* April 17, 2007.

2.6.4 Rates of Return in Historical Perspective

Figures 2.4A and 2.4B, along with Tables 2.5A and 2.5B, present information about returns on several broad asset classes on a worldwide basis and within the United States. The data covers the period 1926–2003. Figure 2.4A gives a graphic presentation of the data contained in Table 2.5A representing the total returns generated over time by investing in the asset categories. Note that the vertical axis is plotted using a log scale that has the property that a time series with a constant annual rate of growth will plot as a straight line. At any point in time we can think about the indices values as representing the cumulative value of $1 invested initially invested in 1926. For example, $1 initially invested at the beginning of 1926 in a diversified portfolio of large U.S. company equities would have grown to approximately $12.09 at the beginning of 1955. The same $1 in 1926 would have grown to $12.00 by the beginning of 1952 if the portfolio had been comprised of small U.S. company equities.

Table 2.5B and Figure 2.4B convert the total return indices into annual rates of returns and allow us to examine the relative volatilities of these annual returns across alternative asset classes. In the U.S. equity category we have divided equity portfolios between companies with large and small values of market capitalization. We have plotted the time series on the same set of axes. Clearly, small stocks have the most volatile series.

The next-to-last column of Table 2.5B shows the one-year rates of return on a policy of rolling over 30-day Treasury bills as they mature. As this rate changes from month to month, it is riskless only for a 30-day holding period. The column labeled Long-Term T-Bonds presents the annual rates of return an investor would have earned by investing in U.S. Treasury bonds with 20-year maturities. The last column gives the annual inflation rates as measured by the rate of change in the consumer price index.

On the final page of the table are several descriptive statistics. The arithmetic and geometric averages of the annual returns are calculated. For T-bills, the arithmetic average is 3.79%; for T-bonds, 5.64%; and for large common stock, 12.25%. These numbers imply an average risk premium (the average rate of return less the average risk-free rate of 3.79%) of 1.85% per year on T-bonds and 8.46% on large stocks.

Another statistic reported at the bottom of Table 2.5B is the standard deviation. The higher the standard deviation, the higher the volatility of the rate of return. The standard deviation of large stock returns has been 20.50%, compared to 8.19% for T-bonds, and 3.18% for T-bills.

The other summary measures in Table 2.5B are the highest and lowest annual rate of return (the range) for each asset over the 78-year period. The size of this range is another possible measure of the relative riskiness of each asset class. It too confirms the ranking of stocks as the riskiest and bills as the least risky of the three asset classes.

Table 2.5B reports on the annual returns on two global portfolios. The World Portfolio of stocks is a diversified portfolio of equities of companies with large capital market valuations coming from 16 developed economies including those of Japanese, European, and American companies. Up until 1986, index weights were proportional to countries' GDP, measured in U.S. dollars. Since 1987 the index weights have been shifted to be proportional to the U.S. dollar–based market valuations of the countries' aggregate equity markets.

The World Portfolio of bonds uses the same 16 countries as for the stock portfolio and includes the countries' long-term government bonds as instruments. We see in the summary statistics of Table 2.5B that the World Equity Index annual returns have a lower average and standard deviation than the U.S. large company equity index with corresponding values of 11.17% versus 12.25% for the average annual returns, and 18.38% versus 20.50% for the standard deviations of the returns. In the long-term bond comparisons the World

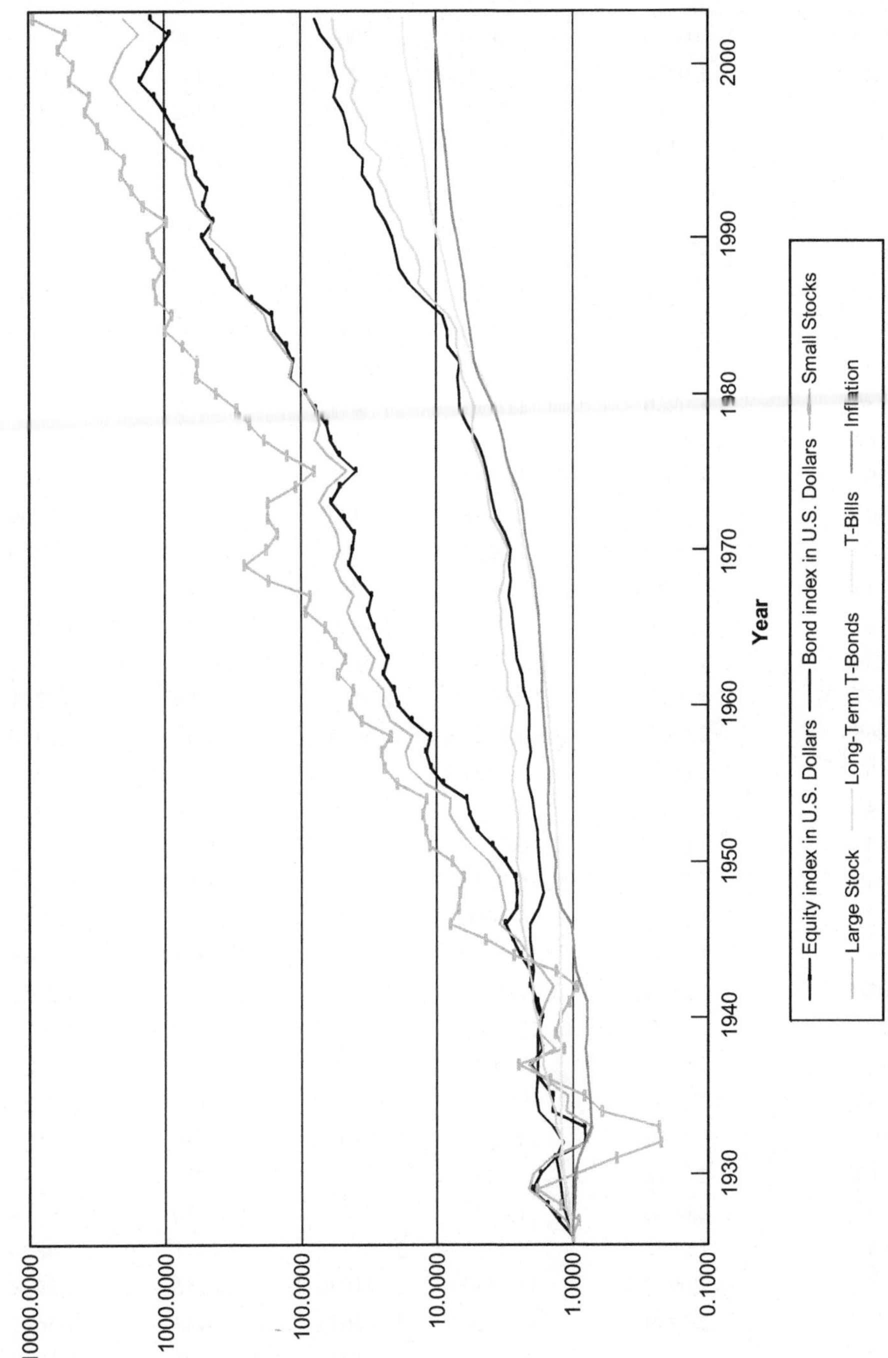

FIGURE 2.4A

Total Return Indices (1926–2004)

TABLE 2.5A Total Return Indices, 1926–2004 (beginning of the year)

	World Portfolio		U.S. Market					
Year	Equity index in U.S. Dollars	Bond index in U.S. Dollars	Small Stocks	Large Stock	Long-Term T-Bonds	T-Bills	Inflation
1926	1.0000	1.0000	1.0000	1.0000	1.0000	1.0000	1.0000
1927	1.2524	1.0776	0.9109	1.1221	1.0454	1.0319	0.9888
1928	1.5423	1.1819	1.2218	1.5259	1.1302	1.0641	0.9665
1929	1.9837	1.2100	1.8367	2.1255	1.1197	1.1047	0.9552
1930	1.7346	1.2513	0.9457	1.9627	1.1690	1.1571	0.9608
1931	1.3426	1.3271	0.4820	1.4543	1.2418	1.1843	0.8993
1932	0.8063	1.1650	0.2257	0.7917	1.1758	1.1964	0.8155
1933	0.8181	1.3794	0.2338	0.7194	1.3156	1.2061	0.7317
1934	1.3974	1.7833	0.6140	1.1119	1.3292	1.2096	0.7373
1935	1.3995	1.8536	0.8228	1.0861	1.4641	1.2114	0.7485
1936	1.7136	1.8250	1.4623	1.5821	1.5370	1.2134	0.7709
1937	2.0364	1.8166	2.5340	2.1129	1.6372	1.2155	0.7821
1938	1.6760	1.8036	1.1616	1.3516	1.6443	1.2194	0.8044
1939	1.7801	1.8093	1.3312	1.7493	1.7306	1.2199	0.7821
1940	1.6804	1.7176	1.2307	1.7307	1.8327	1.2200	0.7821
1941	1.8143	1.9081	1.0615	1.5637	1.9525	1.2193	0.7876
1942	2.0549	2.0128	0.9323	1.3886	1.9719	1.2198	0.8658
1943	2.0434	1.9376	1.3194	1.6774	2.0782	1.2229	0.9440
1944	2.4377	1.9947	2.7356	2.1226	2.1794	1.2271	0.9719
1945	2.7666	2.0532	4.3821	2.5674	2.2576	1.2310	0.9943
1946	3.1462	2.0558	7.9339	3.4946	2.4120	1.2350	1.0167
1947	2.6141	1.7826	6.8993	3.1710	2.4156	1.2393	1.2010
1948	2.5856	1.6354	6.7537	3.3257	2.3869	1.2450	1.3072
1949	2.6648	1.7198	6.3276	3.5016	2.4602	1.2572	1.3462
1950	3.1271	1.7574	7.6696	4.1403	2.6085	1.2711	1.3184
1951	3.8914	1.8006	11.2598	5.4934	2.5835	1.2865	1.3966
1952	5.0078	1.8104	11.9917	6.7827	2.5331	1.3056	1.4804
1953	5.7194	1.8976	12.5709	8.0653	2.5820	1.3270	1.4915
1954	6.0265	1.9671	11.8631	7.9250	2.6809	1.3506	1.5026
1955	8.9313	2.1205	19.4105	12.0895	2.8117	1.3622	1.4915
1956	10.9802	2.1254	24.0826	15.8905	2.7740	1.3835	1.4970
1957	11.9267	2.0338	25.3228	16.9154	2.6320	1.4169	1.5418
1958	11.1085	2.0954	21.6687	15.0310	2.8810	1.4613	1.5865
1959	15.1942	2.0860	35.8271	21.6116	2.7741	1.4820	1.6144
1960	18.9867	2.0952	43.4439	24.4103	2.6756	1.5238	1.6424
1961	20.4506	2.3149	41.2326	24.4567	3.0443	1.5631	1.6647
1962	24.5121	2.3608	53.1736	31.2141	3.0501	1.5969	1.6759
1963	22.7472	2.5879	47.1756	28.4703	3.2578	1.6403	1.6981
1964	26.0114	2.6593	55.7238	34.9132	3.2419	1.6920	1.7260
1965	28.8857	2.7441	66.4562	40.7332	3.3881	1.7516	1.7427

TABLE 2.5A **Continued**

	World Portfolio		U.S. Market				
Year	Equity index in U.S. Dollars	Bond index in U.S. Dollars	Small Stocks	Large Stock	Long-Term T-Bonds	T-Bills	Inflation
1966	31.9158	2.8224	92.4473	45.8249	3.3789	1.8211	1.7762
1967	29.8508	2.9739	86.0407	41.1278	3.5039	1.9069	1.8377
1968	36.9404	2.8752	174.9379	51.0437	3.2443	1.9860	1.8935
1969	44.2989	2.9356	262.8792	56.6585	3.2054	2.0911	1.9829
1970	41.5480	2.8672	180.6506	51.9389	2.9964	2.2289	2.1058
1971	40.3265	3.1479	149.1993	54.0684	3.3766	2.3711	2.2231
1972	48.0772	3.6207	175.9060	61.7299	3.9665	2.4735	2.2958
1973	60.2071	3.9067	176.2930	73.5449	4.1867	2.5697	2.3741
1974	51.5614	4.0747	109.1606	62.6971	4.2453	2.7512	2.5809
1975	39.1815	4.2813	79.5017	46.1450	4.4800	2.9734	2.8994
1976	51.6568	4.6024	126.2646	63.3387	4.8608	3.1465	3.1006
1977	60.3145	5.1192	187.8059	78.5273	5.3989	3.3089	3.2513
1978	64.1928	5.9470	239.3399	72.8262	5.4475	3.4793	3.4691
1979	77.7631	6.7540	298.0978	77.5599	5.2209	3.7336	3.7820
1980	91.7760	6.7837	419.8707	92.1179	5.6918	4.1327	4.2847
1981	119.7035	6.9764	588.1549	122.0378	6.4414	4.6088	4.8211
1982	114.6999	6.7189	579.2738	115.9603	6.6740	5.2937	5.2512
1983	127.6151	8.2079	740.6015	141.5760	7.1091	5.8580	5.4523
1984	158.0640	8.3474	993.2948	173.2465	7.0714	6.3764	5.6589
1985	163.3592	8.9768	891.8794	184.4382	8.1527	7.0115	5.8824
1986	229.3073	12.0477	1151.1487	243.4585	10.8169	7.5500	6.1060
1987	317.7740	15.7416	1195.8133	288.2549	13.4087	8.0075	6.1731
1988	369.2216	18.6931	1029.1169	303.6477	13.0534	8.4383	6.4466
1989	449.8965	19.6558	1220.6356	354.8427	14.1498	8.9716	6.7316
1990	535.1519	20.9177	1331.1031	466.0503	16.9076	9.7091	7.0446
1991	440.6441	23.4237	968.9100	451.1367	18.1132	10.4548	7.4750
1992	524.0580	27.7828	1441.3504	589.4553	21.4442	11.0308	7.7037
1993	491.2520	29.0914	1745.4754	634.9023	23.1147	11.4059	7.9271
1994	592.0078	34.9736	2078.5121	697.5671	26.6928	11.7366	8.1451
1995	631.4947	34.3861	1967.1038	706.5657	24.7763	12.1920	8.3626
1996	761.3300	43.5362	2630.8047	973.0117	32.6229	12.8723	8.5750
1997	854.2123	45.1297	3067.7813	1197.4855	32.3587	13.5340	8.8597
1998	990.6300	48.2301	3799.7540	1594.6914	37.2384	14.2215	9.0103
1999	1194.2045	56.5835	3524.6518	2050.4542	42.2730	14.9013	9.1554
2000	1517.8339	53.4148	4939.7995	2481.8697	38.5783	15.5808	9.4008
2001	1318.9976	57.8483	4651.8092	2256.0196	46.3982	16.4829	9.7194
2002	1110.3322	57.6400	5993.8561	1987.7789	48.3515	17.0961	9.8701
2003	921.3537	70.6897	5297.9694	1548.4797	56.4698	17.3799	10.1050
2004	1269.2568	78.7695	9248.6652	1992.7386	57.8137	17.5554	10.2950

TABLE 2.5B **Annual Rates of Return, 1926–2003 (over the year)**

	World Portfolio		U.S. Market				
Year	Equity Return in U.S. Dollars	Bond Return in U.S. Dollars	Small Stocks	Large Stock	Long-Term T-Bonds	T-Bills	Inflation
1926	25.24	7.76	−8.91	12.21	4.54	3.19	−1.12
1927	23.15	9.68	34.13	35.99	8.11	3.12	−2.26
1928	28.62	2.38	50.33	39.29	−0.93	3.82	−1.16
1929	−12.56	3.41	−48.51	−7.66	4.41	4.74	0.58
1930	−22.6	6.06	−49.03	−25.90	6.22	2.35	−6.40
1931	39.94	−12.22	−53.18	−45.56	−5.31	1.02	−9.32
1932	1.46	18.41	3.58	−9.14	11.89	0.81	−10.27
1933	70.81	29.28	162.67	54.56	1.03	0.29	0.76
1934	0.15	3.94	34.00	−2.32	10.15	0.15	1.52
1935	22.44	−1.54	77.72	45.67	4.98	0.17	2.99
1936	18.84	−0.46	73.29	33.55	6.52	0.17	1.45
1937	−17.7	−0.72	−54.16	−36.03	0.43	0.32	2.86
1938	6.21	0.32	14.60	29.42	5.25	0.04	−2.78
1939	−5.6	−5.07	−7.55	−1.06	5.90	0.01	0.00
1940	7.97	11.09	−13.75	−9.65	6.54	−0.06	0.71
1941	13.26	5.49	−12.17	−11.20	0.99	0.04	9.93
1942	−0.56	−3.74	41.52	20.80	5.39	0.26	9.03
1943	19.3	2.95	107.34	26.54	4.87	0.34	2.96
1944	13.49	2.93	60.19	20.96	3.59	0.32	2.30
1945	13.72	0.13	81.05	36.11	6.84	0.32	2.25
1946	−16.91	−13.29	−13.04	−9.26	0.15	0.35	18.13
1947	−1.09	−8.26	−2.11	4.88	−1.19	0.46	8.84
1948	3.06	5.16	−6.31	5.29	3.07	0.98	2.99
1949	17.35	2.19	21.21	18.24	6.03	1.11	−2.07
1950	24.44	2.46	46.81	32.68	−0.96	1.21	5.93
1951	28.69	0.54	6.50	23.47	−1.95	1.48	6.00
1952	14.21	4.82	4.83	18.91	1.93	1.64	0.75
1953	5.37	3.66	−5.63	−1.74	3.83	1.78	0.75
1954	48.2	7.8	63.62	52.55	4.88	0.86	−0.74
1955	22.94	0.23	24.07	31.44	−1.34	1.56	0.37
1956	8.62	−4.31	5.15	6.45	−5.12	2.42	2.99
1957	−6.86	3.03	−14.43	−11.14	9.46	3.13	2.90
1958	36.78	−0.45	65.34	43.78	−3.71	1.42	1.76
1959	24.96	0.44	21.26	12.95	−3.55	2.82	1.73
1960	7.71	10.49	−5.09	0.19	13.78	2.58	1.36
1961	19.86	1.98	28.96	27.63	0.19	2.16	0.67
1962	−7.2	9.62	−11.28	−8.79	6.81	2.72	1.33
1963	14.35	2.76	18.12	22.63	−0.49	3.15	1.64
1964	11.05	3.19	19.26	16.67	4.51	3.52	0.97
1965	10.49	2.85	39.11	12.50	−0.27	3.97	1.92

TABLE 2.5B **Continued**

Year	World Portfolio: Equity Return in U.S. Dollars	World Portfolio: Bond Return in U.S. Dollars	U.S. Market: Small Stocks	U.S. Market: Large Stock	U.S. Market: Long-Term T-Bonds	U.S. Market: T-Bills	U.S. Market: Inflation
1966	-6.47	5.37	-6.93	-10.25	3.70	4.71	3.46
1967	23.75	-3.32	103.32	24.11	-7.41	4.15	3.04
1968	19.92	2.1	50.27	11.00	-1.20	5.29	4.72
1969	-6.21	-2.33	-31.28	-8.33	-6.52	6.59	6.20
1970	-2.94	9.79	-17.41	4.10	12.69	6.38	5.57
1971	19.22	15.02	17.90	14.17	17.47	4.32	3.27
1972	25.23	7.9	0.22	19.14	5.55	3.89	3.41
1973	-14.36	4.3	-38.08	-14.75	1.40	7.06	8.71
1974	-24.01	5.07	-27.17	-26.40	5.53	8.08	12.34
1975	31.84	7.5	58.82	37.26	8.50	5.82	6.94
1976	16.76	11.23	48.74	23.98	11.07	5.16	4.86
1977	6.43	16.17	27.44	-7.26	0.90	5.15	6.70
1978	21.14	13.57	24.55	6.50	-4.16	7.31	9.02
1979	18.02	0.44	40.85	18.77	9.02	10.69	13.29
1980	30.43	2.84	40.08	32.48	13.17	11.52	12.52
1981	-4.18	-3.69	-1.51	-4.98	3.61	14.86	8.92
1982	11.26	22.16	27.85	22.09	6.52	10.66	3.83
1983	23.86	1.7	34.12	22.37	-0.53	8.85	3.79
1984	3.35	7.54	-10.21	6.46	15.29	9.96	3.95
1985	40.37	34.21	29.07	32.00	32.68	7.68	3.80
1986	38.58	30.66	3.88	18.40	23.96	6.06	1.10
1987	16.19	18.75	-13.94	5.34	-2.65	5.38	4.43
1988	21.85	5.15	18.61	16.86	8.40	6.32	4.42
1989	18.95	6.42	9.05	31.34	19.49	8.22	4.65
1990	-17.66	11.98	-27.21	-3.20	7.13	7.68	6.11
1991	18.93	18.61	48.76	30.66	18.39	5.51	3.06
1992	-6.26	4.71	21.10	7.71	7.79	3.40	2.90
1993	20.51	20.22	19.08	9.87	15.48	2.90	2.75
1994	6.67	-1.68	-5.36	1.29	-7.18	3.88	2.67
1995	20.56	26.61	33.74	37.71	31.67	5.58	2.54
1996	12.2	3.66	16.61	23.07	-0.81	5.14	3.32
1997	15.97	6.87	23.86	33.17	15.08	5.08	1.70
1998	20.55	17.32	-7.24	28.58	13.52	4.78	1.61
1999	27.1	-5.6	40.15	21.04	-8.74	4.56	2.68
2000	-13.1	8.3	-5.83	-9.10	20.27	5.79	3.39
2001	-15.82	-0.36	28.85	-11.89	4.21	3.72	1.55
2002	-17.02	22.64	-11.61	-22.10	16.79	1.66	2.38
2003	37.76	11.43	74.57	28.69	2.38	1.01	1.88

(Continued)

TABLE 2.5B **Continued**

	World Portfolio		U.S. Market				
	Equity Return in U.S. Dollars	Bond Return in U.S. Dollars	Small Stocks	Large Stock	Long-Term T-Bonds	T-Bills	Inflation
Rate of Return Statistics							
Geometric Average	9.41	5.34	11.80	10.23	5.10	3.71	2.98
Arithmetic Average	11.17	6.13	18.43	12.25	5.64	3.79	3.12
Standard Deviation	18.38	9.14	38.11	20.50	8.19	3.18	4.35
Minimum	−39.94	−13.29	−54.16	−45.56	−8.74	−0.06	−10.27
Maximum	70.81	34.21	162.67	54.56	32.68	14.86	18.13
Excess Return Statistics							
Average	7.37	2.34	14.64	8.46	1.85		
Standard Deviation	18.69	8.98	38.72	20.80	8.00		
Minimum	−41.02	−18.40	−54.48	−46.58	−13.30		
Maximum	70.51	28.99	162.38	54.27	26.09		

Sources:
Inflation data: Bureau of Labor Statistics.
Security return data for 1926–1995: Center for Research in Security Prices.
Security return data since 1996: Returns on appropriate index portfolios:
Large stocks: S&P 500
Small stocks: Fama & French 1st quantile
LT Government bonds: Lehman Bros. LT Treasury index.
ST Government bonds: Lehman Bros. Intermediate term Treasury index.
T-bills: Salomon Smith Barney 3-month U.S. T-bill index.

Portfolio of bonds has both a higher average annual return, at 6.13% versus 5.64% for U.S. T-bonds, and a higher standard deviation of returns, at 9.14% versus 8.19% for U.S. T-bonds.

2.6.5 Inflation and Real Interest Rates

People have long recognized that the prices of goods, services, and assets must be corrected for the effects of inflation in order to make meaningful economic comparisons over time. To correct for the effects of inflation, economists distinguish between what they call **nominal prices,** or prices in terms of some currency, and **real prices,** or prices in terms of purchasing power over goods and services.

Just as we distinguish between nominal and real prices, so too we distinguish between *nominal* and *real* interest rates. The **nominal interest rate** on a bond is the promised amount of money you receive per unit you lend. The **real rate of return** is defined as the nominal interest rate you earn corrected for the change in the purchasing power of money. For

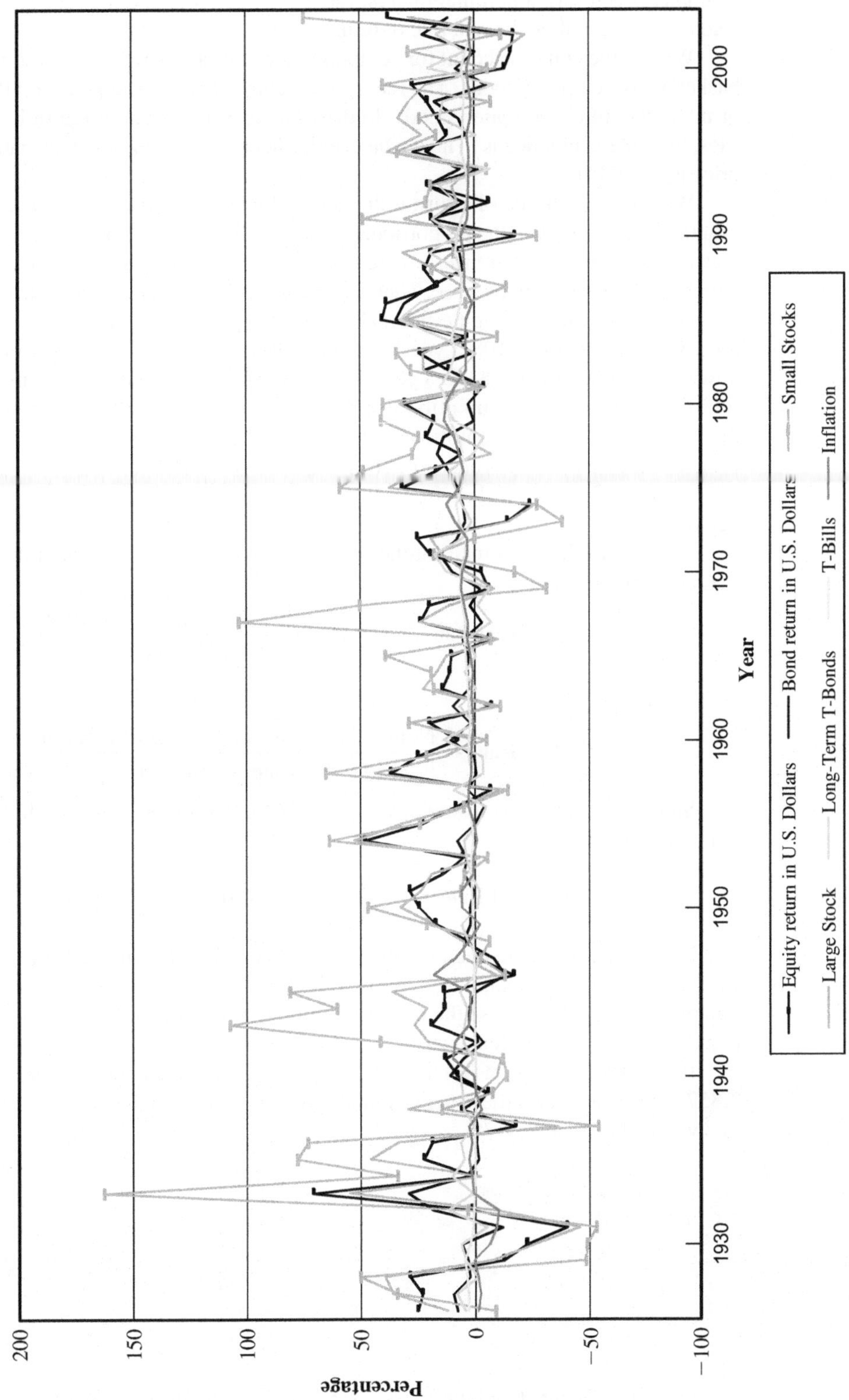

FIGURE 2.4B

Annual Returns (1926–2003)

example, if you earn a nominal interest rate of 8% per year and the rate of price inflation is also 8% per year, then the real rate of return is zero.

What is the unit of account for computing the real rate of return? It is some standardized basket of consumption goods. The real rate of return, therefore, depends on the composition of the basket of consumption goods. In discussions of real rates of return in different countries, the general practice is to take whatever basket is used to compute the national consumer price index (CPI).

What is the real rate of return if the nominal interest rate is 8% per year, and the rate of inflation as measured by the proportional change in the CPI is 5% per year? Intuition suggests that it is simply the difference between the nominal interest rate and the rate of inflation, which is 3% per year in this case. That is approximately correct, but not exactly so.

To see why, let's compute the real rate of return precisely. For every \$100 you invest now, you will receive \$108 a year from now. But a basket of consumption goods, which now costs \$100, will cost \$105 a year from now. How much will your future value of \$108 be worth in terms of consumption goods? To find the answer we must divide the \$108 by the future price of a consumption basket: \$108/\$105 = 1.02857 baskets. Thus, for every basket you give up now, you will get the equivalent of 1.02857 baskets a year from now. The real rate of return (baskets in the future per basket invested today) is, therefore, 2.857% per year.

The general formula relating the real rate of return to the nominal rate of interest and the rate of inflation is:

$$1 + \text{Real Rate of Return} = \frac{1 + \text{Nominal Interest Rate}}{1 + \text{Rate of Inflation}}$$

or equivalently,

$$\text{Real Rate} = \frac{\text{Nominal Interest Rate} - \text{Rate of Inflation}}{1 + \text{Rate of Inflation}}$$

Substituting into this formula, we can confirm that in our example the real rate works out to be 2.857% per year:

$$\text{Real Rate} = \frac{0.08 - 0.05}{1.05} = 0.02857 = 2.857\%$$

Note that a fixed-income instrument that is risk free in nominal terms will not be risk free in real terms. For example, suppose a bank offers depositors a risk-free dollar interest rate of 8% per year. Because the rate of inflation is not known with certainty in advance, the bank account is risky in real terms.

If the expected rate of inflation is 5% per year, then the expected real rate of return is 2.857% per year. But if the rate of inflation turns out to be higher than 5%, the realized real rate will be less than 2.857%.

Quick Check 2-15

Suppose the risk-free nominal interest rate on a one-year U.S. Treasury bill is 6% per year and the expected rate of inflation is 3% per year. What is the expected real rate of return on the T-bill? Why is the T-bill risky in real terms?

To protect against inflation risk, one can denominate interest rates in terms of real goods and services. For example, one can specify that the unit of account for the fixed-income instrument is some commodity.

Some bonds have their interest and principal denominated in terms of the basket of goods and services used to compute the cost of living in a particular country. For example, the government of the United Kingdom has been issuing such **index-linked bonds** since 1981. The U.S. Treasury started issuing such bonds in January 1997. They are called Treasury Inflation Protected Securities (TIPS). The interest rate on these bonds is a risk-free real rate. In September 1998, the U.S. Treasury added inflation-protected savings bonds.

To illustrate how TIPS work, consider one that matures in one year. Assume that it offers a risk-free real rate of interest of 3% per year. The rate of return in dollars is not known with certainty in advance because it depends on the rate of inflation. If the inflation rate turns out to be only 2%, then the realized dollar rate of return will be approximately 5%; if, however, the rate of inflation turns out to be 10%, then the realized dollar rate of return will be approximately 13%.

To summarize, an interest rate is a promised rate of return. Because most bonds offer an interest rate that is denominated in terms of some currency, their real rate of return in terms of consumption goods is uncertain. In the case of inflation-indexed bonds the interest

Box 2.6 Germany's Inflation-Linked Bonds

Inflation can be a bondholder's worst enemy, unless she happens to own a bond that is inflation-protected. Most bonds work in nominal terms: They entitle the holder to a specific amount of money paid some time in the future. If inflation is stable, it can be incorporated into the bond's nominal interest rate and the bondholder can be assured of the real value of her bond when it comes due. However, if inflation increases significantly and unexpectedly, the money received when the bond is redeemed can have a purchasing power that is much less than was anticipated.

Imagine that Jane lends Mark $900 today. Mark promises to pay Jane back $1,000 in one year. Jane anticipates inflation of 1% during the year, so she expects that the real return on her loan to Mark will be about 10%. As the year goes by, something unexpected happens—the inflation rate turns out to be 50%: All prices increase by 50%. Now when Mark pays Jane back, the $1,000 she receives is only worth $500 in purchasing power: Jane has lost $400 on the loan! She is only able to buy five-ninths of what she could have purchased last year had she spent her money instead of lending it to Mark.

Nowadays, many national governments offer bonds that are "inflation-protected." The yield on these bonds is linked to a price index so that if inflation is higher (or lower) than anticipated, the interest rate can adjust accordingly. The real return on these bonds is therefore much less uncertain. Britain introduced inflation-linked bonds in 1981 and the United States followed in 1997. Several other developed countries, like France, Italy, and most recently Germany now also issue inflation-linked bonds.

Germany's situation is particularly interesting. In the 1920s, the Reichsbank—Germany's central bank at the time—got into the habit of printing too much money. Inflation soon followed: it was 1,024% in 1922 and by 1923 it had increased to 105,700,000,000%! By late 1923, one U.S. dollar was worth about 4.2 billion Reichsmarks (the German currency unit), and paper money was the most inexpensive form of heating fuel available. German bonds issued during the First World War became nearly worthless.

To a large extent this inflationary spiral was self-reinforcing: People expected inflation to be high and so prices continued to rise. The Germans blamed inflation-linked financial contracts for feeding expectations, and in 1948 all such contracts were banned. In the 50 years that followed, the Bundesbank—Germany's new Central Bank—developed a reputation as one of the toughest inflation-fighters in the world.

Germany reintroduced inflation-linked bonds in early 2006. As long as inflation remains low, this is one of the cheapest ways for a government to borrow. The bonds can also be attractive to investors who wish to mitigate inflation risk. Pension funds, for example, may have liabilities that are indexed to inflation. Holding inflation-linked bonds eliminates the possibility that inflation will erode away the value of assets.

Source: "Laying the Ghost of 1923," *The Economist,* March 14, 2006.

rate is denominated in terms of some basket of consumer goods and it is a risk-free real rate for that basket.

Quick Check 2-16

Suppose that the real rate of interest on TIPS is 3.5% per year and the expected rate of inflation in the United States is 4% per year. What is the expected nominal rate of return on these bonds?

2.6.6 Interest Rate Equalization

Competition in financial markets ensures that *interest rates* on equivalent assets are the same. Suppose, for instance, that the interest rate the U.S. Treasury currently pays on its one-year T-bills is 4% per year. What interest rate would you expect a major institution such as the World Bank to pay on its one-year dollar-denominated debt securities (assuming they are virtually free of default risk)?

Your answer should be approximately 4% per year.

To see why, suppose that the World Bank offered significantly *less* than 4% per year. Well-informed investors would not buy the bonds issued by the World Bank; instead they would invest in one-year T-bills. Thus, if the World Bank expects to sell its bonds, it must offer at least as high a rate as the U.S. Treasury.

Would the World Bank offer significantly *more* than 4% per year? Assuming that it wants to minimize its borrowing costs, it would offer no more than is necessary to attract investors. Thus, interest rates on any default-free borrowing and lending denominated in dollars with a maturity of one year will tend to be around the same as the 4% per year interest rate on one-year U.S. T-bills.

If there are entities that have the ability to borrow and lend on the *same* terms (e.g., maturity, default risk) at *different* interest rates, then they can carry out **interest-rate arbitrage:** borrowing at the lower rate and lending at the higher rate. Their attempts to expand their activity will bring about an equalization of interest rates.

Quick Check 2-17

Suppose you have $10,000 in a bank account earning an interest rate of 3% per year. At the same time you have an unpaid balance on your credit card of $5,000 on which you are paying an interest rate of 17% per year. What is the arbitrage opportunity you face?

2.6.7 The Fundamental Determinants of Rates of Return

There are four main factors that determine rates of return in a market economy:

- *productivity of capital goods*—expected rates of return on mines, dams, roads, bridges, factories, machinery, and inventories;
- *degree of uncertainty regarding the productivity of capital goods;*
- *time preferences of people*—the preference of people for consumption now versus consumption in the future; and
- *risk aversion*—the amount people are willing to give up in order to reduce their exposure to risk.

Let us briefly discuss each of the four factors.

THE EXPECTED PRODUCTIVITY OF CAPITAL GOODS

The first determinant of expected rates of return is the **productivity of capital goods.** Recall from chapter 1 that *capital goods* are goods produced in the economy that can be used in the production of other goods. Typical examples of capital goods are mines, roads, canals, dams, power stations, factories, machinery, and inventories. In addition to such physical goods (tangible capital), capital also includes patents, contracts, formulas, brand-name recognition, and production and distribution system designs that contribute to output. Such nonphysical goods (*intangible capital*) are often the result of expenditures on research and development and advertising.

Capital's productivity can be expressed as a percentage per year, called the **rate of return on capital.** This return on capital is the source of the dividends and interest paid to the holders of the stocks, bonds, and other financial instruments issued by firms. These instruments represent claims to the return on capital. The expected rate of return on capital varies over time and place according to the state of technology, the availability of other factors of production such as natural resources and labor, and the demand for the goods and services the capital can produce. *The higher the expected rate of return on capital, the higher the level of interest rates in the economy.*

THE DEGREE OF UNCERTAINTY ABOUT THE PRODUCTIVITY OF CAPITAL GOODS

The rate of return on capital is always uncertain for a host of reasons. The uncertainties of the weather affect agricultural output; mines and wells often turn out to be "dry"; machines break down from time to time; the demand for a product may change unpredictably due to changing tastes or the development of substitutes; and above all, technological progress that comes from the development of new knowledge is by its nature unpredictable. Even the simple production process of storing goods in inventory for use at a future date is not risk free because an unknown quantity could go bad or become obsolete.

Equity securities represent claims to the profits earned on capital goods. *The greater the degree of uncertainty about the productivity of capital goods, the higher the risk premium on equity securities.*

TIME PREFERENCES OF PEOPLE

Another factor determining the level of rates of return is the preferences of people for consumption now versus consumption in the future. Economists generally assume that the rate of interest would still be positive even if there were no capital goods to invest in and the only reason for borrowing and lending was that people wanted to alter their patterns of consumption over time. In general, the greater the preference of people for current consumption over future consumption, the higher the rate of interest in the economy.

One reason people may prefer greater consumption in the present than in the future is uncertainty about their time of death. They know they are alive now to enjoy their consumption spending, but there is some uncertainty about whether they will be around to enjoy it in the future.

RISK AVERSION

As discussed, the rate of return on capital is always risky. How then is it possible for people to earn a risk-free rate of interest, and what determines the risk-free rate?

The answer is that the financial system provides contractual mechanisms for people who want to invest in risk-free assets to do so by giving up some of their expected return. People who are more tolerant of risk offer to those who are more averse to risk the opportunity to earn a risk-free rate of interest in return for accepting a rate that is lower than the average expected rate of return on risky assets. The greater the degree of risk aversion of the population, the higher the risk premium required, and the lower will be the risk-free rate of interest.

Quick Check 2-18

What are the fundamental determinants of the rate of interest?

2.7 Financial Intermediaries

Financial intermediaries are firms whose primary business is to provide customers with financial products and services that cannot be obtained more efficiently by transacting directly in securities markets. Among the main types of intermediaries are banks, investment companies, and insurance companies. Their products include checking accounts, loans, mortgages, mutual funds, and a wide range of insurance contracts.

Perhaps the simplest example of a financial intermediary is a mutual fund, which pools the financial resources of many small savers and invests their money in securities. The mutual fund has substantial economies of scale in record keeping and in executing purchases and sales of securities and, therefore, offers its customers a more efficient way of investing in securities than the direct purchase and sale of securities in the markets.

2.7.1 Banks

Banks are today the largest (in terms of assets) and oldest of all financial intermediaries. The earliest banks appeared hundreds of years ago in the towns of Renaissance Italy. Their main function was to serve as a mechanism for clearing and settling payments, thereby facilitating the trade in goods and services that had started to flourish in Italy at that time. The early banks evolved from money changers.[5] Indeed, the word *bank* comes from *banca,* the Italian word for "bench" because money changers worked at benches in converting currencies.

Most firms called banks today, however, perform at least two functions: They take deposits and make loans. In the United States they are called **commercial banks.**

In some countries banks are virtually all-purpose financial intermediaries, offering customers not just transaction services and loans, but also mutual funds and insurance of every kind. In Germany, for example, *universal banks* fulfill virtually all of the functions performed by the more specialized intermediaries to be discussed in the remaining sections of this chapter.

Indeed, it is becoming increasingly difficult to differentiate among the various financial firms doing business around the world on the basis of what type of intermediary or financial service provider they are. Thus, although Deutsche Bank is classified as a universal bank, it performs pretty much the same set of functions around the world as does Merrill Lynch, which is usually classified as a broker/dealer.

2.7.2 Other Depository Savings Institutions

Depository savings institutions, thrift institutions, or simply *thrifts* are the terms used to refer collectively to savings banks, savings and loan associations (S&Ls), and credit unions. In the United States, they compete with commercial banks in both their deposit and lending activities. U.S. thrifts specialize in making home mortgage and consumer loans. In other countries there is a variety of special-purpose savings institutions that are similar to the thrifts and credit unions in the United States.

---

[5]An excellent survey of what historians have discovered about the origins of banking can be found in Raymond de Roover, "New Interpretations of the History of Banking," chapter 5 in *Business, Banking, and Economic Thought in Late Medieval and Early Modern Europe* (Chicago: The University of Chicago Press, 1974).

2.7.3 Insurance Companies

Insurance companies are intermediaries whose primary function is to allow households and businesses to shed specific risks by buying contracts called insurance policies that pay cash compensation if certain specified events occur. Policies that cover accidents, theft, or fire are called *property and casualty* insurance. Policies that cover sickness or the inability to work are called *health and disability* insurance, and policies that cover death are called *life insurance.*

Insurance policies are assets of the households and businesses that buy them, and they are liabilities of the insurance companies that sell them. Payments made to insurance companies for the insurance they provide are called *premiums.* Because customers pay insurance premiums before benefits are received, insurance companies have the use of the funds for periods of time ranging from less than a year to several decades. Insurance companies invest the premiums they collect in assets such as stocks, bonds, and real estate.

2.7.4 Pension and Retirement Funds

The function of a pension plan is to replace a person's preretirement earnings when combined with Social Security retirement benefits and private savings. A pension plan can be sponsored by an employer, a labor union, or an individual.

Pension plans are classified into two types: defined contribution and defined benefit. In a **defined-contribution pension plan,** each employee has an account into which the employer and usually the employee make regular contributions. At retirement, the employee receives a benefit whose size depends on the accumulated value of the funds in the retirement account.

In a **defined-benefit pension plan,** the employee's pension benefit is determined by a formula that takes into account years of service to the employer and, in most cases, wages or salary. A typical benefit formula would be 1% of average retirement salary for each year of service.

The sponsor of a defined-benefit plan or an insurance company hired by the sponsor guarantees the benefits and, thus, absorbs the investment risk. In some countries, such as Germany, Japan, and the United States, a government or quasi-governmental agency backs the sponsor's guarantee of pension benefits up to specified limits.

2.7.5 Mutual Funds

A **mutual fund** is a portfolio of stocks, bonds, or other assets purchased in the name of a group of investors and managed by a professional investment company or other financial institution. Each customer is entitled to a pro rata share of any distributions and can redeem his or her share of the fund at any time at its then current market value.

The company that manages the fund keeps track of how much each investor has and reinvests all distributions received according to the rules of the fund. In addition to divisibility, record keeping, and reinvestment of receipts, mutual funds provide an efficient means of diversification.

There are two types of mutual funds: *open end* and *closed end.* Open-end mutual funds stand ready to redeem or issue shares at their net asset value (NAV), which is the market value of all securities held divided by the number of shares outstanding. The number of shares outstanding of an open-end fund changes daily as investors buy new or redeem old shares.

Closed-end mutual funds do not redeem or issue shares at NAV. Shares of closed-end funds are traded through brokers just like other common stocks, and their prices can, therefore, differ from NAV.

2.7.6 Investment Banks

Investment banks are firms whose primary function is to help businesses, governments, and other entities raise funds to finance their activities by issuing securities. Investment banks also facilitate and sometimes initiate mergers of firms or acquisitions of one firm by another.

Investment banks often *underwrite* the securities they distribute. Underwriting means insuring. In the case of securities, underwriting means committing to buy them at a guaranteed future price.

In many countries, universal banks perform the functions of U.S. investment banks, but in the United States the Glass Steagall Act of 1933 prohibited commercial banks from engaging in most underwriting activities. In recent years, however, commercial banks in the United States have again been permitted to engage in some of these activities.

2.7.7 Venture Capital Firms

Venture capital firms are similar to investment banks, except their clients are startup firms rather than large corporations. Young firms with inexperienced managers often need considerable advice in running their business in addition to financing. Venture capital firms provide both.

Venture capitalists invest their funds in new businesses and help the management team get the firm to the point at which it is ready to "go public"—that is, sell shares of stock to the investing public. Once that point is reached, the venture capital firm will typically sell its stake in the corporation and move on to the next new venture.

2.7.8 Asset Management Firms

Asset management firms are also called *investment management firms.* They advise and often administer mutual funds, pension funds, and other asset pools for individuals, firms, and governments. They may be separate firms or they may be a division within a firm, such as a trust company that is part of a bank, insurance company, or brokerage firm.

2.7.9 Information Services

Many financial service firms provide information as a by-product of their main activities, but there are firms that specialize in providing information. The oldest information service firms are rating agencies, such as Moody's and Standard & Poor's for the securities business and Best's for the insurance industry. A more recent growth sector is the firms or divisions within firms offering analysis of financial data (such as Bloomberg and Reuters) or performance statistics on mutual funds (such as Lipper, Morningstar, and SEI).

2.8 Financial Infrastructure and Regulation

All social activity is conducted within the bounds of certain rules of behavior. Some rules are codified in the law and constrain the financial system as they constrain all other realms of economic activity. Prime among these are laws outlawing fraud and enforcing contracts. Moreover, these laws may differ from country to country and change over time. They are part of the legal infrastructure of a society, and we generally treat them as outside the financial system, although changes in the law are sometimes a response to changing needs for the operation of the financial system.

The financial infrastructure consists of the legal and accounting procedures, the organization of trading and clearing facilities, and the regulatory structures that govern the relations among the users of the financial system. Those who take a historical perspective of several centuries have identified the evolution of the infrastructure of the financial system as a key factor in understanding the economic development of nations.

Some regulatory tasks are performed by private sector organizations and some are performed by governmental organizations. The performance of some regulatory tasks that are legally assigned to government are delegated to private sector organizations. This is true in the United States as well as in other countries. Some of these private sector organizations are professional associations with special expertise such as the Financial Accounting Standards

Board in the United States, some are securities exchanges, and some are trade associations such as the International Swap Dealers Association (ISDA).

As in other areas of the economic system, so too in the financial system, government can play a useful role in promoting economic efficiency. However, successful public policy depends importantly on recognizing the limits of what government can do to improve efficiency and on recognizing when government *inaction* is the best choice.

2.8.1 Rules for Trading

Rules for trading securities are usually established by organized exchanges and then sometimes given the sanction of law. These rules serve the function of standardizing procedures so that the costs of transacting are kept to a minimum. Ideally, the rules are well thought out to promote low-cost trading, but sometimes they are seemingly arbitrary. Even arbitrary rules, however, are usually preferable to no rules at all.

2.8.2 Accounting Systems

To be useful, financial information must be presented in a standard format. The discipline that studies the reporting of financial information is called *accounting*. Accounting systems are perhaps the most important part of the infrastructure of the financial system.

Not surprisingly, the earliest accounting systems developed in parallel with the development of financial contracting. Archaeologists have found elaborate and detailed accounts of financial transactions dating back to ancient Babylon (around 2000 B.C.). The development of *double-entry bookkeeping*—a major leap forward in accounting systems—occurred in Renaissance Italy in response to the need to keep track of the complex financial transactions arising from trade and banking.

2.9 Governmental and Quasi-Governmental Organizations

As the maker and enforcer of a society's laws, government is ultimately responsible to regulate the financial system. As demonstrated in the previous section, there are some regulatory tasks that are delegated to private sector organizations such as trade or industry associations or the securities exchanges. This is true in the United States as well as in other countries.

For example, in the United States, the *Securities Exchange Commission* (SEC) establishes the precise disclosure requirements that must be satisfied for a public offering of securities. Other countries have similar regulatory bodies.

However, in addition to their role as regulators of the financial system, governments use the financial system to achieve other public policy goals. An example is the use of monetary policy to achieve national targets for economic growth or employment. In the following sections we describe some of the main governmental organizations that either seek to regulate the operation of some part of the financial system or use the financial system as the principal means of achieving other economic goals.

2.9.1 Central Banks

Central banks are intermediaries whose primary function is to promote public policy objectives by influencing certain financial market parameters such as the supply of the local currency. In some countries the central bank is subject to the direct control of the executive body of government; in others it is semiautonomous.[6]

[6]In the United States, the central bank has a great deal of autonomy from the government. It consists of 12 regional banks and a seven-member board of governors in Washington, DC. All seven members of the board of governors are, however, appointed by the president of the United States and confirmed by the Senate.

In many countries the central bank is identifiable through its title: the Bank of England, the Bank of Japan, and so on. But in the United States the central bank is called the *Federal Reserve System* (or the "Fed" for short), and in Sweden the *Riksbank.*

A central bank is usually at the heart of a country's payments system. It provides the supply of local currency and operates the clearing system for the banks. An efficient payments system requires at least a moderate degree of price stability. Central banks, therefore, usually view this as their primary goal. But central banks in many countries are also expected to promote the goals of full employment and economic growth. In these countries, central banks must balance the sometimes conflicting goals of price stability and full employment.

2.9.2 Special-Purpose Intermediaries

This group of organizations includes entities that are set up to encourage specific economic activities by making financing more readily available or by guaranteeing debt instruments of various sorts. Examples are government agencies that make loans or guarantee loans to farmers, students, small businesses, new home buyers, and so on.

A different class of governmental organization is the agencies that are designed to insure bank deposits. Their main function is to promote economic stability by preventing a breakdown in part or all of the financial system.

The worst-case scenario is a banking panic. Depositors are content to leave their deposits in banks as long as they are confident that their money is safe and accessible. However, depositors know that the bank is holding illiquid and risky assets as collateral for its obligation to depositors. If they believe that they will not be able to get back the full value of their deposits, then depositors will race to be first in line to withdraw their money.

This forces the bank into liquidating some of its risky assets. If the collateral assets are illiquid, then being forced to liquidate them quickly means that the bank will have to accept less than full value for them. If one bank does not have sufficient funds to pay off its depositors, then contagion can set in, and other banks are then faced with a run. However, such a contagion problem occurs for the banking system as a whole only if there is a "flight to currency," in which people refuse to hold deposits of *any* bank and insist on having currency.

2.9.3 Regional and World Organizations

Several international bodies currently exist for the purpose of coordinating the financial policies of national governments. Perhaps the most important is the Bank for International Settlements (BIS) in Basel, Switzerland, whose objective is to promote uniformity of banking regulations.

In addition, two official international agencies operate in the international financial markets to promote growth in trade and finance: the International Monetary Fund (IMF) and the International Bank for Reconstruction and Development (World Bank). The IMF monitors economic and financial conditions in member countries, provides technical assistance, establishes rules for international trade and finance, provides a forum for international consultation, and most important, provides resources that permit lengthening the time necessary for individual members to correct imbalances in their payments to other countries.

The World Bank finances investment projects in developing countries. It raises funds primarily by selling bonds in developed countries and then makes loans for projects that must meet certain criteria designed to encourage economic development.

Summary

The financial system is the set of markets and intermediaries used by households, firms, and governments to implement their financial decisions. It includes the markets for stocks, bonds, and other securities, as well as financial intermediaries such as banks and insurance companies.

Funds flow through the financial system from entities that have a surplus of funds to those that have a deficit. Often these fund flows take place through a financial intermediary.

There are six core functions performed by the financial system:

- To provide ways to *transfer economic resources* through time, across borders, and among industries.
- To provide ways of *managing risk.*
- To provide ways of *clearing and settling payments* to facilitate trade.
- To provide a mechanism for the *pooling of resources* and for the *subdividing* of shares in various enterprises.
- To provide *price information* to help coordinate decentralized decision making in various sectors of the economy.
- To provide ways of *dealing with the incentive problems* created when one party to a transaction has information that the other party does not or when one party acts as agent for another.

The fundamental economic force behind financial innovation is competition, which generally leads to improvements in the way financial functions are performed.

The basic types of financial assets traded in markets are *debt, equity,* and *derivatives:*

- Debt instruments are issued by anyone who borrows money—firms, governments, and households.
- Equity is the claim of the owners of a firm. Equity securities issued by corporations are called common stocks.
- Derivatives are financial instruments such as options and futures contracts that derive their value from the prices of one or more other assets.

An interest rate is a promised rate of return, and there are as many different interest rates as there are distinct kinds of borrowing and lending. Interest rates vary depending on the unit of account, the maturity, and the default risk of the credit instrument. A *nominal* interest rate is denominated in units of some currency; a *real* interest rate is denominated in units of some commodity or basket of goods and services. Bonds that offer a fixed nominal interest rate have an uncertain real rate of return; and inflation-indexed bonds offering a fixed real interest rate have an uncertain nominal rate of return.

There are four main factors that determine rates of return in a market economy:

- *productivity of capital goods*—expected rates of return on mines, dams, roads, bridges, factories, machinery, and inventories;
- *degree of uncertainty regarding the productivity of capital goods;*
- *time preferences of people*—the preference of people for consumption now versus consumption in the future; and
- *risk aversion*—the amount people are willing to give up in order to reduce their exposure to risk.

Indexing is an investment strategy that seeks to match the returns of a specified stock market index.

Financial intermediaries are firms whose primary business is to provide customers with financial products that cannot be obtained more efficiently by transacting directly in securities markets. Among the main types of intermediaries are banks, investment companies, and insurance companies. Their products include checking accounts, loans, mortgages, mutual funds, and a wide range of insurance contracts.

Key Terms

- over-the-counter markets 24
- flow of funds 25
- moral hazard 31
- adverse selection 32
- life annuities 32
- principal-agent problem 33
- collateralization 33
- fixed-income instruments 36
- money market 36
- capital market 36
- liquidity 36
- residual claim 36
- limited liability 36
- derivatives 36
- call option 37
- put option 37
- forward contracts 37
- mortgage rate 37
- commercial loan rate 37
- unit of account 37
- maturity 37
- default risk 37
- exchange rate 38
- yield curve 38
- yield spread 40
- capital gain 40
- capital loss 40
- nominal prices 52
- real prices 52
- nominal interest rate 52
- real rate of return 52
- index-linked bonds 55
- interest-rate arbitrage 56
- productivity of capital goods 57
- rate of return on capital 57
- commercial banks 58
- defined-contribution pension plan 59
- defined-benefit pension plan 59
- mutual fund 59
- investment banks 59
- market-weighted stock indexes 69

Answers to Quick Check Questions

Quick Check 2-1 A depositor puts $5,000 into a bank account and you take a $5,000 student loan from the bank. Trace this flow of funds in Figure 2.1.

Answer: The funds flow from the depositor (a surplus unit) to a financial intermediary, and then from the intermediary to you (a deficit unit).

Quick Check 2-2 Give an example of a transfer of resources over time that takes place through the financial system. Is there a more efficient way for this transfer of resources to be handled?

Answer: An example would be a young person saving for his or her own retirement by saving money in a bank account. A more efficient way might be for the individual to save for retirement through an insurance company or mutual fund retirement account whose sole function is to provide retirement income.

Quick Check 2-3 Give an example of a transfer of risk that takes place through the financial system.

Answer: Whenever anyone buys an insurance policy, risk is being transferred.

Quick Check 2-4 Would you accept an IOU from me in payment for a good or service that I buy from you? What factors will determine the answer?

Answer: The answer depends upon the size of the transaction and the nature of the IOU. If our transaction is very small in size, I will be less concerned with the riskiness of the IOU, as my exposure is small. However, for larger transactions, I would want a guarantee of your IOU from a financial institution. I would accept payment by credit card because I am sure to receive payment from the bank issuing the credit card, but I might not be willing to accept a personal check unless you are a long-standing customer with whom I have done a lot of business.

Quick Check 2-5 Give an example of an investment that would not be undertaken if it were not possible to pool the savings of many different households.

Answer: Any investment that requires a large minimum investment to complete. One example would be a bridge or a dam.

Quick Check 2-6 Give an example of a financial transaction that provides important information to parties not involved in the transaction.

Answer: Whenever shares of stock are traded on a competitive stock market, information is being conveyed to everyone who can observe the price about how much investors think the stock is worth.

Quick Check 2-7 Give an example of how the problem of moral hazard might prevent you from getting financing for something you want to do. Can you think of a way of overcoming the problem?

Answer: If you ask a bank to lend you 100% of the funds you need to enter a certain business venture, the bank may refuse for fear that you will take large risks with its money. One way of overcoming the problem is to offer the bank additional collateral—your own personal assets—or a third-party guarantee of the loan.

Quick Check 2-8 Suppose a bank offered to make loans to potential borrowers without checking their credit history. What would be true of the types of borrowers they would attract compared with banks that did check credit history? Would such a bank charge the same interest rate on loans as banks that check credit history?

Answer: The bank that did no credit checks would attract borrowers with a higher probability of defaulting on their loans. To survive as a viable business such a bank would have to charge higher interest rates.

Quick Check 2-9 If you get financial planning advice from your insurance agent, how does this give rise to a principal-agent problem? Can you think of a way of overcoming the problem?

Answer: Insurance agents want you to buy insurance products on which they earn commissions, even if those products are not necessarily in your best interest. To avoid this conflict of interest you should seek financial advice from a qualified adviser who does not profit from selling you a particular financial product other than good advice.

Quick Check 2-10 What are the defining features of debt, equity, and derivative securities?

Answer: Debt instruments are issued by anyone who borrows money. Equity is the claim of the owners of a firm. Derivatives are financial instruments that derive their value from the prices of one or more other assets such as equity securities, fixed-income securities, foreign currencies, or commodities.

Quick Check 2-11 In the previous example, what does the change in the exchange rate have to be at year's end for the Japanese investor to earn exactly 3% per year on the investment in U.K. bonds?

Answer:

$$\frac{\left(£109 \times \text{Future Yen Price of Pound}\left(¥/£\right)\right) - ¥15{,}000}{¥15{,}000} = 0.03$$

Solving for the future yen price of the pound we obtain:

$$\text{Future Yen Price of Pound} = 141.74\left(¥/£\right)$$

Quick Check 2-12 Go on-line to Bloomberg.com and discover what the level and shape of the U.S. Treasury yield curve are. Do the same for the Japanese and German Treasury yield curves.

Answer: Answers will vary.

Quick Check 2-13 Look on Bloomberg.com and discover what the yield spreads are between corporate bonds and U.S. treasury bonds.

Answer: Answers will vary.

Quick Check 2-14 You invest a stock costing \$50. It pays a cash dividend during the year of \$1, and you expect its price to be \$60 at year's end. What is your expected rate of return? If the stock's price is actually \$40 at year's end, what is your realized rate of return?

Answer:

$$\text{Expected Rate of Return} = \frac{\$1 + \$60 - \$50}{\$50} = 0.22 \text{ or } 22\%$$

$$\text{Realized Rate of Return} = \frac{\$1 + \$40 - \$50}{\$50} = -0.18 \text{ or } -18\%$$

Quick Check 2-15 Suppose the risk-free nominal interest rate on a one-year U.S. Treasury bill is 6% per year and the expected rate of inflation is 3% per year. What is the expected real rate of return on the T-bill? Why is the T-bill risky in real terms?

Answer:

$$\text{Real Rate} = \frac{\text{Nominal Interest Rate} - \text{Rate of Inflation}}{1 + \text{Rate of Inflation}} = 0.02913 = 2.913\%$$

Because the actual inflation rate is not known when the nominal interest rate is set, investors can never know for certain what their real return will be (it will depend on what inflation actually turns out to be).

Quick Check 2-16 Suppose that the real rate of interest on TIPS is 3.5% per year and the expected rate of inflation in the United States is 4% per year. What is the expected nominal rate of return on these bonds?

Answer: 1 + Nominal Interest Rate = (1 + Real Interest Rate) × (1 + Rate of Inflation) hence, Nominal Interest Rate = (1.035 × 1.04) − 1 = 0.0764 = 7.64%

Quick Check 2-17 Suppose you have \$10,000 in a bank account earning an interest rate of 3% per year. At the same time you have an unpaid balance on your credit card of \$5,000 on which you are paying an interest rate of 17% per year. What is the arbitrage opportunity you face?

Answer: You could take \$5,000 out of your bank account and pay down your credit-card balance. You would give up 3% per year in interest earnings (\$150 per year), but you would save 17% per year in interest expenses ($850 per year). So the arbitrage opportunity is worth $700 per year.

Quick Check 2-18 What are the fundamental determinants of the rate of interest?

Answer:

- The *productivity of capital goods*—expected rates of return on mines, dams, roads, bridges, factories, machinery, and inventories;
- the *degree of uncertainty regarding the productivity of capital goods;*
- *time preferences of people*—the preference of people for consumption now versus consumption in the future; and
- *risk aversion*—the amount people are willing to give up in order to reduce their exposure to risk.

Sources of Financial Data

Thanks to the Internet, there is a vast amount of free information about the financial system that is accessible at the click of a computer mouse. Here is a list of some of them:

Flow of Funds Accounts of the United States
http://www.federalreserve.gov/releases/z1/

Investment Company Fact Book
http://www.icifactbook.org/

U.S. and International Government Yield Curves
http://www.bloomberg.com/markets/rates/

U.S. and International Markets and Funds Data
http://markets.ft.com/markets/overview.asp

Questions and Problems

What Is the Financial System?

1. How does the financial system contribute to economic security and prosperity in a capitalist society?

The Flow of Funds

2. Suppose your great uncle decides to take this month's savings and purchase a bond issued by the Gateway Computer Company to finance an increase in computer components in their new factory. Describe how this exchange can be analyzed in the flow-of-funds framework.

The Functional Perspective

3. Would you be able to get a student loan without someone else offering to guarantee it?
4. Give an example of a new business that would not be able to get financing if insurance against risk were not available.
5. Suppose you invest in a real-estate development deal. The total investment is $100,000. You invest $20,000 of your own money and borrow the other $80,000 from the bank. Who bears the risk of this venture and why?
6. Give an example of how the problem of moral hazard might prevent you from getting financing for something you want to do. Can you think of a way of overcoming this problem?

7. Give an example of how the problem of adverse selection might prevent you from getting financing for something you want to do. Can you think of a way of overcoming this problem?
8. Give an example of how the principal-agent problem might prevent you from getting financing for something you want to do. Can you think of a way of overcoming this problem?
9. Give an example of how each of the six functions of the financial system are performed more efficiently today than they were in the time of Adam Smith (1776).
10. You are living in the United States and are thinking of traveling to Germany 6 months from now. You can purchase an option to buy euros now at a fixed rate of $1.50 per euro 6 months from now. How is the option like an insurance policy?

Financial Innovation and the "Invisible Hand"

11. Do you agree with Adam Smith's view that society can rely more on the "invisible hand" than on government to promote economic prosperity?
12. Why is it that a country's postage stamps are not as good a medium of exchange as its paper currency?
13. Who is hurt if I issue counterfeit U.S. dollars and use them to purchase valuable goods and services?
14. Some say the only criterion to use in predicting what will serve as money in the future is the real resource cost of producing it, including the transaction costs of verifying its authenticity. According to this criterion what do you think will be the money of the future?

Financial Markets

15. *Challenge Question:* Suppose Delta Airlines signs a contract to purchase 50 new Boeing 787 planes at fixed negotiated prices and with fixed delivery dates over the next five years. In addition the contract has a special clause stating that an additional 20 planes may be purchased at the buyer's discretion. The clause gives Delta the ability to buy four more planes each year for a 5 percent premium to the prices set for the original 50 planes. What sort of derivative security does this special clause represent? What is the primary factor that will determine the value of this clause over the life of the contract? What value does this clause have in terms of Delta's risk management?

Financial Market Rates

16. Should all governments issue debt that is indexed to their domestic price level? Is there a moral hazard problem that citizens face with regard to their public officials when government debt is fixed in units of the domestic currency?
17. Use the Internet to answer the following question by navigating to the URL: (http://markets.ft.com/ft/markets/researchArchive.asp?report=Gov&cat=BR). From the data on *bid yields* plot the German, Japanese, and American yield curves and summarize the major differences in the term structure.

Financial Intermediaries

18. Describe your country's system for financing higher education. What are the roles played by households, voluntary nonprofit organizations, businesses, and government?
19. Describe your country's system for financing residential housing. What are the roles played by households, businesses, and government?
20. Describe your country's system for financing new enterprises. What are the roles played by households, businesses, and government?

Financial Infrastructure and Regulation

21. How does a competitive stock market accomplish the result that Adam Smith describes? Should the stock market be regulated? How and why?

Governmental and Quasi-Governmental Organizations

22. The structure of central banking in Europe has undergone a major transformation over the past few years as twelve countries have joined together to operate under the European Union's (EU) Economic and Monetary Union (EMU) and now conduct transactions in a new single currency, the euro. Navigate the Internet to the official Web site of the European Central Bank at the URL: (http://www.ecb.int). Find the background material on the organization of the ECB and describe briefly the makeup and role of it's Governing Council. Name the two EU member states to become the most recent members of the euro area.

APPENDIX

Alternative Stock Market Indexes

In the United States, perhaps the stock index most often cited in the news is the Dow Jones Industrial Index (DJI). It is an index of the prices of 30 stocks of major industrial U.S. corporations. The DJI has two major defects that limit its usefulness as a benchmark for measuring stock performance. One is that it is not broadly diversified enough to accurately reflect the wide spectrum of stocks in the United States. The other is that it corresponds to a portfolio strategy that is unsuitable as a performance benchmark.

Most investment professionals, therefore, prefer to use other indexes such as the Standard and Poor's 500 (S&P 500) as a performance benchmark. The S&P 500 index corresponds to a portfolio of 500 stocks selected from among the largest public corporations in the United States, with dollar amounts invested in each in proportion to their shares of the total market value.

To illustrate the construction of these two types of indexes and to compare them, let us simplify matters by analyzing a hypothetical two-stock index. The two stocks in the index are IBM (International Business Machines) and HPQ (Hewlett-Packard Company). The relevant data on the two stocks are presented in Table 2A.1.

The DJI-type index is computed by taking the average current price of a share, dividing by the average price in the base year, and multiplying the result by 100.

$$\text{DJI-Type Index} = \frac{\text{Average of Current Stock Prices}}{\text{Average of Stock Prices in Base Year}} \times 100$$

Let us say that in the base year the prices were \$100 per share for IBM and \$50 for HPQ. The average price per share, computed by adding the two prices and dividing by 2, is, therefore, \$75. A year later, the prices are \$50 per share for IBM and \$110 per share for HPQ, and the average is \$80. The DJI-type index would, therefore, show a value of 106.67, indicating an increase of 6.67%.

$$\text{DJI-Type Index} = \frac{(50 + 110)/2}{(100 + 50)/2} \times 100 = \frac{80}{75} \times 100 = 106.67$$

The DJI-type index assumes that the benchmark portfolio consists of one share of each stock. Had investors bought one share of IBM stock and one share of HPQ in the base year, then their portfolio would have increased in value by 6.67%. Such a portfolio is not

TABLE 2A.1 **Data for Constructing Stock Price Indexes**

Company	Stock Price: Base Year	Stock Price: Now	Number of Shares	Market Value: Base Year	Market Value: Now
IBM	\$100	\$50	200 million	\$20 billion	\$10 billion
HPQ	\$50	\$110	100 million	\$5 billion	\$11 billion
			Total	\$25 billion	\$21 billion

a natural benchmark for measuring performance, because the total value of all stocks declined from \$25 billion to \$21 billion in our example, which is a 16% decline.

Investment professionals typically use a market-weighted index as a benchmark for measuring the performance of common stock mutual funds. **Market-weighted stock indexes** represent the price performance of a portfolio that holds each stock in proportion to its total market value. In the preceding example, IBM accounted for 80% of the total value of the stock market and HPQ for 20%. A market-weighted index gives each stock these weights:

$$\begin{aligned}\text{S\&P-Type Index} &= \left(\text{Weight of IBM} \times \frac{\text{Current Price of IBM}}{\text{IBM's Price in Base Year}}\right.\\ &\quad \left. + \text{Weight of HPQ} \times \frac{\text{Current Price of HPQ}}{\text{HPQ's Price in Base Year}}\right) \times 100\\ &= (0.8 \times 0.5 + 0.2 \times 2.2) \times 100 = 84\end{aligned}$$

Thus, this index shows a 16% decline, which accurately reflects what has happened to the total market value of all stocks.

Alternative Stock Market Indexes

23. Assume there are only two stocks traded in the stock market, and you are trying to construct an index to show what has happened to stock prices. Let us say that in the base year the prices were \$20 per share for stock 1 with 100 million shares outstanding and \$10 for stock 2 with 50 million shares outstanding. A year later, the prices are \$30 per share for stock 1 and \$2 per share for stock 2. Using the two different methods explained in the chapter, compute stock indexes showing what has happened to the overall stock market. Which of the two methods do you prefer and why?

CHAPTER 3

Managing Financial Health and Performance

OBJECTIVES

- To contrast the economic and accounting models of the firm.
- To show how accounting information can be useful to the financial decision maker when used with care.
- To understand the purpose and process of financial planning.
- To understand why firms need working capital and how to manage it to maximize shareholder value.

CONTENTS

Much of the information about businesses and other organizations available to financial decision makers comes in the form of standard financial statements published in annual and quarterly reports to shareholders. These financial statements—balance sheets, income statements, and statements of cash flow—are prepared according to rules established by the accounting profession, and it is, therefore, important to understand what those rules are. But financial analysts sometimes disagree with how the accounting profession has decided to measure certain key financial variables. The most fundamental disagreement is about how to measure the values of assets and liabilities.

In this chapter we review basic financial statements and show how to use them as templates for financial planning. We begin by reviewing current accounting rules. We then examine how accounting measures of value and income can differ from the underlying economic concepts needed to make good financial decisions. We then construct a financial planning model for a typical manufacturing firm starting from the firm's financial statements for the last few years. Finally, we discuss short-term planning and the management of working capital.

3.1 Functions of Financial Statements

Financial statements serve three important economic functions:

- *They provide information to the owners and creditors of the firm about the company's current status and past financial performance.*

Although published financial statements rarely provide enough information to enable one to form conclusive judgments about a company's performance, they can provide important clues about aspects of a firm's operations that should be examined more carefully. Sometimes through a careful audit of financial statements it is possible to detect mismanagement and even fraud. For example, by analyzing financial statements an accounting professor uncovered fraud in one of his university's investments.

- *Financial statements provide a convenient way for owners and creditors to set performance targets and to impose restrictions on the managers of the firm.*

Financial statements are used by boards of directors to specify performance targets for management. For example, the board might set targets in terms of a growth rate of accounting earnings or return on equity (*ROE*). Creditors often specify restrictions on management's actions in terms of measures like the ratio of current assets to current liabilities.

- *Financial statements provide convenient templates for financial planning.*

By preparing projections of income statements, balance sheets, and statements of cash flow for the company as a whole, managers can check the overall consistency of separate plans made on a project-by-project basis and estimate the firm's total financing requirements. Although other templates can be substituted for standard financial statements in the planning process, a major advantage of using standard income statements and balance sheets is that the people involved are probably familiar with them from their professional education and training.

Quick Check 3-1

What are the three basic economic functions served by financial statements?

Box 3.1 Backdated Options

Corporate executives' enormous payoffs often result from holding a large amount of stock options in a company, and behaving unethically and—unfortunately in today's world—as a combination of both. Supplying executives with a large share of stock options is usually justified as an incentive for the CEOs to make sure their company performs well in the equity market. After all, if the company's stock price increases, so do the returns of the executive. Yet if these options are manipulated so that they are coincidentally awarded to the executive right before a company's stock price increases, this justification seems moot.

Recent investigations have revealed that it is very likely that companies have falsely report when stock options were assigned to top executives. In particular, firms frequently report that shares are dated as of an opportune low moment right before the price of the firms' stock prices jumped. This process of backdating shares may or may not be illegal in certain circumstances, but it certainly calls into question whether stock option compensation provides the best incentive for a corporate executive to do his or her job. An executive can do a number of things to increase the price of a stock, such as supplying fewer dividends to shareholders. This, in combination with backdating, could significantly alter the real motives behind an executive's actions, and cause firms more trouble in the future.

In the end, giving CEOs stock options in lieu of higher salaries may motivate the executives to better serve the firms, but if the executives can determine precisely when these options are dated with the benefit of twenty-twenty hindsight, what's the point?

Source: Adapted from "Time and Money," *The Economist,* May 30, 2006.

3.2 Review of Financial Statements

To explain the three basic financial statements, we will use the hypothetical example of Generic Products Corporation (GPC). GPC is a company that was founded 10 years ago to manufacture and sell generic products for the consumer market.

Tables 3.1, 3.2, and 3.3 show GPC's balance sheet, income statement, and statement of cash flows. They are fairly typical of a U.S. manufacturing firm. Let us consider each in turn.

3.2.1 The Balance Sheet

A firm's balance sheet shows its assets (what it owns) and its liabilities (what it owes) at a point in time. The difference between assets and liabilities is the firm's net worth, also called owners' equity. For a corporation, net worth is called stockholder's equity.

The values of assets, liabilities, and net worth carried on a company's published balance sheet are measured at historical acquisition costs in accordance with generally accepted accounting principles, otherwise known as GAAP. These rules (GAAP) are determined and modified periodically by the Financial Accounting Standards Board. Any U.S. or non-U.S. corporation that wishes to list its shares on an exchange in the United States must conform with the accounting standards and report regularly on its activities by filing financial statements with the Securities and Exchange Commission.

Table 3.1 presents GPC's balance sheet at two different points in time that bracket the year 20x1. Let us first examine the balance sheet on December 31, 20x0, just before the start of 20x1.

The first section of the balance sheet lists the assets of the firm, beginning with its current assets, defined as cash and other items that will be converted into cash within one year. In GPC's case, cash and marketable securities are valued at $100 million. The other current assets consist of $50 million in receivables, which is the amount owed to GPC by customers,

TABLE 3.1 **GPC Balance Sheet on December 31**

Assets	20x0	20x1	Change
Current assets			
Cash and marketable securities	100.0	120.0	20.0
Receivables	50.0	60.0	10.0
Inventories	150.0	180.0	30.0
Total current assets	300.0	360.0	60.0
Property, plant, and equipment (PP&E)	400.0	490.0	90.0
less Accumulated depreciation	100.0	130.0	30.0
Net PP&E	300.0	360.0	60.0
Total assets	600.0	720.0	120.0
Liabilities and Stockholders' Equity			
Current liabilities			
Accounts payable	60.0	72.0	12.0
Short-term debt	90.0	184.6	94.6
Total current liabilities	150.0	256.6	106.6
Long-term debt (8% interest bonds maturing in 20x7)	150.0	150.0	0.0
Stockholders' equity (1 million shares outstanding)	300.0	313.4	13.4
Paid-in capital	200.0	200.0	0.0
Retained earnings	100.0	113.4	13.4
Total liabilities and equity	600.0	720.0	120.0
Other data: Market price per common share	$200.0	$187.2	–$12.8

All figures, except in the final row, are in millions of U.S. dollars.

and $150 million in inventories. Inventories consist of raw materials, goods in process of production, and finished goods.

Next come GPC's noncurrent assets. These consist of property, plant, and equipment. The reported value of these assets net of depreciation is listed as $300 million. Total assets are $600 million.

Next come GPC's liabilities. Liabilities that must be paid off within a year are called current liabilities. For GPC these consist of $60 million in accounts payable, which is the amount owed to its suppliers, and $90 million in short-term debt.

The difference between a firm's current assets and its current liabilities is called net working capital. It does not explicitly appear as an item on the balance sheet. GPC's net working capital at the end of 20x0 was $150 million: current assets of $300 million less current liabilities of $150 million.

The next liability item on GPC's balance sheet is long-term debt, which consists of bonds with a face value of $150 million maturing in 20x7. The interest rate on these bonds is fixed at 8% per year, which means that each year the interest expense associated with them is $12 million. This interest expense shows up on GPC's income statement.

The final category on GPC's balance sheet is shareholders' equity. The paid-in capital, which is the amount that GPC raised in the past by issuing common stock, is $200 million, and the retained earnings, which is the cumulative amount of past earnings that have been retained in the business, is $100 million.

Let us now consider the changes in GPC's balance sheet between December 31, 20x0, and December 31, 20x1. During the year assets grew by 20%, as did accounts payable. GPC's short-term debt increased by $94.6 million, and its long-term debt remained fixed at $150 million. Shareholders' equity increased by $13.4 million, which was the net income retained in the business. No new shares were issued, so paid-in capital stayed the same.

Quick Check 3-2

What difference would it have made to the end-of-year balance sheet if GPC had issued an additional $50 million in long-term debt during the year and added that amount to its holdings in cash and marketable securities?

3.2.2 The Income Statement

The income statement summarizes the profitability of the firm over a period of time, in this case a year. Income, profit, and earnings all mean the same thing—the difference between revenues and expenses. The income statement is also known as the statement of earnings or the statement of profit and loss. Table 3.2 shows that in 20x1 GPC had sales revenue of $200 million, and its net income was $23.4 million.

GPC's expenses are broken down into four major categories. The first is cost of goods sold, which was $110 million. This is the expense GPC incurred in producing the products it sold during the year, and includes the materials and labor used to manufacture them. The difference between revenues and cost of goods sold is called gross margin. GPC's gross margin in 20x1 was $90 million.

The second expense category is general, administrative, and selling (GS&A) expense. This represents the expenses incurred in managing the firm (such as the salaries of the managers) and in marketing and distributing the products produced during the year. The difference between gross margin and GS&A expenses is called operating income. GPC's GS&A expenses in 20x1 were $30 million, and its operating income was, therefore, $60 million.

TABLE 3.2 GPC Income Statement for 20x1

Sales revenue	$200.0
Cost of goods sold	(110.0)
Gross margin	90.0
General, selling, and administrative expenses	(30.0)
Operating income	60.0
Interest expense	(21.0)
Taxable income	39.0
Income tax	(15.6)
Net income	23.4
Allocation of net income:	
Dividends	10.0
Change in retained earnings	13.4
Earnings per share (1 million shares outstanding)	$23.4

All figures, except those in the final row, are in millions of U.S. dollars.

The third category of expense is the interest expense on GPC's debt, and in 20x1 it was \$21 million. After deducting interest expense, GPC's taxable income (i.e., its income subject to corporate income tax) was \$39 million.

The fourth and last category of expense is corporate income taxes. GPC paid taxes at an average rate of 40% on its taxable income in 20x1 and, therefore, its corporate income tax was \$15.6 million. GPC's net income after taxes was, therefore, \$23.4 million. Because there were 1 million shares of GPC stock outstanding, the earnings per share were \$23.40.

The income statement also shows that GPC paid cash dividends of \$10 million in 20x1. This means that \$13.4 million of the net income is retained in the business and shows up as an increase in shareholders' equity in the balance sheet at the end of 20x1. It is important to note that this latter figure (\$13.4 million) is not an addition to the cash balance of the firm because net income is not the same as cash flow.

Quick Check 3-3

What difference would it have made to the income statement and the end-of-year balance sheet if GPC had retained all of its net income instead of paying out cash dividends of \$10 million?

3.2.3 The Cash Flow Statement

The statement of cash flows shows all of the cash that flowed into and out of the firm during a period of time. It differs from the income statement, which shows the firm's revenues and expenses.

The cash flow statement is a useful supplement to the income statement for two reasons. First, it focuses attention on what is happening to the firm's cash position over time. Even very profitable firms can experience financial distress if they run out of cash. Paying attention to the cash flow statement allows the firm's managers and outsiders to see whether the firm is building up or drawing down its cash and to understand why. Often, for example, rapidly growing, profitable firms run short of cash and have difficulty meeting their financial obligations.

The cash flow statement is also useful because it avoids the judgments about revenue and expense recognition that go into the income statement. The income statement is based on accrual accounting methods according to which not every revenue is an inflow of cash and not every expense is an outflow. A firm's reported net income is affected by many judgments on the part of management about issues such as how to value its inventory and how quickly to depreciate its tangible assets and amortize its intangible assets.

The statement of cash flows is not influenced by these accrual accounting decisions. Therefore, by examining the differences between the firm's cash flow statement and its income statement an analyst is able to determine the impact of these accounting decisions.

Let us illustrate by examining Table 3.3, which presents GPC's cash flow statement for 20x1. It organizes cash flows into three sections: operating activities, investing activities, and financing activities. Let us look at each section in turn.

Cash flow from operating activities (or cash flow from operations) consists of the cash inflows from selling the firm's products less the cash outflows for expenses such as materials and labor. GPC's cash flow from operations in 20xl is \$25.4 million, whereas its net income is \$23.4 million. Why are these two numbers different?

There are four items that explain the difference between a firm's net income and its cash flow from operations: depreciation charges, the change in accounts receivable, the change in inventories, and the change in accounts payable. Let us consider each of these items for the case of GPC in 20x1.

TABLE 3.3 **GPC Cash Flow Statement for 20x1**

Cash Flow from Operating Activities	
Net income	\$23.4
+ Depreciation	+30.0
− Increase in accounts receivable	−10.0
− Increase in inventories	−30.0
+ Increase in accounts payable	+12.0
Total cash flow from Operations	25.4
Cash Flow from Investing Activities	
− Investment in plant and equipment	−90.0
Cash Flow from Financing Activities	
− Dividends paid	−10.0
+ Increase in short-term debt	+94.6
Total change in cash and marketable securities	20.0

First, depreciation charges for 20xl were \$30 million. This was a noncash expense deducted from revenues in computing net income. The cash outlays for the plant and equipment that gave rise to the depreciation charges occurred when they were originally purchased, but the depreciation charges are recognized as an expense in each period over their assumed useful life. Therefore, to get from net income to cash flow from operations, we have to add back the depreciation charges.

The second item is an increase in accounts receivable of \$10 million. This is the difference between the revenue recognized during the year and the actual cash collected from customers. The revenue figure of \$200 million on the income statement means that \$200 million worth of goods and services were shipped and billed to customers in 20x1, but only \$190 million in cash was collected. Therefore, to get from net income to cash flow from operations, we have to subtract the \$10 million increase in accounts receivable.

The third item is an increase in inventories of \$30 million. This means the value of inventories at the end of the year was \$30 million more than at the beginning. Thus, \$30 million in cash was used to purchase or to produce goods that went into inventory. This cash outlay was not accounted for in computing net income. Therefore, to get from net income to cash flow from operations, we have to subtract the \$30 million increase in inventories.

The fourth item is an increase in accounts payable of \$12 million. This is the difference between GPC's cost of goods sold during the year (\$110 million) and the amount of cash it paid to its suppliers and employees. In computing net income, the full \$110 million was deducted, but in computing cash flow from operations only the \$98 million in cash that it paid out should be deducted. Therefore, to go from net income to cash flow from operations, \$12 million must be added back.

Thus, we can see that there is no reason to expect equality between cash flow from operations and net income. To reconcile the two measures, we must adjust net income for the four items detailed previously. Cash flow statements can be particularly important in making comparisons of companies reporting their net income in different countries that have different accrual accounting standards.

The second section of Table 3.3—cash flows from investing activities—shows GPC's \$90 million cash outlay on new plant and equipment in 20x1. The third section—cash flows

TABLE 3.4 **Summary of Financial Statements**

Balance Sheet	
Assets = Liabilities + Stockholders' Equity	• A snapshot at a point in time of the value of the firm's assets and liabilities. • Long-term assets given at historic cost, depreciated over time.
Income Statement	
Net Income = Revenues − Expenses	• A record of the flow of revenues and related expenses over the period. • Use of accrual principles implies that net income usually does not equal net cash flow.
Statement of Cash Flows	
Total Cash Flow = Cash from Operating Activities + Cash from Financing Activities + Cash from Investing Activities	• A flow statement showing how much cash has flowed into and out of the firm over the period. • Each source and use of cash is placed in one of three categories.

from financing activities—shows that GPC paid out $10 million in cash dividends to shareholders and raised $94.6 million in cash by increasing its short-term debt.

To summarize, the net impact on GPC's cash balances of its operating, investing, and financing activities was to increase cash by $20 million. GPC's operating activities produced $25.4 million in cash, and GPC increased its borrowing by $94.6 million, so a total of $120 million in cash flowed in. Of that amount, $90 million in cash was used to purchase new plant and equipment and $10 million was used to pay dividends.

Quick Check 3-4

What difference would it have made to the cash flow statement if GPC had retained all of its net income instead of paying out cash dividends of $10 million?

Table 3.4 presents a summary of the features of each of the three main financial statements.

3.2.4 Notes to Financial Statements

When a corporation publishes its financial statements, it includes notes providing greater detail about the accounting methods it has used and the financial condition of the company. Frequently there is more information relevant to understanding the true financial condition of the company in the notes to the financial statements than in the statements themselves.

Some of the specific items commonly found in the notes are the following:

- *An explanation of accounting methods used.* Because firms are allowed some latitude in how to report certain costs (e.g., straight-line versus accelerated depreciation charges or LIFO versus FIFO inventory costing methods), the notes must explain which specific methods the company has actually employed. Moreover, accounting standards often change, and companies restate prior year results in the notes using the new standards.
- *Greater detail regarding certain assets or liabilities.* Notes provide details regarding the conditions and expiration dates for long- and short-term debt, leases, and the like.

Box 3.2 Pensions Crunch

Actuaries in the world of corporate finance are frequently called on to assess the liabilities associated with a pension fund, and determine what sort of asset portfolio will be required to meet the demands of those liabilities. This process is complex, has had a variable success rate, and has altered the way in which firms provide pensions.

Actuaries make predictions about the many things that could affect the welfare of a pension fund, or at least this is what they are supposed to do. Yet across the world, corporate pension funds have fared terribly in the market. These funds have encountered unforeseen liabilities that have had to be paid, resulting in fewer net gains for the overall fund.

Are all the actuaries in the world incompetent? Well, no. The variables that an actuary must consider are staggering—interest rates, life expectancies, rates of return on alternative investments. All these things and more are considered when making a prediction as to what assets a firm will need in the future to cover a given pension fund's set of liabilities.

Actuaries in the past have tended to recommend that pension funds invest in assets that generated high returns in the short run, but proved risky in the long term. Actuaries' predictions about the assets needed to cover future liabilities therefore proved more variable. The losses associated with some of the funds' performance have led firms to restructure who qualifies for pension benefits. These past results and the resulting worker, and executive, dissatisfaction have produced a new set of ideas among actuaries about how to provide more consistent returns for a pension fund.

These ideas include some basic observations: The amount you make out of a particular fund will not alter the amount that you will owe in the future. For example, if a firm borrows to invest in an asset, the fact that an asset generates a return doesn't affect the fact that the initial liability must be paid off. More generally, many policies that actuaries are now considering involve ways to control and reduce risk. Actuaries now consider liability-driven investing, or investment techniques that reduce the risk associated with large liabilities—if large liabilities have less risk, the predictions about what future assets are required of a firm will be more accurate.

If these policies are properly prudent, the returns from pension funds should be less variable, the predictions actuaries make will be more accurate, and future policies regarding pension fund distribution will be more consistent for workers.

Source: Adapted from "When the Spinning Stops," *The Economist,* January 26, 2006.

- *Information regarding the equity structure of the firm.* Notes explain conditions attached to the ownership of shares, and these can be particularly useful for assessing the vulnerability of the firm to takeovers.
- *Documentation of changes in operations.* Two main activities that can have a great impact on financial statements are acquisitions and divestitures, and the notes explain the impact of these.
- *Off-balance-sheet items.* Financial contracts entered into by the firm that do not appear on the balance sheet, but that can profoundly affect its financial condition, are often disclosed in the notes. Among these are derivative contracts such as forward contracts, swaps, and options, which are typically used to reduce certain risk exposures.

Quick Check 3-5

What potentially important information about a firm can be found in the footnotes to its financial statements?

Box 3.3 What Is Fair Value?

Accountants are expected to make fair and accurate reports about a firm's finances, and these reports are supposed to be in a standardized form so that they can be easily compared to the financial statements of other firms. One way that financial statements can be standardized is if all the assets and liabilities a firm owns are reported at a fair value. That is, if the firm's assets and liabilities are reported at existing market prices, individuals can make reasonable comparisons across the assets and liabilities numerous firms hold.

This can become complicated and controversial when firms are asked to assign market prices to particular types of financial instruments and pension liabilities. For example, structured derivative transactions may be assigned market prices, even though complex derivative arrangements are often not traded on secondary markets. The models that firms use to assign market prices to these types of transactions can vary widely from firm to firm—which makes it almost impossible to argue that standardization has taken place.

This modeling-based problem also exists for pension accountants. Some investors are applying pressure on firms to more fully detail the assumptions behind the valuation models, in an effort to make more reasonable comparisons across companies. In the end, standardizing these reporting methods may have to be done in a way that combines fair market prices, as well as some other method of calculating these prices, so investors can increase the confidence in comparisons across firms' assets and liabilities mixes.

Source: Adapted from "Complexity Dogs the Benefits of Fair Value," *Financial Times*, January 12, 2006.

3.3 Market Values versus Book Values

The official accounting values of assets and shareholders' equity are called **book values**. A company's book value per share is the number we get if we divide the total dollar amount in the shareholders' equity account of the firm's official balance sheet by the number of shares of common stock outstanding.[1]

Thus, in Table 3.1 we see that the book value per share of GPC stock at the end of 20x1 was $313.40. But the market price of a share of GPC stock at the end of 20x1 was only $187.50. This was the price that investors were willing to pay for a share of GPC common stock. The market value of the stock does not appear on the official balance sheet.

Why doesn't the market price of a company's stock equal its book value? And which of the two values is more relevant to the financial decision maker? We now turn our attention to these important questions.

There are essentially two reasons why the market price of a company's stock does not necessarily equal its book value:

- The book value does not include all of a firm's assets and liabilities.
- The assets and liabilities included on a firm's official balance sheet are (for the most part) valued at original acquisition cost less depreciation, rather than at current market values.

Let us consider each of these reasons separately.

First, the accounting balance sheet often omits some economically significant assets. For example, if a firm builds up a good reputation for the quality and reliability of its products, this will not appear as an asset on the balance sheet. Similarly, if a firm builds up

[1] Note that shares outstanding do not include Treasury stock, which are shares of stock that the firm has repurchased.

a knowledge base as the result of past research and development spending or as the result of training its workforce, these too will not appear as assets. These kinds of assets are called **intangible assets,** and clearly they add to the firm's market value and are relevant in decision making.

Accountants do report some intangible assets on the balance sheet, but not at their market values. For example, if a firm buys a patent from another firm, the value of that patent is recorded as an asset and amortized over time. Also, when one firm acquires another firm for a price that exceeds its book value, accountants will record an intangible asset called **goodwill** on the balance sheet of the acquiring firm. The value of goodwill is the difference between the market price of the acquisition and its book value. Despite these cases of intangible assets that are recorded on the accounting balance sheet, many others are not.

The accounting balance sheet also omits some economically significant liabilities. For example, if the firm has lawsuits pending against it, these will not appear on the balance sheet. The existence and amount of such contingent liabilities will at best only be disclosed in the footnotes to the financial statements.

Now let us consider whether it is market value or book value that is relevant for financial decision making. In almost all cases, book values are irrelevant. For example, say three years ago IBM purchased equipment needed for molding computer shells for $3.9 million and today the equipment is carried on its books at $2.6 million, after three years of depreciation. But today, owing to technological change in the manufacture of computer shells, the market value of the machine has fallen to $1.2 million.

Now suppose you are considering replacing the equipment with more modern equipment. What is the relevant value to use to compare the alternatives? If we ignore tax considerations for the moment, we know from first principles in economics that the relevant value is the asset's opportunity cost, which is the asset's value in the best alternative use. Clearly, this value is best approximated by the market value of the equipment of $1.2 million, whereas the book value is essentially irrelevant.

As another example, let us consider your inventory of copper to be used in the manufacturing process of heating furnaces. You paid $29,000 at the beginning of the year for the copper, but today its market value has risen to $60,000. What is the relevant cost to include for the copper in your production decisions? Again, the original cost of $29,000 is not meaningful because the copper could be sold and to replace the inventory will cost $60,000. If you use the copper in production, you are actually using up $60,000 worth of resources.

The difference in value between the two measures can vary drastically depending on the situation. For example, in the case of cash there is literally no difference between book value and market value. In the case of fixed assets, such as specialized plant and equipment, the difference can be, and often is, huge. Thus, the difference between the market and book values of an asset depends on the type of asset. Again, for decision-making purposes, the correct value to use is the market value, whenever available.

It is worth noting that the accounting profession has moved slowly toward market-value–based accounting in an effort to be more relevant to decision makers. For example, assets held by corporations in their pension funds are now reported at current market values rather than acquisition cost. Revaluing and reporting a firm's assets and liabilities at their current market prices is called **marking to market.**

Quick Check 3-6

Why does the market price of a firm's stock usually differ from its book value?

3.4 Accounting versus Economic Measures of Income

The distinctions made about market values and book values carry over to our notions of income. A commonsense definition of income is the amount that you could spend during the period while maintaining the wealth with which you started the period. That is, what you could spend from incoming cash and still have the amount you started with remaining at the end of the period. Loosely speaking, this is the definition that the English Nobel Prize–winning economist John R. Hicks used in his classic treatise on the subject and the one that is generally used today by economists.[2] The accounting definition of income or earnings or profits (which all mean the same thing) ignores unrealized gains or losses in the market values of assets and liabilities, such as the increase or decrease in value of your shares of stock or the value of your property over the period.

As an example, suppose your net wages over the year were \$100,000, which you spent on your family consumption, but your assets overall declined in value by \$60,000. Generally speaking, accountants would ignore the decline in the market value of your assets because it is unrealized. The economist, on the other hand, would say that the decline in value must be counted in the income calculation because it affects your consumption possibilities, which are currently \$60,000 less than at the beginning of the year. Thus, your income is only \$40,000.

One other feature, often overlooked, is that accounting income allows as an income deduction the interest expense for the cost of borrowed funds, but not a comparable deduction for the equity funds employed. For example, if a company earned \$2 million but used \$50 million in shareholders' equity to finance the firm's assets at an approximate cost of 10% then from an economic perspective the firm incurred a loss of about \$3 million (i.e., $\$2\text{ m} - \$50\text{ m} \times 0.10 = -\$3\text{ m}$). Here is a case in which the accounting profit is positive but the firm is not covering its basic costs, including its costs of capital.

Box 3.4 Measuring EVA

Economic Value Added (EVA) is a method of measuring the economic performance of a firm. EVA can be thought of as the earnings a company has after accounting for required capital costs. The idea behind this measurement is that a company increases in value only if the return on its capital is greater than the opportunity cost of the capital investment. EVA is one of many measures that firms are using to diagnose their financial health. This measure is very clear, and is easily generated: It is either positive or negative, and is clearly based on standard measurements and not hidden assumptions. That is, the opportunity costs and returns on capital are known statistics that are little disputed.

EVA also makes the full costs a firm faces much more transparent, as well as the additional opportunities a firm has for investment. The problem with EVA is that it is a measure that bases its calculations on the historical record of past expenditures. Thus the calculation provides little information as to how a firm's current investments will likely impact on the future returns a firm will receive. Some argue that such a basis of measurement has a tendency to reward shortsighted decision making.

If the earnings of a firm are currently high, the EVA of the firm will also be high and this doesn't provide an additional incentive to make prudent long-run investments. Thus while EVA is an alternative method of examining economic performance, it isn't a method that, if adopted, will necessarily transform how a firm operates for the better.

Source: Adapted from "A Star to Sail By?," *The Economist*, July 31, 1997.

[2] J. R. Hicks, *Value and Capital*, 2nd ed. (New York: Oxford University Press, 1946), p. 172.

3.5 Returns to Shareholders versus Return on Book Equity

When shareholders of a corporation ask how well their company performed in a particular period (a quarter, a year, or several years), they mean by how much did the company add to their personal wealth in that period. A direct way to measure this is to compute the rate of return on an investment in the company's stock over the period. Recall from chapter 2 that we defined the rate of return from investing in a firm's stock as:

$$r = \frac{\text{Ending Price of a Share} - \text{Beginning Price} + \text{Cash Dividend}}{\text{Beginning Price}}$$

This is called **total shareholder returns**.

For example, consider the case of GPC Corp. From observed market data, we know that at the beginning of 20x1 GPC had a market price of \$200 per share and at the end of the year after paying dividends the market price was \$187.20 per share. Cash dividends for the year were \$10; the rate of return on an investment in GPC's stock in 20x1 was, therefore, 1.4% computed as follows:

$$\text{Total Shareholder Returns} = \frac{\$187.20 - \$200 + \$10}{\$200} = -0.014 \text{ or } -1.4\%$$

Traditionally, however, corporate performance has also been measured by looking at a ratio called the *return on equity* (*ROE*). *ROE* is defined as net profit (the bottom line from the company's income statement) divided by the book value of shareholders' equity (the bottom line from the firm's balance sheet).

For GPC's *ROE* we get:

$$ROE = \frac{\text{Net Income}}{\text{Shareholders' Equity}} = \frac{\$23.4 \text{ million}}{\$300 \text{ million}} = 0.078 \text{ or } 7.8\%$$

Thus, we see that there need be no correspondence between a firm's *ROE* in any year and the total rate of return earned by shareholders on their investment in the company's stock.

Quick Check 3-7

In 20x7 VGI corporation reported earnings per share of \$5 and paid a cash dividend to shareholders of \$3.00 per share. Its beginning-of-year book value per share was \$30, and its market price was \$40. At the end of the year, the book value per share was \$32 and the market price was \$35. Compare VGI's *ROE* and total shareholder returns.

3.6 Analysis Using Financial Ratios

Despite the differences between accounting and finance principles and practices listed previously, a firm's published financial statements can often offer some clues about its financial condition and insights into its past performance that may be relevant for the future.

Box 3.5 Sarbanes-Oxley

After Enron and other well-known corporate scandals, Congress responded to public outcry for reform by passing the Sarbanes-Oxley statute. The effectiveness and overall worth of this action remains up for debate. The law created the Public Company Accounting Oversight Board, an institution that monitors the work of auditors, largely as a result of Arthur Anderson LLP's actions with regard to the Enron scandal.

The statute also instituted provisions meant to reduce corporate corruption: Corporations can't make loans to executives; executives must certify the account records of their respective firms; and, if someone believes any corruption is occurring and blows the whistle, these individuals can't be persecuted. The law also holds managers and auditors more accountable for their routine actions. In order to comply with the law, however, firms have had to spend tremendous amounts of money. Some estimate the aggregate costs of compliance in the trillions of dollars.

These costs have become a significant problem as today four firms—Ernst & Young, Deloitte, PricewaterhouseCoopers, and KPMG—are responsible for auditing 97% of all large companies in America. The higher prices these auditing firms are now charging, to meet the demand to be in compliance with the law have caused a spillover, increasing the auditing costs for small firms as well. Of course these small firms have fewer additional options outside of using any of the "final four." Some analysts have claimed that the costs associated with adhering to the law will discourage foreign companies from listing on the New York exchange and that the law overly penalizes regular types of business errors.

Many of the costs associated with these legal compliance issues may be expected to decrease once auditors are accustomed to the new regulations. Only time will tell, however, when it comes to seeing how effective Sarbanes-Oxley will be in preventing corporate malfeasance, and whether the costs associated with the law are worthwhile.

Source: Adapted from "A Price Worth Paying?" *The Economist*, May 19, 2005.

In analyzing a firm's performance using its financial statements, it is helpful to define a set of ratios to facilitate comparisons over time and across companies.

We can analyze five main aspects of the firm's performance through ratios: profitability, asset turnover, financial leverage, liquidity, and market value. In Table 3.5 we present these ratios, and calculate them for GPC.

First are *profitability* ratios. Profitability can be measured with respect to sales (return on sales), assets (return on assets), or its equity base (return on equity). Income here is taken as earnings before interest and taxes (*EBIT*) in the case of return on sales and return on assets, but as net income in the case of return on equity. Also, whenever a financial ratio contains one item from the income statement, which covers a period of time, and another from the balance sheet, which is a "snapshot" at a point in time, the practice is to take the average of the beginning and end-of-year balance sheet figures, and use this average as the denominator.

Second are *asset turnover* ratios, which assess the firm's ability to use its assets productively in generating revenue. Asset turnover is a broad measure, whereas receivable turnover and inventory turnover are specific measures for these particular asset categories.

Third, *financial leverage* ratios highlight the capital structure of the firm, and the extent to which it is burdened with debt. The debt ratio measures the capital structure, and the times interest earned measure indicates the ability of the firm to cover its interest payments.

Fourth, *liquidity* ratios measure the ability of the firm to meet its short-term obligations, or to pay its bills and remain solvent. The main ratios for measuring liquidity are the current ratio and the more stringent quick ratio or acid test, which considers only the most liquid of current assets: cash and marketable securities.

TABLE 3.5 Classification of Financial Ratios

Ratio	Formula	Calculation	
Profitability			
Return on sales (*ROS*)	$\frac{EBIT}{\text{Sales}}$	$\frac{\$60}{\$200}$	= 30%
Return on assets (*ROA*)	$\frac{EBIT}{\text{Average Total Assets}}$	$\frac{\$60}{(\$600 + \$720)/2}$	= 9.1%
Return on equity (*ROE*)	$\frac{\text{Net Income}}{\text{Stockholders' Equity}}$	$\frac{\$23.4}{(\$300 + \$313.4)/2}$	= 7.6%
Asset Turnover			
Receivables turnover	$\frac{\text{Sales}}{\text{Average Receivables}}$	$\frac{\$200}{(\$50 + \$60)/2}$	= 3.6 times
Inventory turnover	$\frac{\text{Cost of Goods Sold}}{\text{Average Inventory}}$	$\frac{\$110}{(\$150 + \$180)/2}$	= 0.7 times
Asset turnover	$\frac{\text{Sales}}{\text{Average Total Assets}}$	$\frac{\$200}{(\$600 + \$720)/2}$	= 0.3 times
Financial Leverage			
Debt	$\frac{\text{Total Debt}}{\text{Total Assets}}$	$\frac{\$406.6}{\$720}$	= 57%
Times interest earned	$\frac{EBIT}{\text{Interest Expense}}$	$\frac{\$60}{\$21}$	= 2.9 times
Liquidity			
Current	$\frac{\text{Current Assets}}{\text{Current Liabilities}}$	$\frac{\$360}{\$256.6}$	= 1.4 times
Quick, or acid test	$\frac{\text{Cash + Receivables}}{\text{Current Liabilities}}$	$\frac{\$180}{\$256.6}$	= 0.7 times
Market Value			
Price to earnings	$\frac{\text{Price per Share}}{\text{Earnings per Share}}$	$\frac{\$187.2}{\$23.4}$	= 8.0
Market to book	$\frac{\text{Price per Share}}{\text{Book Value per Share}}$	$\frac{\$187.2}{\$313.4}$	= 0.6

Fifth are *market value* ratios, which measure the relation between the accounting representation of the firm and the market value of the firm. The two most common ratios are price to earnings (*P/E*) and market to book (*M/B*).[3]

When analyzing a firm's financial ratios, we need first to establish two things:

- whose perspective to adopt—shareholders, creditors, or some other group of stakeholders.
- what standard of comparison to use as a benchmark.

---

[3]A measure similar to the market to book (M/B) ratio is Tobin's Q ratio, which is named for the American Nobel Prize–winning economist, James Tobin. The ratio is defined as:

$$Q = \text{Market Value of Assets/Replacement Cost}$$

The denominator includes an adjustment to the original cost of assets for inflation.

Benchmarks can be of three types:

- financial ratios of other companies for the same period of time.
- financial ratios of the company itself in previous time periods.
- information extracted from financial markets such as asset prices or interest rates.

A variety of sources are available that produce ratios for a number of industries, including (1) Dun & Bradstreet, (2) *Annual Statement Studies* by Robert Morris Associates, (3) the Commerce Department's *Quarterly Financial Report,* and (4) trade associations. Additionally, these data have become available on-line via the Internet.

Quick Check 3-8

What are the five types of financial ratios used to analyze a company's performance?

3.6.1 The Relations among Ratios

It is useful to decompose a firm's *ROA* into the product of two ratios as follows:

$$\begin{aligned} ROA &= \frac{EBIT}{\text{Sales}} \times \frac{\text{Sales}}{\text{Assets}} \\ &= \text{Return on Sales} \times \text{Asset Turnover} \\ &= ROS \times ATO \end{aligned}$$

The decomposition of *ROA* into *ROS* and *ATO* highlights the fact that firms in different industries can have vastly different *ROS* and turnover ratios yet the same return on assets. Thus, a supermarket typically has a low profit margin on sales and a high asset turnover, whereas a high-priced jewelry store typically has a high profit margin and a low turnover. Both may have the same *ROA.*

To illustrate, let us take two firms with the same *ROA* of 10% per year. The first is a supermarket chain, the second a public utility company. As Table 3.6 shows, the supermarket chain has a "low" *ROS* of 2% and achieves a 10% *ROA* by "turning over" its assets five times per year. The capital-intensive utility, on the other hand, has a "low" *ATO* of only 0.5 times per year and achieves its 10% *ROA* by having an *ROS* of 20%.

The point here is that a "low" *ROS* or *ATO* ratio need not be a sign of a troubled firm. Each of these ratios must be interpreted in light of industry norms. Even in the same industry systematic differences may exist. For example, a Rolls Royce dealership will almost certainly have a higher margin and lower turnover than a Chevrolet dealership, even though both may have the same *ROA.*

Quick Check 3-9

If firm A has a higher *ROA* than firm B but the same *ATO,* what must be true of its *ROS?*

TABLE 3.6 **Difference Between *ROS* and *ATO* Across Industries**

	ROS	×	ATO	=	ROA
Supermarket chain	0.02		5.0		0.10
Public utility	0.20		0.5		0.10

3.6.2 The Effect of Financial Leverage

Financial leverage simply means the use of borrowed money. The shareholders of a firm use financial leverage in order to boost their *ROE,* but in so doing they increase the sensitivity of *ROE* to fluctuations in the firm's underlying operating profitability as measured by its *ROA.* In other words, by making use of financial leverage, the firm's shareholders are subjected to financial risk as well as to the operating risk of the firm.

An increase in a firm's financial leverage will increase its *ROE* if and only if its *ROA* exceeds the interest rate on the borrowed funds. This makes intuitive sense. If *ROA* exceeds the borrowing rate, then the firm earns more on the capital it employs than it pays to its creditors. The surplus is thus available to the firm's shareholders, and so raises *ROE.* If, on the other hand, *ROA* is less than the interest rate, the shareholders would have been better off not borrowing at all.

For example, Halfdebt Co. uses financial leverage, whereas Nodebt Co. does not. Let us compare their *ROE* under two different assumptions about the interest rate: (1) 10% per year, and (2) 15% per year. The results are given in Table 3.7.

Increased financial leverage magnifies the variability that firms experience in their *ROE* over the business cycle and increases the likelihood of bankruptcy. Table 3.8 illustrates the behavior of *ROA* and *ROE* under three scenarios, representing phases of the business cycle. We assume that the interest rate on Halfdebt's debt is 10% per year.

TABLE 3.7 Effect of Interest Rate on *ROE*

	Nodebt	Halfdebt
Total Assets	$1,000,000	$1,000,000
Equity	1,000,000	500,000
Debt	0	500,000
EBIT	120,000	120,000
ROA (EBIT/ASSETS)	12.0%	12.0%
Case (1): Borrowing at an interest rate of 10% per year		
EBIT	120,000	120,000
Interest Expense	0	50,000
Taxable Income	120,000	70,000
Taxes (@ 40%)	48,000	28,000
Net Income	72,000	42,000
Equity	1,000,000	500,000
ROE	7.2%	8.4%
Case (2): Borrowing at an interest rate of 15% per year		
EBIT	120,000	120,000
Interest Expense	0	75,000
Taxable Income	120,000	45,000
Taxes (@ 40%)	48,000	18,000
Net Income	72,000	27,000
Equity	1,000,000	500,000
ROE	7.2%	5.4%

TABLE 3.8 **Effect of Business Cycle on *ROE***

		ROE	
Economic Conditions	*ROA*	Nodebt	Halfdebt
Bad year	1.0%	0.6%	−4.8%
Normal year	12.0	7.2	8.4
Good year	30.0	18.0	30.0

The exact relationship between *ROE, ROA,* and leverage can be summarized in the following equation:

$$ROE = (1 - \text{Tax Rate}) \times \left[ROA + \left(\left({}^{\text{Debt}}\!/\!_{\text{Equity}} \right) \times (ROA - \text{Interest Rate}) \right) \right]$$

This equation has the following implications. If a firm's *ROA* exceeds the interest rate that it pays to its creditors, then its *ROE* will exceed (1 − tax rate) times *ROA* by an amount that will be greater the higher the debt/equity ratio.

From the perspective of a creditor, an increase in a firm's debt ratio is generally a negative sign. Bond-rating agencies, such as Moody's and Standard and Poors Corporation, will often downgrade a firm's securities if its debt ratio goes up. But from the shareholder's perspective, it might be positive for the firm to increase its debt ratio.

Quick Check 3-10

What is the effect of increased leverage on a firm's *ROE* if the interest rate on its debt is equal to its *ROA*?

3.6.3 Limitations of Ratio Analysis

Finally, the user of ratios must be aware of their limitations. The basic problem is there is no absolute standard by which to judge whether the ratios are too high or too low. Moreover, ratios are comprised of accounting numbers, often calculated in arbitrary ways. Furthermore, it is difficult to define a set of comparable firms because firms, even within the same industry, are often quite different. For example, firms vary in their level of diversification, in their size, in their age, in the extent to which they are international, and in the accounting methods used (e.g., their inventory and depreciation methods may differ). The punch line of financial ratio analysis, then, is that it may provide a rough guide that should not be relied upon exclusively for decisions.

3.7 The Financial Planning Process

Financial planning is a dynamic process that follows a cycle of making plans, implementing them, and revising them in the light of actual results. The starting point in developing a financial plan is the firm's strategic plan. Strategy guides the financial planning process by establishing overall business development guidelines and growth targets. Which lines of business does the firm want to expand, which to contract, and how quickly?

For example, ITT Corporation decided in 1995 to quit the insurance business and to concentrate on expanding its gaming and resort businesses. This decision meant that its financial plans starting in that year would be based on redeploying its assets. For several years there would not be any growth in total sales at the corporate level. Indeed, there would be significant "downsizing."[4]

The length of the *planning horizon* is another important element in financial planning. In general, the longer the horizon, the less detailed the financial plan. A five-year financial plan will typically consist of a set of forecasted income statements and balance sheets showing only general categories with few details. On the other hand, a financial plan for next month will show detailed forecasts of revenues and expenses for specific product lines and detailed projections of cash inflows and outflows. Multiyear plans are usually revised on an annual basis, and annual plans on a quarterly basis.

The financial planning cycle can be broken down into several steps:

1. Managers forecast the key external factors that determine the demand for the firm's products and its production costs. These factors include the level of economic activity in the markets in which the firm sells its products, inflation, exchange rates, interest rates, and the output and prices charged by the firm's competitors.
2. Based on these external factors and their own tentative decisions regarding investment outlays, production levels, research and marketing expenditures, and dividend payments, managers forecast the firm's revenues, expenses, and cash flows, and estimate the implied need for external financing. They check that the firm's likely future financial results are consistent with their strategic plan for creating value for shareholders and that financing is available to implement the plan. If there are any inconsistencies, then managers revise their decisions until they come up with a workable plan, which becomes a blueprint for the firm's operating decisions during the year. It is good practice to make contingency plans in case some of the forecasts turn out to be wrong.
3. Based on the plan, senior managers establish specific performance targets for themselves and their subordinates.
4. Actual performance is measured at regular intervals (either monthly or quarterly), compared to the targets set in the plan, and corrective actions are taken as needed. Management may adjust targets during the year to take into account large deviations from forecast values.
5. At the end of each year, rewards (e.g., bonuses or raises) are distributed and the planning cycle starts again.

3.8 Constructing a Financial Planning Model

Financial plans are usually embodied in quantitative models derived in whole or in part from a firm's financial statements. For example, let us construct a one-year financial plan for Generic Products Corporation (GPC), the same hypothetical firm whose financial statements we analyzed earlier in this chapter. GPC is a company that was founded 10 years ago to manufacture and sell generic products for the consumer market. Table 3.9 shows GPC's income statements and balance sheets for the last three years.

Let us assume that these financial statements are the only information about the company available. How could one formulate a plan for the coming year? The simplest approach is to make a forecast of sales for the next year and assume that most of the items on the income statement and balance sheet will maintain the same ratio to sales as in the previous year. This is called the **percent-of-sales method**. Let us illustrate the method with GPC.

The first step is an examination of past financial data to determine which items on the income statement and balance sheet have maintained a fixed ratio to sales. This enables us to

[4]The stock market reacted quite favorably to this shift in strategy. ITT's stock price rose dramatically compared to the change in the S&P 500 index. ITT's stock price tripled over the period from 1991 to 1995, during which its new strategy was formulated and ultimately implemented.

TABLE 3.9 **GPC Financial Statements: 20x1–20x3**

Income Statement		20x1	20x2	20x3
Sales		$200.00	$240.00	$288.00
Cost of goods sold		110.00	132.00	158.40
Gross margin		90.00	108.00	129.60
Selling, general, and administrative expenses		30.00	36.00	43.20
EBIT		60.00	72.00	86.40
Interest expense		30.00	45.21	64.04
Taxes		12.00	10.72	8.94
Net income		18.00	16.07	13.41
Dividends		5.40	4.82	4.02
Change in shareholders' equity		12.60	11.25	9.39
Balance Sheet	**20x0**	**20x1**	**20x2**	**20x3**
Assets	600.00	720.00	864.00	1,036.80
Cash and equivalents	10.00	12.00	14.40	17.28
Receivables	40.00	48.00	57.60	69.12
Inventories	50.00	60.00	72.00	86.40
Property, plant, and equipment	500.00	600.00	720.00	864.00
Liabilities	300.00	407.40	540.15	703.56
Payables	30.00	36.00	43.20	51.84
Short-term debt	120.00	221.40	346.95	501.72
Long-term debt	150.00	150.00	150.00	150.00
Shareholders' equity	$300.00	$312.60	$323.85	$333.24

In millions of U.S. dollars.

decide which items can be forecast strictly on the basis of our projected sales and which have to be forecast on some other basis. In the case of GPC, it is clear from the record that costs, *EBIT*, and assets have maintained fixed ratios to sales. However, interest expense, taxes, net income, and most liabilities (with the exception of payables) have not. This is shown in Table 3.10.

The second step is to forecast sales. Because so many items are linked to sales, it is important to have an accurate sales forecast and later to test the sensitivity of the plan to variations in sales. For GPC we will assume that sales will continue to grow by 20% next year, so that sales for 20x4 are forecast to be $345.6 million.

The third step is to forecast those items on the income statement and balance sheet that are assumed to maintain a constant ratio to sales. Thus, because cost of goods sold has historically been 55% of sales, the 20x4 forecast is 0.55 × $345.6 million, which is $190.08 million. Because total assets at the end of the year have been 3.6 times annual sales, the total asset figure forecast for the end of 20x4 is $1,244.16 million.

The final step is to fill in the missing items in the income statement and balance sheet (i.e., the items that do not maintain a fixed ratio to sales). Let us assume that the interest rate on the long-term debt is 8% per year and on the short-term debt 15% per year. Then our forecast for interest expense is 8% times the amount of long-term debt plus 15% times the amount of short-term debt outstanding at the beginning of the year (i.e., at the end of 20x3). Thus, total interest expense for 20x4 will be $87.26 million. Taxes are assumed to be 40% of

TABLE 3.10 **GPC Common-Size Financial Statements: 20x1–20x3**

Income Statement	20x1	20x2	20x3
Sales	100.0%	100.0%	100.0%
Cost of goods sold	55.0	55.0	55.0
Gross margin	45.0	45.0	45.0
Selling, general, and administrative expenses	15.0	15.0	15.0
EBIT	30.0	30.0	30.0
Interest expense	15.0	18.8	22.2
Taxes	6.0	4.5	3.1
Net income	9.0	6.7	4.7
Dividends	2.7	2.0	1.4
Change in shareholders' equity	6.3	4.7	3.3
Balance Sheet	**20x1**	**20x2**	**20x3**
Assets	360.0%	360.0%	360.0%
Cash and equivalents	6.0	6.0	6.0
Receivables	24.0	24.0	24.0
Inventories	30.0	30.0	30.0
Property, plant, and equipment	300.0	300.0	300.0
Liabilities	203.7	225.1	244.3
Payables	18.0	18.0	18.0
Short-term debt	110.7	144.6	174.2
Long-term debt	75.0	62.5	52.1
Shareholders' equity	156.3	134.9	115.7

All figures are percentages of sales for the respective years.

income after interest expense, or \$6.57 million. Net income after taxes is, therefore, \$9.85 million. The income statement for 20x4 will be as shown in the last column of Table 3.11.

Now let us consider the balance sheet at the end of 20x4. Because GPC will pay out 30% of net income as dividends, shareholders' equity will increase by \$6.9 million (from \$333.24 million to \$340.14 million). Total assets will increase by \$207.36 million, and payables will increase by \$10.37 million. To find the total need for additional funds to be raised either by issuing new stock or by increased borrowing, we subtract the increase in retained earnings and the increase in payables from the change in assets as follows:

$$\text{Additional Financing Needed} = \text{Change in Assets}$$
$$- \text{Increase in Retained Earnings} - \text{Increase in Payables} = \$207.36 \text{ million}$$
$$- \$6.9 \text{ million} - \$10.37 \text{ million} = 190.09 \text{ million}$$

Thus, there will be a need for an additional \$190.09 million in external financing. In the balance sheet data of Table 3.11, we have assumed that all of this financing will be in the form of an increase in short-term debt, which therefore increases from \$501.72 million to \$691.81 million.

Quick Check 3-11

If the sales revenue forecast for 20x4 is \$360 million instead of \$345.60, what will be the need for additional external financing?

TABLE 3.11 **GPC Forecast Income Statement and Balance Sheet for 20x4**

Income Statement		20x1	20x2	20x3	20x4e
Sales		$200.00	$240.00	$288.00	$345.60
Cost of goods sold		110.00	132.00	158.40	190.08
Gross margin		90.00	108.00	129.60	155.52
Selling, general, and administrative expenses		30.00	36.00	43.20	51.84
EBIT		60.00	72.00	86.40	103.68
Interest expense		30.00	45.21	64.04	87.26
Taxes		12.00	10.72	8.94	6.57
Net income		18.00	16.07	13.41	9.85
Dividends		5.40	4.82	4.02	2.96
Change in equity		12.60	11.25	9.39	6.90
Balance Sheet	**20x0**	**20x1**	**20x2**	**20x3**	**20x4e**
Assets	$600.00	$720.00	$864.00	$1,036.80	$1,244.16
Cash and equivalents	10.00	12.00	14.40	17.28	20.74
Receivables	40.00	48.00	57.60	69.12	82.94
Inventories	50.00	60.00	72.00	86.40	103.68
Property, plant, and equipment	500.00	600.00	720.00	864.00	1,036.80
Liabilities	300.00	407.40	540.15	703.56	904.02
Payables	30.00	36.00	43.20	51.84	62.21
Short-term debt	120.00	221.40	346.95	501.72	691.81
Long-term debt	150.00	150.00	150.00	150.00	150.00
Equity	300.00	312.60	323.85	333.24	340.14

In millions of U.S. dollars.

3.9 Growth and the Need for External Financing

We now know that if GPC's sales grow by 20% during 20x4, it will need to raise an additional $190.09 million in funds from external sources. Management may decide to raise this money either by increasing its short-term borrowing (as assumed in Table 3.11), by increasing its long-term debt, or by issuing new stock. Let us now see how sensitive this external financing need is to the assumed growth rate of sales.

One way to carry out such a sensitivity analysis is to repeat the procedure we just did in the previous section using different growth rates of sales. This can easily be done by creating an automated spreadsheet model with a computer program such as the one at this textbook's companion Web site.[5] The result is shown in Figure 3.1.

3.9.1 The Firm's Sustainable Growth Rate

Figure 3.1 tells us the amount of external financing the firm needs in order to achieve a certain targeted growth rate of sales. But we can ask the reverse question: How fast can a firm grow if it is constrained in the amount of external financing available to it?

[5]See www.prenhall.com/bodie.

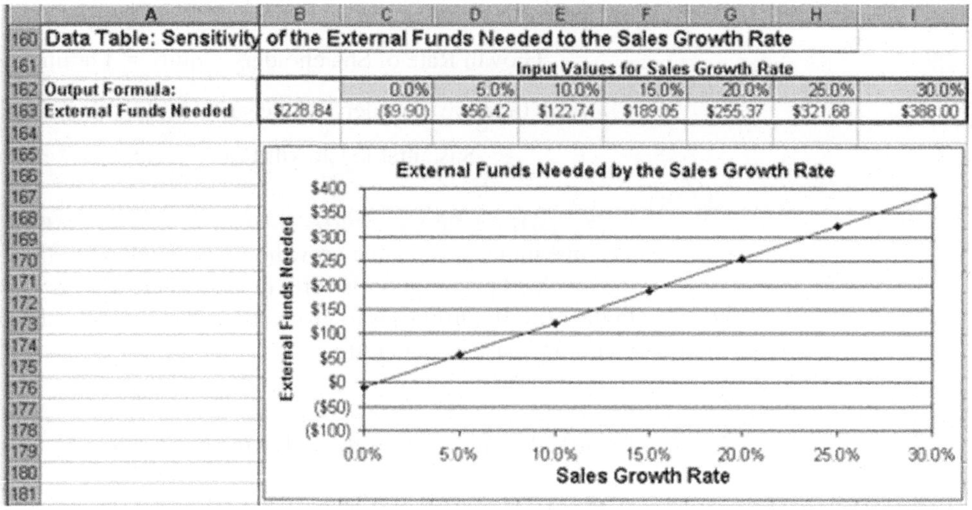

FIGURE 3.1

External Funds Needed as a Function of the Growth Rate

To address this question we assume that the financing constraint takes the following form:

- The firm will not issue any new equity shares, so that growth in equity capital occurs only through the retention of earnings.
- The firm will not increase its ratio of debt to equity, so that external debt financing will grow at the same rate as equity grows through retained earnings.

Under these circumstances, the firm cannot grow any faster than the growth rate in owners' equity, which is called the firm's **sustainable growth rate.** The formula for the sustainable growth rate is:

$$\text{Sustainable Growth Rate} = \text{Earnings Retention Rate} \times ROE$$

DERIVATION OF THE SUSTAINABLE GROWTH EQUATION

$$\text{Sustainable Growth Rate} = \text{Growth Rate of Shareholders' Equity}$$

Without the issuance of new shares, the rate of growth in shareholders' equity is just the increase in retained earnings divided by the beginning-of-year shareholders' equity:

$$\begin{aligned}&\text{Growth Rate of Shareholders' Equity}\\&= \text{Increase in Retained Earnings} \div \text{Shareholders' Equity at Beginning of Year}\end{aligned}$$

But:

$$\begin{aligned}&\text{Increase in Retained Earnings}\\&= \text{Earnings Retention Rate} \times \text{Net Income}\end{aligned}$$

The earnings retention rate is the proportion of net income not paid out in dividends or used to repurchase outstanding shares of stock. By definition it is equal to:

$$\begin{aligned}&\text{Earnings Retention Rate}\\&= 1 - \text{Dividend Payout Ratio} - \text{Share Repurchase Rate}\end{aligned}$$

Therefore, by substitution:

$$\begin{aligned}&\text{Growth Rate of Shareholders' Equity}\\&= \text{Earnings Retention Rate} \times \text{Net Income} \div \text{Shareholders' Equity}\end{aligned}$$

or in other words:

$$\text{Growth Rate of Shareholders' Equity} = \text{Earnings Retention Rate} \times ROE$$

And, thus, we have derived the sustainable growth equation:

$$\text{Sustainable Growth Rate} = \text{Earnings Retention Rate} \times ROE$$

IMPLICATIONS OF THE SUSTAINABLE GROWTH EQUATION

The maximum sustainable growth rate is equal to the firm's *ROE,* and it is achieved when the dividend payout ratio is zero, that is, when all of net income is retained and reinvested in the firm. If a firm tries to grow faster than this rate, then it will have to issue new shares and/or increase its debt ratio.

EXAMPLE OF SUSTAINABLE GROWTH

Rapid Industries (RI) has the following fixed ratios:

Asset Turnover = 0.5 Times per Year

Debt/Equity Ratio = 1.0

Dividend Payout Ratio = 0.4

ROE = 20% per Year

Last year sales were $1 million. That means that assets were $2 million, and debt and shareholders' equity were $1 million each. Because *ROE* was 20%, net income must have been $200,000, of which $80,000 was paid out in dividends and $120,000 retained as new equity capital. With a debt/equity ratio of 1, RI could increase its assets by $240,000 and its sales by as much as $120,000.

The sustainable growth rate of sales is, therefore:

$$g = \frac{\$120{,}000}{\$1 \text{ million}} = 0.12 \text{ or } 12\%$$

We get the same answer by applying the formula:

$$\begin{aligned} g &= ROE \times (1 - \text{Dividend Payout Ratio}) \\ &= 20\% \times (1 - 0.4) \\ &= 12\% \end{aligned}$$

The financial statements of Rapid Industries for three years of sustainable growth are shown in Table 3.12.

Quick Check 3-12

What are the implications for financing if a firm grew at a rate less than its sustainable rate?

3.10 Working Capital Management

In most businesses cash must be paid out to cover expenses before any cash is collected from the sale of the firm's products. As a result, a typical firm's investment in assets such as inventories and accounts receivable exceeds its liabilities such as accrued expenses and accounts payable. The difference between these current assets and current liabilities is called **working capital.** If a firm's need for working capital is permanent rather than seasonal,

TABLE 3.12 Rapid Industries Financial Statements for 20x1–20x3

Income Statements		20x1	20x2	20x3
Sales		$1,000,000	$1,120,000	$1,254,400
Net income		200,000	224,000	250,880
Dividends		80,000	89,600	100,352
Increase in retained earnings		120,000	134,400	150,528
Balance Sheets	**20x0**	**20x1**	**20x2**	**20x3**
Assets	$2,000,000	$2,240,000	$2,508,800	$2,809,856
Debt	1,000,000	1,120,000	1,254,400	1,404,928
Equity	1,000,000	1,120,000	1,254,400	1,404,928

it usually seeks long-term financing for it. Seasonal financing needs are met through short-term financing arrangements, such as a loan from a bank.

The main principle behind the efficient management of a firm's working capital is to minimize the amount of the firm's investment in nonearning assets such as receivables and inventories and maximize the use of "free" credit such as prepayments by customers, accrued wages, and accounts payable. These three sources of funds are free to the firm in the sense that they usually bear no explicit interest charge.[6]

Policies and procedures that shorten the lag between the time that the firm sells a product and the time that it collects cash from its customers reduce the need for working capital. Ideally, the firm would like its customers to pay in advance. The firm can also reduce its need for working capital by extending the time between when it purchases its inputs and when it pays cash for them.

To gain a clearer understanding of the relation between these time lags and the firm's investment in working capital, consider Figure 3.2.

The **cash cycle time** is the number of days between the date the firm must start to pay cash to its suppliers and the date it begins to receive cash from its customers. From Figure 3.2, we see that the cash cycle time is the difference between the sum of the inventory and receivables periods on the one hand and the payables period on the other.

$$\text{Cash Cycle Time} = \text{Inventory Period} + \text{Receivables Period} - \text{Payables Period}$$

The firm's required investment in working capital is directly related to the length of its cash cycle time. If the payables period is long enough to cover the sum of the inventory and receivables periods, then the firm needs no working capital at all.

FIGURE 3.2

The Cash Flow Cycle

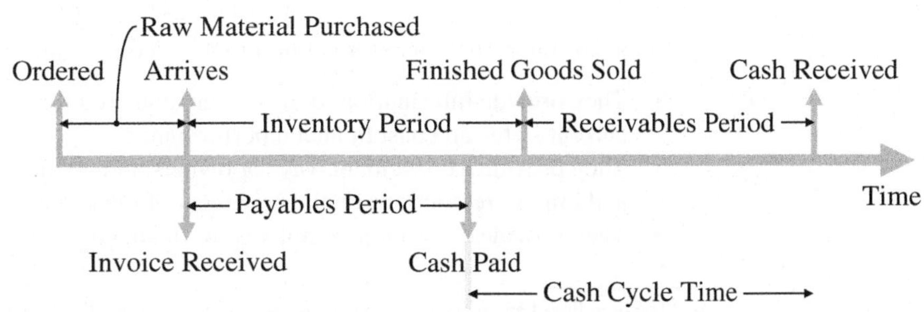

[6]If, however, the firm gives price discounts on its products to customers who pay in advance, then the size of this discount represents an implicit interest charge. Similarly, if the firm forgoes a discount from its suppliers by delaying payment to them, this forgone discount represents an implicit interest charge.

What kinds of actions can a firm take to reduce its need for working capital? From the equation for cash cycle time, we can see that a firm can reduce its need for working capital by:

- *reducing the amount of time that goods are held in inventory.* This can be accomplished by improving the inventory control process or by having suppliers deliver raw materials exactly when they are needed in the production process.
- *collecting accounts receivable more quickly.* Among the methods available to speed up the collection process are improving the efficiency of the collection process, offering discounts to customers who pay faster, and charging interest on accounts that are overdue.
- *paying its own bills more slowly.*

Quick Check 3-13

How can a firm reduce its need for working capital?

3.11 Liquidity and Cash Budgeting

There is an apocryphal story about how the billionaire Howard Hughes found himself without any cash or credit cards in a place where no one recognized him. Without any means to pay for food, drink, shelter, or transportation, the billionaire nearly died of starvation and exposure. The same point applies to corporations: A firm that is profitable in the long run can experience serious difficulties and even fail if it runs out of cash or credit in the short run. Rarely does a firm become spectacularly successful simply by managing well the short-term flows of cash into and out of the business, but failure to manage them properly can lead to ruin.

Howard Hughes's problem was that he became temporarily illiquid. **Liquidity** means that one has the means to make *immediate* payment for some purchase or to settle a debt that has come due. *Illiquidity* is a situation in which one has sufficient wealth to afford the purchase or to settle the debt, but one does not have the means to pay immediately.[7]

To avoid the difficulties caused by illiquidity, firms need to forecast their cash outflows and inflows carefully. A plan that shows these forecasts is called a **cash budget**.

Quick Check 3-14

Why is liquidity important to a firm?

Summary

Financial statements serve three important economic functions:

- They provide information to the owners and creditors of the firm about the company's current status and past financial performance.
- They provide a convenient way for owners and creditors to set performance targets and impose restrictions on the managers of the firm.
- They provide convenient templates for financial planning.

[7]The liquidity of an asset can be defined as one's ability to immediately convert it into cash at full value. A good measure of an asset's liquidity is the cost of buying it and then immediately reselling it. Thus, the liquidity of a new car that you buy is the gap between the price you paid for it and the price you could get for it if you sold it to someone else the next instant. For an asset that is traded in a dealer market this cost is its bid-asked spread. Cash is defined as the asset with a zero bid-asked spread.

The basic accounting statements reviewed are the income statement, the balance sheet, and the statement of cash flows. The *income statement* reports the results of operations over the period and is based on the model of revenues minus costs (including depreciation and taxes) equals net income or earnings. The *balance sheet* shows the assets (both current and long-term or fixed assets) on the one hand, and the claims against them (i.e., the liabilities and equity) on the other. The *statement of cash flows* gives a summary of cash flows from operating, investing, and financing activities for the period.

A firm's accounting balance sheet differs from an economic balance sheet because:

- it omits some economically significant assets and liabilities, and
- it does not report all assets and liabilities at their current market values.

Analysts use financial ratios as one mode of analysis to better understand the company's strengths and weaknesses, whether its fortunes are improving, and what its prospects are. These ratios are often compared with the ratios of a comparable set of companies and to ratios of recent past periods. The five types of ratios are profitability, turnover, financial leverage, liquidity, and market value ratios. Finally, it is helpful to organize the analysis of these ratios in a way that reveals the logical connections among them and their relation to the underlying operations of the firm.

The purpose of financial planning is to assemble the firm's separate divisional plans into a consistent whole, to establish concrete targets for measuring success, and to create incentives for achieving the firm's goals. The tangible outcome of the financial planning process is a set of "blueprints" in the form of projected financial statements and budgets. The longer the time horizon, the less detailed the financial plan.

In the short run, financial planning is concerned primarily with the management of working capital. The need for working capital arises because for many firms cash needed to conduct production and selling activities starts to flow out before cash flows in. The longer this time lag, which is called the length of the cash flow cycle, the more the amount of working capital the firm needs.

A firm's need for working capital is measured as the sum of cash equivalents, prepaid expenses, receivables, and inventories minus the sum of customer advances, payables, and accrued expenses. The main principle behind the efficient management of a firm's working capital is to minimize the amount of the firm's investment in low-earning current assets such as receivables and inventories and maximize the use of low-cost financing through current liabilities such as customer advances and accounts payable.

Cash management is important because even a profitable firm can get into financial distress or even go bankrupt if it becomes illiquid.

Key Terms

- book values 80
- intangible assets 81
- goodwill 81
- marking to market 81
- total shareholder returns 83
- percent-of-sales method 89
- sustainable growth rate 93
- working capital 94
- cash cycle time 95
- liquidity 96
- cash budget 96

Answers to Quick Check Questions

Quick Check 3-1 What are the three basic economic functions served by financial statements?

Answer:

- They provide information to the owners and creditors of the firm about the company's current status and past financial performance.
- They provide a convenient way for owners and creditors to set performance targets and to impose restrictions on the managers of the firm.
- Financial statements provide convenient templates for financial planning.

Quick Check 3-2 What difference would it have made to the end-of-year balance sheet if GPC had issued an additional $50 million of long-term debt during the year and added that amount to its holdings of cash and marketable securities?

Answer: The liability, long-term debt, and the asset, cash and marketable securities, would both have increased by $50 million, and shareholder's equity would have remained unchanged.

Quick Check 3-3 What difference would it have made to the income statement and the end-of-year balance sheet if GPC had retained all of its net income instead of paying out cash dividends of $10 million?

Answer: Net income would have been the same. The end-of-year balance sheet, however, would have shown an increase of $10 million in cash and in shareholders' equity.

Quick Check 3-4 What difference would it have made to the cash flow statement if GPC had retained all of its net income instead of paying out cash dividends of $10 million?

Answer: If GPC had not paid a cash dividend of $10 million, it could have borrowed $10 million less. Therefore, the cash flow statement would have showed no dividend and an increase in debt of only $84.6 million.

Quick Check 3-5 What potentially important information about a firm can be found in the footnotes to its financial statements?

Answer:

- An explanation of accounting methods used.
- Greater detail regarding certain assets or liabilities.
- Information regarding the equity structure of the firm.
- Documentation of changes in operations.
- Off-balance-sheet items.

Quick Check 3-6 Why does the market price of a firm's stock usually differ from its book value?

Answer: The book value does not include all of a firm's assets and liabilities. The assets and liabilities included on a firm's official balance sheet are not marked to market.

Quick Check 3-7 In 20x7 VGI corporation reported earnings per share of $5 and paid a cash dividend to shareholders of $3.00 per share. Its beginning-of-year book value per share was $30, and its market price was $40. At the end of the year, the book value per share was $32 and the market price was $35. Compare VGI's *ROE* and total shareholder returns (*TSR*).

Answer:

$$ROE = 5/30 = 16.67\%$$

$$TSR = (3 + 35 - 40)/40 = -5\%$$

Quick Check 3-8 What are the five types of financial ratios used to analyze a company?

Answer: The five ratios are profitability, activity, financial leverage, liquidity, and market price ratios.

Quick Check 3-9 If firm A has a higher *ROA* than firm B but the same *ATO*, what must be true of its *ROS*?

Answer: Firm A's *ROS* must be higher than B's.

Quick Check 3-10 What is the effect of increased leverage on a firm's *ROE* if the interest rate on its debt is equal to its *ROA*?

Answer: The firm's *ROE* will not change.

Quick Check 3-11 If the sales revenue forecast for 20x4 is $360 million instead of $345.60, what will be the need for additional external financing?

Answer: The total asset figure forecast for the end of 20x4 is now 3.6 × $360 million, which is $1,296 million. So the change in assets for the year is $1,296 − $1,036.8, which is $259.20. This growth in assets will be partially financed from the increase in retained earnings and the growth in payables, but the rest of the financing needed will have to come from external sources. Payables will increase by 18% (the ratio of payables to sales) times the increase in sales, which is 0.18 × $72 million or $12.96 million. Now let us forecast the firm's net income. *EBIT* is 0.3 × $360 million, which is $108 million. Total interest expense is unchanged at $87.26 million. Taxes are 40% of income after interest expense: Taxes = 0.4 × (108 − 87.26) = $8.296 million. Net income after taxes is, therefore, 0.6 × (108 − 87.26) = $12.444 million. Because GPC will pay out 30% of net income as dividends, the increase in retained earnings will be 0.7 × $12.444 = $8.711 million.

Additional Financing Needed =
Change in Assets − Increase in Retained Earnings − Increase in Payables =
$259.2 million − $8.711 million − $12.96 million = $237.529 million

Quick Check 3-12 What are the implications for financing if a firm grows at a rate less than its sustainable rate?

Answer: The firm will be able to lower its debt ratio or repurchase its own shares.

Quick Check 3-13 How can a firm reduce its need for working capital?

Answer: By either reducing inventories, speeding up collections, or slowing down the payment of its own bills.

Quick Check 3-14 Why is liquidity important to a firm?

Answer: A firm that is profitable in the long run can experience serious difficulties and even fail if it runs out of cash or credit in the short run.

Questions and Problems

Review of Financial Statements

1. Suggest if and how the following assets and liabilities would be recorded on their owner's balance sheets.
   a. a lottery ticket
   b. a successful song
   c. an unsuccessful movie
2. Show how the following events and transactions should appear on your personal income statement, balance sheet, and cash flow statement.
   a. On July 1, 200X, you receive $20,000 in gifts upon graduation from school and pay off a $10,000 student loan.

b. On August 1, 200X, you get a job as a finance intern at General Financial Services Inc. You are promised a salary of $4,000 per month, payable on the last day of each month.

c. On August 31, you receive your first statement of GFS salary and benefits showing the following items:

Gross salary	$4,000
Income tax withholding	1,400
Social Security and Medicare tax	500
Health care premium	150
Contribution to pension plan	200
Employer Social Security tax	300
Employer contribution to pension plan	200
Employer contribution to health care	150
Amount credited to employee checking account at GFS Bank	1,750
Total employer benefit	650

d. On September 1, you purchase a new car for $20,000. You make a down payment of $5,000 and borrow the remaining $15,000 from GFS bank at a monthly interest rate of 1%. Your monthly payment is $498.21 for 36 months.

e. As an individual or a household, why might you want to maintain a balance sheet? How often would you update it? Should you mark-to-market or leave your assets and liabilities at their historical values?

Problems 3 through 10 are based on the following information:
The Ruffy Stuffed Toy Company's balance sheet at the end of 20x1 is given below.

Assets		Liabilities and Shareholders' Equity	
Cash	$27,300	Payable	
Accounts Receivable	35,000	Accounts payable	$65,000
Inventory	57,000	Salary Payable	3,000
Total current assets	119,300	Utilities Payable	1,500
Property, Plant, and Equipment		Loans (Long-term debt)	25,000
Equipment	25,000	*Total Liabilities*	94,500
Less Accumulated Depreciation	(2,500)	Common Stock	45,000
Net Equipment	22,500	Retained Earnings	16,300
Furniture	16,000	*Total Shareholders' Equity*	61,300
Less Accumulated Depreciation	(2,000)	**Total Liabilities & Equity**	**155,800**
Net Furniture	14,000		
Total Prop, Plant, and Equipment	36,500		
Total Assets	**155,800**		

During 20x2, the Ruffy Stuffed Toy Company recorded the following transactions:

- Early in the year, purchased a new toy stuffing machine for $9,000 cash and signed a 3-year note for the balance of $12,000.
- Had cash sales of $115,000 and sales on credit of $316,000.
- Purchased raw materials from suppliers for $207,000.

- Made payments of $225,000 to its raw materials suppliers.
- Paid rent expenses totaling $43,000.
- Paid insurance expenses totaling $23,000.
- Paid utility bills totaling $7,500; $1,500 of this amount reversed the existing payable from 20x1.
- Paid wages and salaries totaling $79,000; $3,000 of this amount reversed the payable from 20x1.
- Paid other miscellaneous operating expenses totaling $4,000.
- Collected $270,000 from its customers who made purchases on credit.
- The interest rate on the loan payable is 10% per year. Interest was paid on 12/31/20x2.

Other information:

- The equipment has been estimated to have a useful life of 20 years, with no salvage value. Two years have been depreciated through 20x1.
- The existing furniture has been estimated to have a useful life of 8 years (no salvage value), of which one year has been depreciated through 20x1.
- The new stuffing machine has been estimated to have a useful life of 7 years, and will probably have no salvage value.
- The corporate income tax rate is 35% and taxes are paid on 12/31/20x2.
- Dividend payout, if possible, will be 10% of net income.
- Cost of Goods Sold for the year's sales were $250,000.
- Accounts Receivable Ending Balance = Beginning Balance − cash received from credit customers + sales on credit.
- Accounts Payable Ending Balance = Beginning Balance + purchases − cash payments to suppliers
- Inventory Ending Balance = Beginning Balance + purchases of raw material – cost of goods sold
- The company's stock price at market close on 12/31/20x2 was 4.625. It has 20,000 shares outstanding.

3. Construct the balance sheet for the Ruffy Stuffed Toy Company as of 12/31/20x2.
4. Construct the income statement for operations during the year 20x2.
5. Construct a cash flow statement for the year 20x2.

Analysis Using Financial Ratios

6. Calculate the following Profitability Ratios: Return on Sales, Return on Assets, Return on Equity.
7. Calculate the following Asset Turnover Ratios: Receivables turnover, Inventory turnover, Asset turnover.
8. Calculate the following Financial Leverage and Liquidity Ratios: debt, times interest earned, current ratio, quick (acid) test.
9. What is the Ruffy's book value per share at the end of 20x2?

Market Values versus Book Values

10. Calculate the firm's price-to-earnings ratio and the ratio of its market share price to its book value per share.

Analysis Using Financial Ratios

11. You have the following information taken from the 2001 financial statements of Computronixs Corporation and Digitek Corporation: (*All figures are in $ millions except for the second and final three rows.*)

	Computronix	Digitek
Net income	153.7	239.0
Dividend payout ratio	40%	20%
EBIT	317.6	403.1
Interest expense	54.7	4.8
Average assets	2,457.9	3,459.7
Sales	3,379.3	4,537.0
Average shareholders' equity	1,113.3	2,347.3
Market price of the common stock:		
beginning of year	$15	$38
end of year	$12	$40
Shares of common stock outstanding	200 million	100 million

Compare and contrast the financial performance of the two companies using the financial ratios discussed in this chapter.

Review of Financial Statements

12. You are thinking of taking a trip to Florida for your spring vacation, which begins two months from now. You use Excite's free preview Travel service on the Internet to find the cheapest round trip fare from Boston to Fort Lauderdale. It tells you that the cheapest airline is AirTran. You have never heard of this airline before and are concerned that it may go out of business before you can use your ticket two months from now. How can you use financial data available on the Internet (e.g., at http://www.quicken.com) to investigate the risk to you of buying an AirTran ticket? Which firms are in the relevant "benchmark" group for your purposes?
13. Using the income statements and balance sheets (see below):
    a. Determine which items varied in constant proportion to sales between 20x6 and 20x7.
    b. Determine the rate of growth in sales that was achieved from 20x6 to 20x7.
    c. What was the firm's return on equity for 20x7? Can you calculate it for 20x6?
    d. What was the firm's external (additional) funding requirement determined to be for 20x7? How was the funding obtained?
14. *Challenge Problem:* Prepare financial statements for 20x8 with the following assumptions:
    - Rate of growth in sales = 15%.
    - The firm intends to pay down $100,000 of its short-term debt on Jan. 1, 20x8.
    - Interest rates on debt are as stated in the balance sheet, and are applied to the start-of-year (20x8) balances for short-term and long-term debt. Remember that the firm intends to pay down part of the short-term loan on 1/1/20x8.
    - The firm's dividend payout in 20x8 will be reduced to 30%.

    What would be the firm's forecasted return on equity for 20x8? How much additional funding will the firm need for 20x8? The firm will close 40% of any additional funding gap by issuing new stock. It will then use up to $100,000 of long-term debt, with the remainder coming from 9% short-term borrowing. Complete the balance sheet for 20x8. Suppose the firm anticipates an increase in the corporate tax rate to 38%. Determine the amount of additional funding that would be required.
15. *Challenge Problem:* Take the financial statements (with tax rate = 35%) developed in the previous problem, and: Revise them assuming a growth rate in sales from 20x7 to 20x8 of 10%. What is the additional funding required for 20x8 under this scenario?

Refer to the following financial statements for Problems 13, 14, and 15:

INCOME STATEMENT	20x6	20x7	20x8
Sales	$1,200,000	$1,500,000	
Cost of Goods Sold	$750,000	$937,500	
Gross Margin	$450,000	$562,500	
Operating Expenses			
Advertising Expense	$50,000	$62,500	
Rent Expense	$72,000	$90,000	
Salesperson Commission Expense	$48,000	$60,000	
Utilities Expense	$15,000	$18,750	
EBIT	$265,000	$331,250	
Interest Expense	$106,000	$113,000	
Taxable Income	$159,000	$218,250	
Taxes (35%)	$55,650	$76,388	
Net Income	$103,350	$141,863	
Dividends (40% payout)	$41,340	$56,745	
Change in Retained Earnings	$62,010	$85,118	

BALANCE SHEET	20x6	20x7	20x8
Assets			
Cash	$300,000	$375,000	
Receivables	$200,000	$250,000	
Inventory	$700,000	$875,000	
Property, Plant, Equipment	$1,800,000	$2,250,000	
Total Assets	$3,000,000	$3,750,000	
Liabilities and Shareholders' Equity			
Liabilities			
Payables	$300,000	$375,000	
Short-term debt (10% interest)	$500,000	$989,882	
Long-term debt (7% interest)	$800,000	$900,000	
Shareholders' Equity			
Common Stock	$1,100,000	$1,100,000	
Retained Earnings	$300,000	$385,118	
Total Liabilities and Equity	$3,000,000	$3,750,000	

Now, develop financial statements for 20x9 assuming a growth rate in sales of 20% from 20x8 to 20x9. What is the additional funding needed for 20x9? The firm plans to use 9% short-term debt to cover this entire amount.

Growth and the Need for External Financing

16. Suppose that after analyzing the results of 20x8 and forecasting the financial statements for 20x9, the Give Me Debt Company anticipates an increase in total assets of $50, an increase in retained earnings of $25, and an increase in payables of $40. Assume that other than the payables, the firm's liabilities include short-term and long-term debt, and that its equity includes common stock and retained earnings. The Chief Financial Officer of the company asks you to determine the required amount of external funding in 20x9. What do you tell the CFO?

What actions can Give Me Debt Co. undertake to address the situation you have found?

The Financial Planning Process

17. Place the following planning events in their likely order of occurrence within the planning cycle:

—Funding needs for implementation of tactical plans are estimated.
—The final firm-wide plan and budgets are completed
—CEO and top management team establish strategic objectives for the firm (ex: increase market share from 10% to 12%)
—Line managers devise action plans to support strategic objectives
—Revisions are made to the strategic plan and divisional budgets based on feedback from divisional managers with regard to resource (money, people) requirements
—Decisions are made as to which sources of external financing to tap
—Integration of divisional budgets into a preliminary firm-wide budget by CEO and top management team
—The firm determines the amount of required external financing
—Tactical plans and budgets are reviewed with division management; priorities are assigned to planned activities
—Division managers review the strategic objectives with their line (or tactical) management

Constructing a Financial Planning Model

18. Suppose that the sharply abbreviated actual 20x8 and forecasted 20x9 income statement and balance sheet for Cones 'R' Us, an ice-cream retailer, appear as follows:

INCOME STATEMENT	20x8	20x9
EBIT		$100
Interest Expense		25
Taxable Income		75
Net Income (33% tax rate)		50
Dividends		20
Change in Retained Earnings		30
BALANCE SHEET		
Assets	$800	$1,000
Liabilities		
Payables	80	100
Debt	300	450
Shareholders' Equity	420	450

The \$25 interest expense projected for 20x9 is based on a rate of 8.33% applied to the outstanding debt balance of \$300 at the end of 20x8. Debt increases from \$300 to \$450 because of external financing that is obtained to close the gap exhibited in the relationship:

Additional Financing Needed = Change in Assets − Increase in Retained Earnings − Increase in Payables

a. What problems are created in using the forecasted statements to determine the required amount of additional (external) financing if the debt that will be used to satisfy the funding need is acquired in total at the beginning of 20x9, rather than at the end of 20x9 as is implied in these statements?

b. Is this problem likely to be significant? Why?

Growth and the Need for External Financing

19. The sustainable growth rate is given by the expression: g = ROE(1 − Dividend Payout Ratio) Substitution of the definitions of ROE and the Dividend Payout Ratio allows the growth rate to be expressed as:

g = (Net Income/Shareholders' Equity) (Retention Ratio)
= (Net Income)(Retention Ratio)/(Shareholder's Equity)

How then can a firm ensure its sustainable growth rate will be zero?

20. Assume a firm has net income in 20x9 of \$20 and its end-of-year 20x8 total assets were \$450. Further assume that the firm has a standing requirement to maintain a debt/equity ratio of 0.8, and that its managers are prohibited from further borrowing or stock issuance.

a. What is this firm's maximum sustainable growth rate?

b. If the firm pays \$6 of the \$20 net income as a dividend, and plans to maintain this payout ratio into the future, now what is its maximum sustainable growth rate?

c. If the firm uses \$12 of the \$20 net income to repurchase some of its outstanding shares, and plans to maintain the use of this ratio of net income for future repurchases, now what is its maximum sustainable growth rate?

d. If the firm takes action as described in parts (b) and (c), what would its maximum sustainable growth rate be?

Working Capital Management

21. Suppose it is 3/13/x2, and you just received your monthly credit card statement with a new balance of \$2,000. The payment is due on 4/5/x2, but your spouse panics at the sight (and size) of the balance and wants to pay it immediately. If you practice the principles of cash cycle time management in your personal finances, when would you make the payment? Why? What danger exists in adopting this strategy?

22. Suppose you own a firm that manufactures pool tables. Thirty days ago, you hired a consultant to examine your business and suggest improvements. The consultant's proposal, if implemented, would allow your firm to shorten the time between each sale and the subsequent cash collection by 20 days, slightly lengthen the time between inventory purchase and sale by only 5 days, but shorten the time between inventory purchase and your firm's payment of the bill by 15 days. Would you implement the consultant's proposal? Why?

23. In general, the principles of cash cycle time management call for a firm to shorten (minimize) the time it takes to collect receivables, and lengthen (maximize) the time it takes to pay amounts it owes to suppliers. Explain what tradeoffs need to be managed if the firm offers discounts to customers who pay early, and the firm also foregoes discounts offered by its suppliers by extending the time until it pays invoices.

24. Some furniture companies conduct highly advertised annual sale events in which customers can either take an up-front discount for a cash (or credit card) purchase, or defer finance charges for up to one year on their purchases by charging it to the company's credit account. Assume that the two options do not present a time value of money advantage for the company. In terms of cash cycle management: (1) Why does the company offer the discount? (2) Why might the company be willing to forego cash collection for one year if a customer chooses to defer? What risk does the company assume in the deferment case that it does not assume in the discount case?

Liquidity and Cash Budgeting

25. Compare the frequency with which you think a firm may monitor its working capital situation, and move to correct a problem, with the frequency of the firm's planning exercise in forecasting future sales and determining the need for additional financing. If a firm were to monitor its working capital situation closely, what problem might it be looking to avoid?

PART II TIME AND RESOURCE ALLOCATION

CHAPTER 4

Allocating Resources Over Time

OBJECTIVES

- To explain the concepts of compounding and discounting, and future value and present value.
- To show how these concepts are applied in making financial decisions.

CONTENTS

As we saw in chapter 1, financial decisions involve costs and benefits that are spread over time. Financial decision makers in households and firms all have to evaluate whether investing money today is justified by the expected benefits in the future. They must, therefore, compare the values of sums of money at different dates. To do so requires a thorough understanding of the **time value of money** concepts and **discounted cash flow** techniques presented in this chapter.

The time value of money (*TVM*) refers to the fact that money (a dollar, a euro, or a yen) in hand today is worth more than the expectation of the same amount to be received in the future. There are at least three reasons why this is true. The first is that you can invest it, earn interest, and end up with more in the future. The second is that the purchasing power of money can change over time because of inflation. The third is that the receipt of money expected in the future is, in general, uncertain.

In this chapter we study how to take account of the first of these: interest. We leave the study of how to deal with inflation and uncertainty to later chapters.

4.1 Compounding

We begin our study of the time value of money and discounted cash flow analysis with the concept of **compounding**—the process of going from today's value, or **present value** (*PV*), to **future value** (*FV*). Future value is the amount of money an investment will grow to at some date in the future by earning interest at some compound rate. For example, suppose you put $1,000 (the *PV*) into an account earning an interest rate of 10% per year. The amount you will have in five years, assuming you take nothing out of the account before then, is called the future value of $1,000 at an interest rate of 10% per year for five years.

Let us define our terms more precisely:

PV = present value or beginning amount in your account. Here, it is $1,000.

i = interest rate, usually expressed in percent per year. Here, it is 10% (or 0.10 as a decimal).

n = number of years the account will earn interest.

FV = future value at the end of n years.

Now let's calculate the future value in this example one step at a time. First, how much will you have after the first year? You will have your original $1,000 plus interest of $100 (10% of $1,000 or 0.1 × $1,000). Your future value at the end of year 1 will, therefore, be $1,100:

$$FV = \$1{,}000 \times 1.10 = \$1{,}100$$

If you redeposit this entire sum of $1,100 for another year, how much will you have at the end of year 2? During year 2 you will earn 10% interest on the entire $1,100. The interest earned is, thus, 0.10 × $1,100 or $110. You will, therefore, have $1,210 at the end of year 2.

To gain a good understanding of the nature of compound interest, we can break this future value of $1,210 into its three components. First, there is the original principal of $1,000. Next, there is the interest on this principal—$100 in the first year and another $100 in the second year. The interest on the original principal is called **simple interest** ($200 in our example). Finally, there is $10 of interest earned in the second year on the $100 of interest earned in the first year. Interest earned on interest already paid is called **compound interest.** The total interest earned ($210) is the sum of the simple interest ($200) plus the compound interest ($10).

Practically speaking, you do not care how much of your total interest of $210 is simple interest and how much is compound interest. All you really care about is how much you will have in your account in the future, that is, the future value. The most direct way to calculate the future value at the end of year 2 is to recognize that it is the original principal multiplied by 1.1 (here we drop the zero from 1.10 to shorten our equations) and then multiplied by 1.1 again:

$$FV = \$1{,}000 \times 1.1 \times 1.1 = \$1{,}000 \times 1.1^2 = \$1{,}210$$

After three years you will have:

$$FV = \$1{,}000 \times 1.1 \times 1.1 \times 1.1 = \$1{,}000 \times 1.1^3 = \$1{,}331$$

By this chain of reasoning, we can find future value after five years by repeated multiplication:

$$\$1{,}000 \times 1.1 \times 1.1 \times 1.1 \times 1.1 \times 1.1 = \$1{,}100 \times 1.1^5 = \$1{,}610.51$$

Thus, we have our answer to the original question. The future value of $1,000 at an interest rate of 10% per year for five years is $1,610.51. The total interest earned over the five years is $610.51, of which $500 is simple interest and $110.51 is compound interest.

Quick Check 4-1

If the interest rate is only 5% per year in the previous example, what is the future value? What are the simple interest and the compound interest?

To help in understanding the effect of compounding, look at Table 4.1, which shows the growth of the amount in your account over the five-year period. The table shows clearly that the total interest earned each year is equal to the beginning amount multiplied by the interest rate of 10%. When the information in the table is graphed in Figure 4.1, it shows the part of the growth in the account that is due to simple interest and the part that is due to compound interest. Although the cumulative total of simple interest grows each year by the same $100, the cumulative total of compound interest grows by larger and larger amounts each year. This is because the compound interest is 10% of the sum of all previous interest earned.

More generally, if i is the interest rate and n is the number of years, the future value of the $1,000 is given by the formula:

$$FV = \$1{,}000(1 + i)^n \tag{4.1}$$

TABLE 4.1 Future Value and Compound Interest

Year	Beginning Amount	Interest Earned	Ending Amount
1	$1,000.00	$100.00	$1,100.00
2	$1,100.00	$110.00	$1,210.00
3	$1,210.00	$121.00	$1,331.00
4	$1,331.00	$133.10	$1,464.10
5	$1,464.10	$146.41	$1,610.51
	Total Interest Earned	$610.51	

Note: Table 4.1 and Figure 4.1 show the future value of $1,000 at 10% per year. Simple interest in the graph is the cumulative total of $100 per year. Compound interest in the graph is the cumulative total of all compound interest earned up to that point.

FIGURE 4.1

Future Value and Compound Interest

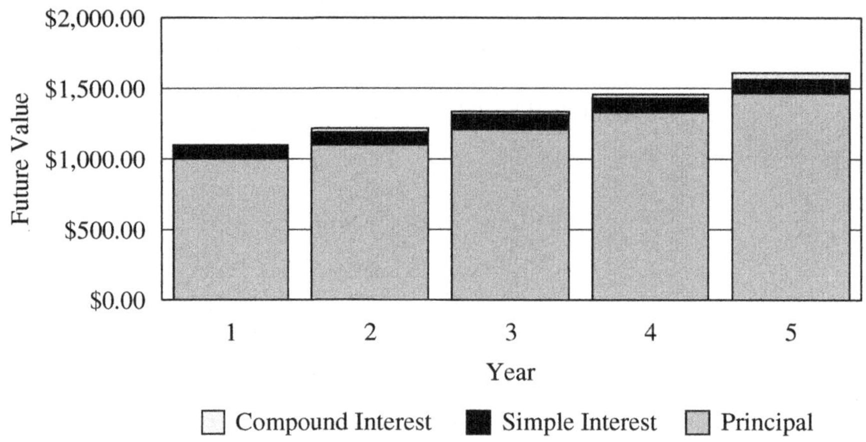

In general, for any present value invested, the **future value factor** is given by:

$$FV = (1+i)^n$$

The future value factor is greater the higher the interest rate and the longer the time the investment is held. Table 4.2 and the graph in Figure 4.2 illustrate this relationship for various interest rates and holding periods.

4.1.1 Calculating Future Values

There are also special-purpose financial calculators available designed to make doing the calculations even easier. By pressing the appropriately labeled keys, you enter (in any order you please) the values for the number of periods (n), the interest rate (i), and the amount of the investment (PV), and then compute future value (FV). Like magic, the answer appears in the calculator's display. Similarly, spreadsheet programs have a simple and convenient way to compute future values. In an Excel spreadsheet the future value is calculated using the built-in *FV function: FV(i, n,* 0, *−PV).* In Excel cash inflows and outflows are represented with positive and negative signs respectively. This requires that the entry for the

TABLE 4.2 **Future Value of $1 for Different Periods and Interest Rates**

	Interest Rate, *i*					
Number of Periods, *n*	2%	4%	6%	8%	10%	12%
1	1.0200	1.0400	1.0600	1.0800	1.1000	1.1200
2	1.0404	1.0816	1.1236	1.1664	1.2100	1.2544
3	1.0612	1.1249	1.1910	1.2597	1.3310	1.4049
4	1.0824	1.1699	1.2625	1.3605	1.4641	1.5735
5	1.1041	1.2167	1.3382	1.4693	1.6105	1.7623
10	1.2190	1.4802	1.7908	2.1589	2.5937	3.1058
15	1.3459	1.8009	2.3966	3.1722	4.1772	5.4736
20	1.4859	2.1911	3.2071	4.6610	6.7275	9.6463

Note: Table 4.2 and Figure 4.2 show the future value of $1 for different holding periods at various interest rates. The higher the interest rate, the faster the future value grows.

FIGURE 4.2

Future Value of $1 at Interest Rates from 2% to 12%

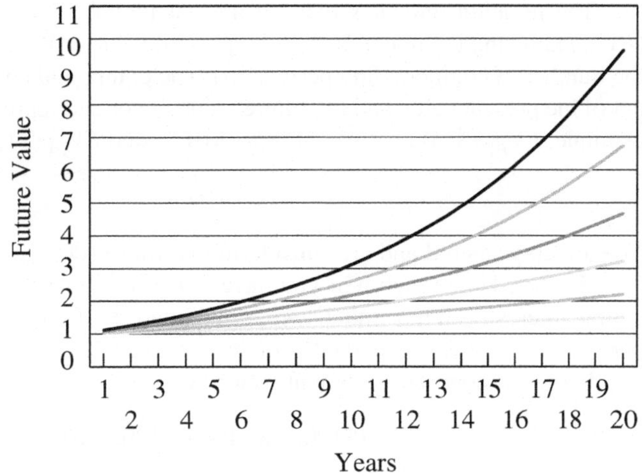

present value be negative. The built-in Excel function can be used directly in a single spreadsheet cell by entering = *FV*(10%, 5, 0, −$1,000) and $1,610.51 would be displayed or in a tabled format to allow for sensitivity analysis and quick recalculations. For example, changing the interest rate in Cell A1 from 10% to 15% would return a new *FV* in Cell A4 equal to $2,011.36

	A	B
1	10%	*i*
2	5	*n*
3	($1,000.00)	*PV*
4	=*FV*(A1, A2, 0, A3) RETURNS $1,610.51	*FV*

1. We can use tables of future value factors, such as those in Table 4.2, to compute future values. In our example, we would look for the factor corresponding to *n* of 5 and an interest rate of 10%. The table shows 1.6105 as the appropriate future value factor. We then multiply our $1,000 by this factor.
2. Finally, there is a handy rule of thumb that can help you estimate future values when you do not have your calculator or a table available. It is called the **Rule of 72.** This rule says that the number of years it takes for a sum of money to double in value (the "doubling time") is approximately equal to the number 72 divided by the interest rate expressed in percent per year:

$$\text{Doubling Time} = \frac{72}{\textit{Interest Rate}}$$

So at an interest rate of 10% per year, it should take approximately 7.2 years to double your money. If you start with $1,000, you will have $2,000 after 7.2 years, $4,000 after 14.4 years, $8,000 after 21.6 years, and so on.

From this point on we shall use a straightforward notation to aid our time value of money computations. To compute the future value of a present amount we will use the **compound amount factor** defined as:

$$FV_{PV}(PV, i, n) = PV(1+i)^n$$

The notation indicates that we are calculating a future value from a present value (FV_{PV}) knowing the magnitude of the present value (PV), the periodic interest rate (i), and the number of compounding periods (n). The compound amount factor is the simple product of the present value and the future value factor and represents the total future value. For example, FV_{PV} (\$1,000, 10%, 5) = \$1,610.51 and FV_{PV}(\$1,000, 12%, 5) = \$1,762,34.

4.1.2 Saving for Old Age

You are 20 years old and are considering putting \$100 into an account paying 8% per year for 45 years. How much will you have in the account at age 65? How much of it will be simple interest, and how much compound interest? If you could find an account paying 9% per year, how much more would you have at age 65?

Using the compound amount factor, we find:

$$FV_{PV}(\$100,\ 8\%,\ 45) = \$100 \times 1.08^{45} = \$3{,}192.04$$

Because the original principal is \$100, total interest earned is \$3,092.04. The simple interest is 45 × 0.08 × \$100 or \$360, whereas the compound interest is \$2,732.04.

At an interest rate of 9% per year, we find:

$$FV_{PV}(\$100,\ 9\%,\ 45) = \$100 \times 1.09^{45} = \$4{,}832.73$$

Thus, a seemingly small increase of 1% in the interest rate results in an extra \$1,640.69 (\$4,832.73 − \$3,192.04) at age 65. This is more than a 50% increase $\left(\frac{\$1{,}640.69}{\$3{,}192.04} = 0.514\right)$.

The general point of this example is that a small difference in interest rates can make a big difference in future values over long periods of time.

Note that the Rule of 72 can help us to find a pretty good approximate answer to our questions. At an interest rate of 8% per year, your \$100 would double about every nine years. Thus, after 45 years, it would double five times, giving an approximate future value of \$3,200:

$$\$100 \times 2 \times 2 \times 2 \times 2 \times 2 = \$100 \times 2^5 = \$100 \times 32 = \$3{,}200$$

which is not too far from the exact answer of \$3,192.04.

At an interest rate of 9% per year, your money would double about every eight years. In 45 years it would double about 5.5 times. Therefore, the future value should be about 50% greater than when the interest rate is 8% per year: Again, this is not too far from the exact answer of \$4,832.73.

4.1.3 Reinvesting at a Different Rate

You are faced with the following investment decision. You have \$10,000 to invest for two years. You have decided to invest your money in bank certificates of deposit (CDs). Two-year CDs are paying 7% per year and one-year CDs are paying 6%. What should you do?

To make this decision you must first decide what you think the interest rate on one-year CDs will be next year. This is called the **reinvestment rate,** that is, the interest rate at which money received before the end of your planning horizon can be reinvested. Suppose you are sure that it will be 8% per year.

Now you can use the concept of future value to make this investment decision. You compute the future value under each investment alternative and choose the one giving the most money at the end of two years. With the two-year CD, the future value will be:

$$FV_{PV}(\$10{,}000,\ 7\%,\ 2) = \$10{,}000 \times 1.07^2 = \$11{,}449$$

With the sequence of two 1-year CDs, the future value will be:

$$FV = \$10{,}000 \times 1.06 \times 1.08 = \$11{,}448$$

Thus, you are slightly better off if you invest in the two-year CD.

4.1.4 Paying Back a Loan

Fifty years after graduation, you get a letter from your college notifying you that they have just discovered that you failed to pay your last student activities fee of \$100. Because it was your college's oversight, it has decided to charge you an interest rate of only 6% per year. Your college would like you to pay it back at the coming fiftieth reunion of your graduating class. As a loyal alumnus, you feel obliged to pay. How much do you owe them?

Using any of the methods discussed earlier, we find:

$$FV_{PV}(\$100, 6\%, 50) = \$100 \times 1.06^{50} = \$1{,}842.02$$

Quick Check 4-2

In 1626, Peter Minuit purchased Manhattan Island from the Native Americans for about \$24 worth of trinkets. If the tribe had taken cash instead and invested it to earn 6% per year compounded annually, how much would they have had in 2006, 380 years later?

4.2 The Frequency of Compounding

Interest rates on loans and saving accounts are usually stated in the form of an **annual percentage rate** (*APR*), (e.g., 6% per year) with a certain frequency of compounding (e.g., monthly). Because the frequency of compounding can differ, it is important to have a way of making interest rates comparable. This is done by computing an **effective annual rate** (*EFF*), defined as the equivalent interest rate, *if compounding were only once per year.*

For example, suppose your money earns interest at a stated annual percentage rate (*APR*) of 6% per year compounded monthly. This means that interest is credited to your account every month at 1/12th the stated *APR*. Thus, the true interest rate is actually 1/2% per month (or 0.005 per month as a decimal).

We find the *EFF* by computing the future value at the end of the year per dollar invested at the beginning of the year. In this example we get:

$$FV = 1.005^{12} = 1.0616778$$

The effective annual rate is just this number minus one.

$$EFF = 1.0616778 - 1 = 0.0616778 \text{ or } 6.16778\% \text{ per year}$$

The general formula for the effective annual rate is:

$$EFF(APR, m) = \left(1 + \frac{APR}{m}\right)^m - 1 \qquad (4.2)$$

where *APR* is the annual percentage rate, and *m* the number of compounding periods per year. Table 4.3 presents the effective annual rates corresponding to an annual percentage rate of 6% per year for different compounding frequencies.

TABLE 4.3 Effective Annual Rates for an *APR* of 6%

Compounding	*m*	*EFF*
Annually	1	6.00000%
Semiannually	2	6.09000%
Quarterly	4	6.13636%
Monthly	12	6.16778%
Weekly	52	6.17998%
Daily	365	6.18313%
Continuously	∞	6.18365%

If compounding is done once per year, then the effective annual rate is the same as the annual percentage rate. As the compounding frequency increases, the effective annual rate gets larger and larger but approaches a limit. With this modification the compound amount factor becomes $FV_m\left(PV, APR, m, n\right) = PV \cdot \left(1+\frac{APR}{m}\right)^{mn}$ where $\frac{APR}{m}$ is the interest rate per compounding period and mn the total number of compounding periods over the n years. As m grows without limit, $\left(1+\frac{i}{m}\right)^{mn}$ approaches e^{in} where e is the constant 2.71828 (rounded off to the fifth decimal place). So with continuous compounding the future value is calculated as: $FV_{con}(PV, i, n) = PV \cdot e^{i \cdot n}$. In the above example, $e^{0.06} = 1.0618365$. Therefore, if interest is continuously compounded at 6%, the *EFF* = 0.0618365 or 6.18365% per year.

In Excel the effective annual rate can be calculated using the built-in EFFECT function. The arguments for the function are EFFECT(*APR, m*). In an Excel cell, entering =EFFECT(10%, 4) would return 0.1038129, which says that a 10% annual percentage rate with quarterly compounding corresponds to an effective annual rate of 10.38129%. The symmetric Excel built-in NOMINAL function calculates the annual percentage rate corresponding to a given effective annual rate and number of compounding periods per year. The functional structure is NOMINAL(*EFF, m*). Thus entering = NOMINAL(12%, 12) in an Excel cell will return 0.1138655. This is interpreted to say that to produce an effective annual rate of 12% under monthly compounding, the *APR* must be 11.38655%.

Quick Check 4-3

You take out a loan at an *APR* of 12% with monthly compounding. What is the effective annual rate on your loan?

4.3 Present Value and Discounting

When we compute future values, we are asking questions like "How much will we have in 10 years if we invest $1,000 today at an interest rate of 8% per year?" (The answer is: *FV* = $2,158.92. Check it!)

But suppose we want to know how much to invest today in order to reach some target amount at a date in the future. For example, if we need to have $15,000 for a child's college education eight years from now, how much do we have to invest now? To find the answer to this kind of question, we need to calculate the present value of a given future amount.

Calculating present values is the reverse of calculating future values. That is, it tells us the amount you would have to invest today to have a certain amount in the future. Let's take a look at calculating *PV* step by step.

Suppose we want to have \$1,000 one year from now and can earn 10% interest per year. The amount we must invest now is the present value of \$1,000. Because the interest rate is 10%, we know that for every dollar we invest now we will have a future value of \$1.1. Therefore, we can write:

$$PV \times 1.1 = \$1{,}000$$

Then the present value is given by:

$$PV = \frac{\$1{,}000}{1.1} = \$909.09$$

So if the interest rate is 10% per year, we need to invest \$909.09 in order to have \$1,000 a year from now.

Now suppose the \$1,000 is not needed until two years from now. Clearly, the amount we need to invest today at an interest rate of 10% is less than \$909.09, because it will earn interest at the rate of 10% per year for two years. To find the present value, we use our knowledge of how to find future values:

$$\$1{,}000 = PV \times 1.1^2 = PV \times 1.21$$

In our example the present value is:

$$PV = \frac{\$1{,}000}{1.1^2} = \$826.45$$

Thus, \$826.45 invested now at an interest rate of 10% per year will grow to \$1,000 in two years.

Calculating present values is called *discounting,* and the interest rate used in the calculation is often referred to as the *discount rate.* Thus, discounting in finance is very different from discounting in retailing. In retailing it means reducing the price in order to sell more goods; in finance it means computing the present value of a future sum of money. To distinguish the two kinds of discounting in the world of business, the calculation of present values is called *discounted cash flow* (*DCF*) analysis.

The general formula for the present value of \$1 to be received *n* periods from now at a discount rate of *i* (per period) is:

$$PV = \frac{1}{(1+i)^n} \tag{4.3}$$

This is called the **present value of \$1** at an interest rate of *i* for *n* periods.

The present value of \$1 to be received five years from now at an interest rate of 10% per year is:

$$PV = \frac{1}{1.1^5} = 0.62092$$

To find the present value of \$1,000 to be received in five years at 10%, we simply multiply this factor by \$1,000 to get \$620.92.

TABLE 4.4 Present Value of $1 for Different Periods and Interest Rates

Number of Periods, n	Interest Rate, i 2%	4%	6%	8%	10%	12%
1	0.9804	0.9615	0.9434	0.9259	0.9091	0.8929
2	0.9612	0.9246	0.8900	0.8573	0.8264	0.7972
3	0.9423	0.8890	0.8396	0.7938	0.7513	0.7118
4	0.9238	0.8548	0.7921	0.7350	0.6830	0.6355
5	0.9057	0.8219	0.7473	0.6806	0.6209	0.5674
10	0.8203	0.6756	0.5584	0.4632	0.3855	0.3220
15	0.7430	0.5553	0.4173	0.3152	0.2394	0.1827
20	0.6730	0.4564	0.3118	0.2145	0.1486	0.1037

Because discounting is just the reverse of compounding, we could use the same table (see Table 4.2) that we used before for future value factors to find present values of $1. Instead of multiplying by the factor, however, we would divide by it. Thus, we can find the present value of $1,000 to be received in five years at 10% by looking up the future value factor of 1.6105 in Table 4.2 and dividing $1,000 by it:

$$\frac{\$1{,}000}{1.6105} = \$620.92$$

For convenience, there are tables of present values of $1 such as the one shown as Table 4.4 containing the reciprocals of the factors in Table 4.2. Look in Table 4.4 for the present value of $1 for an interest rate of 10% and five periods, and verify that it is 0.62092.

The general formula for the present value of $1 is:

$$PV = \frac{1}{(1+i)^n}$$

where i is the interest rate expressed as a decimal fraction and n is the number of periods.

By going down any column in Table 4.4, note how present values decline the further in the future the $1 is to be taken out of the account. At an interest rate of 10%, for example, the present value of $1 to be received in one year is $0.9091, but the present value of $1 to be received in 20 years is only $0.1486.

Consistent with our previous notation for time value of money computations, we can calculate the present value of a future amount using the **present value factor** defined as:

$$PV_{FV}(FV,\ i,\ n) = \frac{FV}{(1+i)^n}$$

The notation indicates that we are calculating a present value from a future value (PV_{FV}) knowing the magnitude of the future value (FV), the periodic interest rate (i), and the number of compounding periods (n). The present factor is the simple product of the future value and the present value of $1 and represents the total present value. For example, PV_{FV} ($1,000, 10%, 5) = $620.92 and PV_{FV} ($1,000, 12%, 5) = $567.43.

4.3.1 When a $100 Gift Is Not Really $100

It is your brother's tenth birthday, and he receives a $100 savings bond maturing in five years. This type of bond pays nothing until its maturity date. In adding up the value of his birthday "loot," he mistakenly writes down $100 for this bond. How much is it really worth if the discount rate is 8% per year and the bond does not mature for another five years? How could you explain your brother's mistake to him, so that he would understand?

We are looking for the present value of $100 to be received in five years at a discount rate of 8% per year. There are several ways we could compute it. The formula is:

$$PV = \frac{\$100}{1.08^5} = \$68.06$$

On an ordinary calculator, we could find this present value by dividing 100 by 1.08 five times to find that it is 68. On a financial calculator, we would enter the values for *n*, *i*, and *FV*, and then compute the present value by pressing the key labeled *PV*. Or we could use the present value factor of $1 in Table 4.4. The table entry corresponding to an interest rate of 8% and five periods is 0.6806. Multiply this factor by $100 to find the present value of $68.

Explaining the answer to your brother is a tough assignment. Probably the best way to do it is to use the idea of future value rather than present value. You could explain to him that his $100 savings bond is worth only $68 because all he has to do to get $100 five years from now is to put $68 into a savings account paying interest of 8% per year.

Quick Check 4-4

What is the present value of $100 to be received in four years at an interest rate of 6% per year?

4.3.2 Discounting with Compounding More Frequently Than Annually

When interest is compound more frequently than on an annual basis we need to make the appropriate adjustments in the method for discounting. Here the formula for present value would be modified to $PV_m\left(FV, APR, n, m\right) = \frac{FV}{\left(1 + \frac{APR}{m}\right)^{mn}}$ where *APR* is the annual percentage rate and *m* is the number of compounding periods per year. For example, the present value of $500 in 5 years with semiannual compounding at a 10% annual rate would be: $PV_m(\$500,\ 10\%,\ 5,\ 2) = \frac{\$500}{\left(1+\frac{10\%}{2}\right)^{10}} = \$306.96$. Note that, using Excel, we could perform the compounding adjustment directly and convert the 10% annual rate into a 5% semiannual rate over 10 six-month periods into the built-in present value function and enter =*PV*(5%, 10, 0, −$500).[1] This would return an entry equal to $306.96.

In the continuous discounting case, the present value formula is $PV_{con} = FV \cdot e^{-APR \cdot n}$. Suppose a T-bill matures in six months with a face value of $10,000 and a competitive continuously compounding rate of return is 5%. What is the present value of the T-bill? Discounting the $10,000 on a continuous basis we would have: $PV = \$10{,}000 \cdot e^{-0.10 \cdot \frac{1}{2}} = \$9{,}512.29$.

[1]The Excel *PV* function has the form: *PV*(*i*, *n*, *PMT*, *FV*).

Quick Check 4-5

Suppose a \$10,000 T-bill that will mature in 3 months is currently selling for \$9,800. If you purchase and hold the T-bill to maturity what rate of return would you earn on this investment computed as a continuously compounding annual rate (over the 3-month period)?

4.4 Alternative Discounted Cash Flow Decision Rules

The discounted cash flow concepts that we have studied so far in this chapter provide a powerful set of tools for making investment decisions. The essential ideas are captured in the equation relating future value, present value, the interest rate, and the number of periods:

$$FV = PV(1+i)^n \tag{4.4}$$

Given any three of the variables in this equation, we can find the fourth and formulate an investment decision rule based on it. The most common decision rule is the **net present value** (*NPV*) rule. This rule is not only widely used and universally applicable (i.e., correctly used it never leads to the wrong decision), but it is also very intuitive. Simply put, the *NPV* rule sounds almost obvious: *Accept any project with a present value of future cash flows that exceed the initial investment.* The only trick is to make sure that one does not compare apples to oranges. Thus, when calculating the future cash flows (which happens some time from now), we must use their present value in order to make them comparable.

Formally, the *NPV* rule says the following:

> The *NPV* is the difference between the present value of all future cash inflows minus the present value of all current and future cash outflows. Accept a project if its *NPV* is positive. Reject a project if its *NPV* is negative.

For example, suppose that a \$100 savings bond maturing in 5 years is selling for a price of \$75. Your next best alternative for investing is an 8% bank account. Is the savings bond a good investment? Let's show how to use the *NPV* decision rule in evaluating this investment. The initial investment for the savings bond is \$75 (this happens today, no discounting necessary). What is the present value of the cash inflows that the bond generates? It is simply the present value of \$100 to be received in five years from now. The relevant interest rate is the rate that the money could earn if it were not invested in the bond.

In general, for the *NPV* calculation of any investment, we use the **opportunity cost of capital** (also called the *market capitalization rate*) as the interest rate. The opportunity cost of capital is simply the rate that we could earn somewhere else if we did not invest it in the project under evaluation. In this example, the opportunity cost of capital of investing in the savings bond is the rate that we could earn if we put our money in a bank instead—8% per year in this case.

For convenience in keeping track of the calculations (especially if they are being done in a spread sheet or on a financial calculator), we organize our information in the following table:

Time Value of Money (*TVM*) Calculation Table	
10%	*i*
5	*n*
?	*PV*
100	*FV*
PV = \$68.06	**Result**

A question mark indicates the variable that has to be computed.

In this case we use three of the variables, *FV*, *n*, and *i*, to compute the fourth, *PV*. We then compare this computed present value to the known initial investment of the savings bond. Using the formula, we find:

$$PV = \frac{\$100}{1.08^5} = \$68.06$$

Comparing the \$68.06 to the \$75 necessary to obtain the bond, we conclude that investing in the bond is not worthwhile. In other words, the *NPV* of the investment is negative.

The *NPV* is a measure of how much your *current* wealth changes as a result of your choice. Clearly, if the *NPV* is negative, it does not pay to undertake the investment. In this case, if you choose to invest in the bond, your current wealth decreases by approximately \$7.

Another way to arrive at the same conclusion is to use a slightly different rule known as the *future value rule.* Simply stated, it says to *invest in the project if its future value is greater than the future value that will obtain in the next best alternative.* This rule is actually slightly more intuitive (and leads to the same decision as the *NPV* rule). The reason it is not used as often in practice is that in many circumstances (as will be shown later in the book) the future value of an investment cannot be computed whereas the *NPV* rule can still be used. Let us illustrate how the future value rule would have worked in the same example just used to illustrate the *NPV* rule.

Investing in a savings bond (initial investment \$75, future value of cash flows \$100 in five years) clearly leads to a future value of \$100. Putting the money into a bank at 8% is the next best thing we can do with the money. Does the savings bond have a higher future value than we could get from the bank? Again, we organize our information in the table:

Time Value of Money (*TVM*) Calculation Table	
8%	*i*
5	*n*
\$75.00	*PV*
?	*FV*
FV = \$110.20	**Result**

Using the formula, we get that the future value from the bank account is given by

$$FV = \$75 \times 1.08^5 = \$110.20$$

This is clearly better than the \$100 future value of the savings bond. Again, we find that the savings bond is an inferior investment.

There are other decision rules that are also used in practice. Each has its own intuition and each is useful for certain problems. It should be noted, however, that none of the rules are as universally applicable as the *NPV* rule. Here is another widely used rule, which in many circumstances is also equivalent to the *NPV* rule:

Accept an investment if its return is greater than the opportunity cost of capital.

This rule is (clearly) based on the concept of rate of return. Recall that in our example the opportunity cost of capital from putting the money into the bank is 8% per year.

By investing \$75 in the savings bond today, you can get \$100 five years from now. What interest rate would you be earning? In other words, we want to find i that solves the equation:

$$\$75 = \frac{\$100}{(1+i)^5}$$

This is called the bond's **yield to maturity** or **internal rate of return** (*IRR*). The internal rate of return is the discount rate that makes the present value of the future cash inflows equal to the present value of cash outflows. In other words, the *IRR* is exactly that interest rate at which the *NPV* is equal to zero. Thus, if the rate at which the *NPV* is zero (the *IRR*) is higher than the opportunity cost of capital, then we know that the *NPV* at the opportunity cost of capital itself must be positive. In other words, if the *IRR* is (say) 10% (i.e., the *NPV* at 10% is zero), then the *NPV* at the opportunity cost of capital (say) 8% must be positive. Why? We know that the *NPV* calculation discounts future cash flows. We also know that the present value of future cash flows is greater when the discount rate is small. Thus, if the *NPV* is zero at 10%, it will be positive at 8%. Hence, having a 10% *IRR* and an 8% opportunity cost of capital is equivalent to saying that the *NPV* must be positive.[2]

To find i (the *IRR*) on a financial calculator, enter *PV, FV,* and n and compute i:

Time Value of Money (*TVM*) Calculation Table	
?	i
5	n
(\$75.00)	*PV*
\$100.00	*FV*
i = 5.92%	**Result**

We have put brackets (representing a negative sign) around the \$75 in the table column labeled *PV* because it signifies an investment (i.e., a cash outflow). Most financial calculators and spreadsheets require you to enter the initial investment or cash outflow as negative. It should not be surprising that the model assumes that an investment (negative cash flow) is needed in order to earn a positive cash flow in the future. If all cash flows were positive, we would have created a money machine and that, sadly, is an impossibility.

If you don't have a spreadsheet, you can solve for i using some algebra:

$$\$100 = 75 \times (1+i)^5$$

$$(1+i)^5 = \frac{\$100}{\$75}$$

$$i = \left(\frac{\$100}{\$75}\right)^{\frac{1}{5}} - 1 = 0.0592 = 5.92\%$$

Thus, the yield to maturity (*IRR*) on the bond is 5.92% per year. This should be compared to the 8% per year you could earn by putting your money in the bank. Clearly, you are better off putting your money in the bank.

The rate of return decision rule is equivalent to the *NPV* rule in evaluating a single investment for which there are no negative future cash flows. Even with that condition, it

[2]This conclusion applies only if all future cash flows are positive.

will not in general produce the same rankings from best to worst among several investment opportunities.

When you have to choose among several alternative investments, choose the one with the highest *NPV*.

There is one more variable in this example for which we can solve with our calculator in order to arrive at a decision: *n* (the number of years). Let us do this for the savings bond. We know that the *FV* is \$100, the *PV* is \$75, and the opportunity cost of capital is 8%; what is *n*?

$$\$75 = \frac{\$100}{1.08^n}$$

On the financial calculator we input *PV, FV,* and *i* and compute *n:*

n	*i*	*PV*	*FV*	Result
?	8	−\$75	\$100	*n* = 3.74

We find that *n* is 3.74 years. Now, what does this mean? It means that if we put the money into the bank (at 8%), it would take 3.74 years for \$75 to grow to \$100. With the savings bond, it takes five years for the \$75 to grow to \$100. This observation has suggested to some the following rule:

Choose the investment alternative with the shortest payback period.

In other words, choose the investment in which you can "get your money back", or meet your growth goal, (i.e., turn the \$75 investment into \$100) in the shortest period of time.

This rule, however, applies only in special cases. As with the *IRR* rule, the "payback" rule is not a reliable one for general investment choice purposes. Although these alternative rules are sometimes used in practice, stick with the *NPV* rule as the safe and universal rule of choice.

4.4.1 Investing in Land

You have the opportunity to buy a piece of land for \$10,000. You are sure that five years from now it will be worth \$20,000. If you can earn 8% per year by investing your money in the bank, is this investment in the land worthwhile?

Invest in a project if its net present value (*NPV*) is positive. Do not invest if the *NPV* is negative.

What is the present value of having \$20,000 (the future cash flow) in five years from now? In this case we input *FV, n,* and *i,* and compute *PV.* We then compare this computed present value to the \$10,000 initial outlay, and make our decision based on which one is greater.

n	*i*	*PV*	*FV*	Result
5	8	?	\$20,000	*PV* = \$13,612

Thus, the investment in the land has a present value of \$13,612. Comparing this to the \$10,000 cost of the land, it clearly seems like a bargain. Its *NPV* is \$3,612.

Quick Check 4-6

Show that the alternative decision criteria presented previously lead to the same result—that the investment is worthwhile.

4.4.2 Other's People Money

In the preceding example, we considered an investment in which you are required to lay out money in the present and receive cash at some future date. But often financial decisions involve just the reverse. For example, suppose that you need to borrow $5,000 to buy a car. You go to a bank and they offer you a loan at an interest rate of 12% per year. You then go to a friend who says he will lend you the $5,000 if you pay him $9,000 in four years. What should you do?

First, let's identify the project that you need to evaluate. The cash flow that you want to evaluate is the $5,000 (today) you can borrow from your friend (a cash inflow). The investment you must make is the present value of the $9,000 repayment (a cash outflow) after four years.

The way to proceed is to calculate the *NPV* of the project. The opportunity cost of capital is 12% (the bank's rate, your next best alternative). The cash flows are given. What is the *NPV*?

n	*i*	*PV*	*FV*	Result
4	12	?	−$9,000	*PV* = $5,719.66

We find that the present value of the cash outflow is $5,719.66. Thus, the *NPV* of the project is −$719.66. Hence, the project of borrowing from your friend is not worthwhile. You are better off borrowing from the bank.

What is the implied interest rate that your friend is charging you? The answer is to solve the present value equation for *i*:

$$\$5,000 = \frac{\$9,000}{(1+i)^4}$$

Using a financial calculator:

n	*i*	*PV*	*FV*	Result
4	?	$5,000	−$9,000	*i* = 15.83%

We find that the interest rate is 15.83% per year. You are better off borrowing from the bank.

Note that the rate you have just computed is the *IRR* of borrowing from your friend. It is 15.83%. Now, in the previous examples we stated that the *IRR* rule works as follows: *Invest* in a project if the *IRR* is *greater* than the opportunity cost of capital. This rule works for projects that have the feature of a one-time investment (i.e., the initial cash flow is negative and the future cash flows are positive).

However, it should be clear that for projects that have the feature of borrowing (i.e., the initial cash flow is positive and the future repayment cash flow is negative) the rule must be turned on its head: *Borrow* from a source if the *IRR* of the loan is *less* than the opportunity cost of capital.

As noted previously, a major potential problem with the *IRR* rule rears its head whenever there are multiple cash inflows. In such cases the *IRR* may not be unique (e.g., there are many) or the *IRR* may not exist at all. More on this problem later.

4.5 Multiple Cash Flows

So far we have considered situations in which there is a single cash flow in the future. What happens if there is more than one? For example, suppose you want to save for a child's college education or for your own retirement by putting a certain amount each year into an interest-bearing account; or you are evaluating an investment such as a bond that offers a stream of future payments; or you are considering taking a loan that requires you to make periodic installment payments. To deal with all of these more complicated situations we need only extend the concepts already presented.

4.5.1 Time Lines

A useful tool in analyzing the timing of cash flows is a diagram known as a **time line.** It is illustrated in Figure 4.3.

A negative sign in front of a cash flow means that you put in that amount of money (a cash *outflow* from you), whereas no sign means that you take out that amount (cash *inflow* to you). In our example, you put in 100 at time 0 and take out 20 at the end of the first period, 50 at the end of the second, and 60 at the end of the third.

4.5.2 Future Value of a Stream of Cash Flows

We begin with a savings decision and the concept of future value. Each year you deposit \$1,000 into an account paying an interest rate of 10% per year starting immediately. How much will you have after two years if you do not withdraw any money before then?

The original \$1,000 grows to \$1,100 at the end of the first year. Then you add another \$1,000, so there is \$2,100 in the account at the beginning of the second year. By the end of the second year there is \$2,100 × (1.1) or \$2,310 in the account.

An alternative way to find this future value of \$2,310 is to calculate the future values of each of the two \$1,000 deposits separately and then add them together. The future value of the first deposit is:

$$\$1,000 \times 1.1^2 = \$1,210$$

The future value of the second deposit will be:

$$\$1,000 \times 1.1 = \$1,100$$

Adding the two together, we get the same \$2,310 that we found by multiplying each year's accumulation by 1.1.

Quick Check 4-7

Suppose you deposit \$1,000 now and then \$2,000 a year from now. How much will you have two years from now, if the interest rate is 10% per year?

FIGURE 4.3

Time Line

Time	0	1	2	3
Cash Flow	−100	20	50	60

4.5.3 Present Value of a Stream of Cash Flows

Often we need to compute the present value rather than the future value of a series of cash flows. For example, suppose you want to have \$1,000 one year from now and then \$2,000 in two years. If the interest rate is 10% per year, how much would you have to put into an account today in order to satisfy your requirement?

In this case we have to compute the present value of the two cash flows depicted in Figure 4.4. Just as the future value of a stream of cash flows is the sum of the future values of each, so too with the present value.

4.5.4 Investing with Multiple Cash Flows

Suppose you are offered an opportunity to invest in a project that will pay you \$1,000 a year from now and another \$2,000 two years from now. The project requires you to invest \$2,500 now. You are convinced that the project is completely free of risk. Is it a worthwhile investment if you can earn 10% per year on your money by leaving it in the bank?

Note that this problem bears a striking resemblance to the previous one. The cash flows that this project will generate are the same as depicted in Figure 4.4—\$1,000 a year from now and \$2,000 two years from now. We already know that if you put your money in the bank, it would take \$2,562 to generate the same future cash flows. Because the outlay required on the project is only \$2,500, it has a net present value of \$62. As we saw earlier in this chapter, an investment with a positive *NPV* should be undertaken.

4.6 Annuities

Often the future cash flows in a savings plan, an investment project, or a loan repayment schedule are the same each year. We call such a level stream of cash flows or payments an **annuity.** The term comes from the life insurance business, in which an annuity contract is one that promises a stream of payments to the purchaser for some period of time. In finance it is applied more generally and applies to any level stream of cash flows. Thus, the stream of payments on an installment loan or a mortgage is called an annuity, too.

If the cash flows start immediately, as in a savings plan or a lease, it is called an **immediate annuity.** If the cash flows start at the end of the current period rather than immediately, it is called an **ordinary annuity.** A mortgage is an example of an ordinary annuity. There are some convenient formulas, tables, and calculator functions for computing the present and future values of annuities, which come in handy when the stream of cash flows lasts for many periods.

4.6.1 Future Value of Annuities

For example, suppose that you intend to save \$100 each year for the next three years. How much will you have accumulated at the end of that time if the interest rate is 10% per year? If you start saving immediately, you will have:

$$FV = \$100 \times 1.1^3 + \$100 \times 1.1^2 + \$100 \times 1.1$$

FIGURE 4.4

Present Value of Multiple Cash Flows

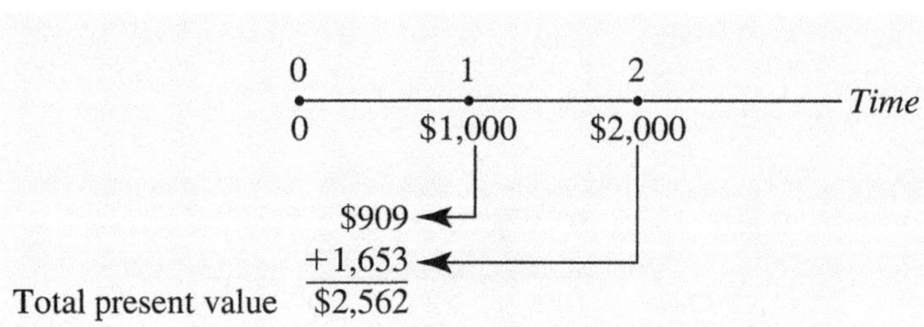

Factoring out the constant annual cash flow of \$100, we get:

$$FV = \$100 \times (1.1 + 1.1^2 + 1.1^3)$$

The result is a future value of \$364.10. The factor multiplying the \$100 is the future value of a \$1 payment per year for three years. Although tables containing such future value factors for various interest rates and numbers of periods are available, most people today use financial calculators. The calculator key used to input the periodic contribution is labeled *PMT* (short for *payment*) on most models.

In our example, we know *i, n,* and *PMT,* and want to compute *FV.* We enter the givens in the appropriate cells of the table and insert a ? (question mark) for the entry that we want to compute.

n	*i*	*PV*	*FV*	*PMT*	Result
3	10	0	?	\$100	*FV* = \$364.10

In computing the future value of an annuity it matters, of course, whether it is an immediate annuity, as in our current example, or whether it is an ordinary annuity. In the case of an ordinary annuity, the first \$100 contribution is made at the end of the first period. Figure 4.5 shows a time line that contrasts the two situations.

Although in both cases there are the same number of payments, under the immediate annuity pattern the entire amount earns interest for an additional year. Thus, an immediate annuity would have an *FV* equal to that of the ordinary annuity multiplied by $1 + i$. For an ordinary annuity of \$1 per year the formula for future value is:

$$FV = \frac{(1+i)^n - 1}{i}$$

We find that the future value of our savings plan of \$100 per year for three years is \$364.10 if the first deposit is made immediately (an immediate annuity), and \$331 if delayed until the end of the first year (an ordinary annuity).

Some financial calculators have a special key to press to let the calculator know whether the annuity payments start at the beginning or end of the first period.

4.6.2 Present Value of Annuities

Often we want to compute the present value rather than the future value of an annuity stream. For example, how much would you have to put into a fund earning an interest rate of 10% per year to be able to take out \$100 per year for the next three years? The answer is the present value of the three cash flows.

The present value of the annuity is the sum of the present values of each of the three payments of \$100:

$$PV = \frac{\$100}{1.1} + \frac{\$100}{1.1^2} + \frac{\$100}{1.1^3}$$

FIGURE 4.5

Cash Flow Diagram of Annuities

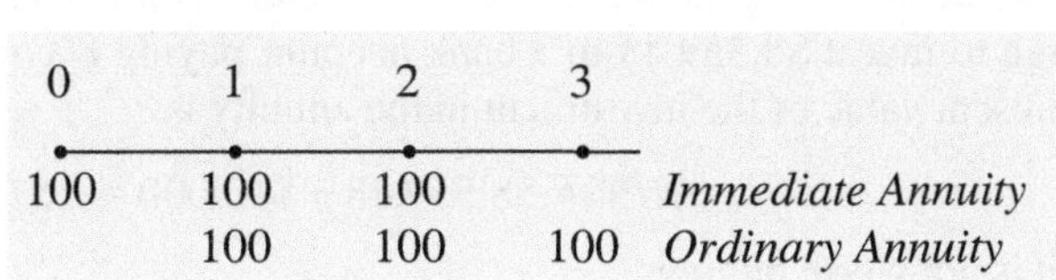

TABLE 4.5 **Proof That Putting in $248.69 Allows You to Take Out $100 per Year for 3 Years**

Year	Amount at Beginning of Year	Multiply by	Amount at End of Year	Subtract $100
1	$248.69	1.1	$273.56	$173.56
2	$173.56	1.1	$190.91	$90.91
3	$90.91	1.1	$100.00	$0.00

Factoring out the constant payment of $100 per year, we get:

$$PV = \$100 \times \left(\frac{1}{1.1} + \frac{1}{1.1^2} + \frac{1}{1.1^3} \right)$$

The result is a present value of $248.69. The factor multiplying the $100 payment is the present value of an ordinary annuity of $1 for three years at an interest rate of 10%.

Table 4.5 verifies that indeed $248.69 is all you would have to put in the account to be able to take out $100 each year for the next three years.

The formula for the present value of an ordinary annuity of $1 per period for n periods at an interest rate of i is:

$$PV = \frac{1-(1+i)^{-n}}{i}$$

On a financial calculator, we would enter the values for *n, i,* and *PMT,* and compute the *PV.*

n	*i*	*PV*	*FV*	*PMT*	Result
3	10	?	0	$100	$PV = \$248.69$

4.6.3 Buying an Annuity

You are 65 years old and are considering whether it pays to buy an annuity from an insurance company. For a cost of $10,000 the insurance company will pay you $1,000 per year for the rest of your life. If you can earn 8% per year on your money in a bank account and expect to live until age 80, is it worth buying the annuity? What implied interest rate is the insurance company paying you? How long must you live for the annuity to be worthwhile?

The most direct way to make this investment decision is to compute the present value of the payments from the annuity and compare it to the annuity's $10,000 cost. Assuming it is an ordinary annuity, then it is expected to make 15 payments of $1,000 each starting at age 66 and ending at age 80. The present value of these 15 payments at a discount rate of 8% per year is $8,559.48.

n	*i*	*PV*	*FV*	*PMT*	Result
15	8	?	0	$1,000	$PV = \$8{,}559.48$

In other words, to generate the same 15 annual payments of $1,000 each, it would be enough to invest $8,559.48 in a bank account paying 8% interest per year. Therefore, the net present value of the investment in the annuity is:

$$NPV = \$8{,}559.48 - \$10{,}000 = -\$1{,}440.52$$

and it is not worth buying.

To compute the implied interest rate on the annuity, we need to find the discount rate that makes the *NPV* of the investment zero. The correct answer is 5.56% per year. On a financial calculator we find it by entering the values for *n, PMT,* and *PV,* and computing *i.*

n	*i*	*PV*	*FV*	*PMT*	Result
15	?	−$10,000	0	$1,000	$i = 5.56\%$

In other words, if a bank were offering you an interest rate of 5.56% per year, you could deposit $10,000 now and be able to withdraw $1,000 per year for the next 15 years.

To find the number of years one would have to live to make this annuity worthwhile, we must ask what value of *n* would make the *NPV* of the investment zero. The correct answer is 21 years. On a financial calculator we find it by entering the values for *i, PMT,* and *PV,* and computing *n.*

n	*i*	*PV*	*FV*	*PMT*	Result
?	8	−$10,000	0	$1,000	$n = 20.91$

Looking at it differently, if you live for 21 years rather than 15, the insurance company would wind up paying you an implied interest rate of 8% per year.

4.6.4 Taking a Mortgage Loan

Now let's look at an example of a financing decision. You have just decided to buy a house and need to borrow $100,000. One bank offers you a mortgage loan to be repaid over 30 years in 360 monthly payments. If the interest rate is 12% per year, what is the amount of the monthly payment? (Although the interest rate is quoted as an annual percentage rate, the rate is actually 1% per month.) Another bank offers you a 15-year mortgage loan with a monthly payment of $1,100. Which loan is the better deal?

The monthly payment on the 30-year mortgage is computed by using a monthly period ($n = 360$ months) and a monthly interest rate of 1%. The payment is $1,028.61 per month. It is calculated as follows:

n	*i*	*PV*	*FV*	*PMT*	Result
360	1	−$100,000	0	?	*PMT* = $1,028.61

At first glance, it might seem as if the 30-year mortgage is a better deal because the $1,028.61 monthly payment is less than the $1,100 for the 15-year mortgage. But the 15-year mortgage is finished after only 180 payments. The monthly interest rate is 0.8677%, or an annual percentage rate of 10.4%. To find this rate:

n	*i*	*PV*	*FV*	*PMT*	Result
180	?	−$100,000	0	$1,100	$i = 10.41\%$

The 15-year mortgage is, therefore, the better deal in this case.

4.7 Perpetual Annuities

An important, special type of annuity is a perpetual annuity or **perpetuity.** A perpetuity is a stream of cash flows that lasts forever. The classic example is the "consol" bonds issued by the British government in the nineteenth century, which pay interest each year on the stated face value of the bonds but have no maturity date. Another example, and perhaps a more relevant one, is a share of preferred stock that pays a fixed cash dividend each period (usually every quarter year) and never matures.

A disturbing feature of any perpetual annuity is that you cannot compute the future value of its cash flows because it is infinite. Nevertheless, it has a perfectly well-defined and determinable present value. It might at first seem paradoxical that a series of cash flows that lasts forever can have a finite value today. But consider a perpetual stream of \$100 per year. If the interest rate is 10% per year, how much is this perpetuity worth today?

The answer is \$1,000. To see why, consider how much money you would have to put into a bank account offering interest of 10% per year in order to be able to take out \$100 every year forever. If you put in \$1,000, then at the end of the first year you would have \$1,100 in the account. You would take out \$100, leaving \$1,000 for the second year. Clearly, if the interest rate stayed at 10% per year, and you had a fountain of youth nearby, you could go on doing this forever.

More generally, the formula for the present value of a level perpetuity is:

$$PV \text{ of a Level Perpetuity} = \frac{C}{i}$$

where C is the periodic payment and i is the interest rate expressed as a decimal fraction. This is the present value of an ordinary annuity with $n = \infty$.

4.7.1 Investing in Preferred Stock

Suppose you are currently earning a nominal interest rate of 8% per year on your money. The preferred stock of Boston Gas and Electric Co. offers a cash dividend of \$10 per year, and it is selling at a price of \$100 per share. Should you invest some of your money in BG&E preferred stock?

The first step is to compute the yield on the preferred stock. To do so, we need only divide the cash dividend of \$10 per share by the price of \$100:

$$\text{Yield on Preferred Stock} = \frac{\textit{Annual Dividend}}{\textit{Price}}$$

In this case the yield is 10% per year (i.e., the 10% yield on the preferred stock exceeds the 8% interest rate you are currently earning). To make your investment decision, however, you must also consider risk, a subject we will consider in detail later in the text.

Often one encounters situations in which the cash flows from an investment grow at a constant rate. For example, suppose that you are considering investing in a property for which you expect the first year's cash flow to be \$1,000, and you expect it to grow by 4% each year in perpetuity. To evaluate such an investment you need a formula for computing the present value of a **growth perpetuity.** That formula is:

$$PV = \frac{C_1}{i-g}$$

where C_1 is the first year's cash flow and g is the growth rate.

In the example at hand suppose that the discount rate is 9%. Then the present value of the property would be:

$$PV = \frac{\$1{,}000}{0.09 - 0.04} = \frac{\$1{,}000}{0.056} = \$20{,}000$$

If you can purchase the property for less than $20,000, it would be a worthwhile investment.

4.7.2 Investing in Common Stock

You have the opportunity to buy stock in a company that is known to pay a cash dividend that grows by 3% every year. The next dividend will be $1 per share, and is to be paid a year from now. If you require a 10% per year rate of return, how much should you be willing to pay for the stock?

The answer is that you should be willing to pay the *PV* of the expected future cash flows discounted at 10% per year. The stream of expected future cash dividends is a growth perpetuity. Using the formula for a growth perpetuity:

$$PV = \frac{\$1}{0.10 - 0.03} = \frac{\$1}{0.07} = \$14.29$$

4.8 Loan Amortization

Many loans, such as home mortgage loans and car loans, are repaid in equal periodic installments. Part of each payment is interest on the outstanding balance of the loan and part is repayment of principal. After each payment, the outstanding balance is reduced by the amount of principal repaid. Therefore, the portion of the payment that goes toward the payment of interest is lower than the previous period's interest and the portion going toward repayment of principal is greater than the previous period's principal payment.

For example, let us assume you take a $100,000 home mortgage loan at an interest rate of 9% per year to be repaid with interest in three annual installments. First, we calculate the annual payment by finding the *PMT* that has a *PV* of $100,000 when discounted at 9% for three years:

n	*i*	*PV*	*FV*	*PMT*	Result
3	9	−$100,000	0	?	*PMT* = $39,505.48

So the annual payment is $39,505.48. In the first year, how much of the $39,505.48 is interest and how much is repayment of principal? Because the interest rate is 9% per year, the interest portion of the first payment must be or $9,000. The remainder of the $39,505.48, or $30,505.48, is repayment of the original $100,000 principal. The remaining balance after the first payment is, therefore, $100,000 − $30,505.48 or $69,494.52. The process of paying off a loan's principal gradually over its term is called loan **amortization.**

In the second year, how much of the $39,505.48 is interest and how much is repayment of principal? Because the interest rate is 9% per year, the interest portion of the second payment must be ($69,494.52(0.09)) or $6,254.51. The remainder of the $39,505.48, or $33,250.97, goes toward the repayment of the outstanding $69,494.52 balance remaining after the first payment. The remaining balance after the second payment is, therefore ($69,494.52 − $33,250.97), or $36,243.55.

The third and final payment covers both interest and principal on this remaining $36,243.55 (i.e., Table 4.6 contains all of this information in what is called an

TABLE 4.6 **Amortization Schedule for 3-Year Loan at 9%**

Year	Beginning Balance	Total Payment	Interest Paid	Principal Paid	Remaining Balance
1	$100,000	$39,505	$9,000	$30,505	$69,495
2	$69,495	$39,505	$6,255	$33,251	$36,244
3	$36,244	$39,505	$3,262	$36,244	($0)
	Totals	$118,516	$18,516	$100,000	

amortization schedule for the mortgage loan. Its breakdown shows how with each successive payment of $39,505.48, the portion that pays interest declines and the portion that repays principal increases.

4.8.1 A Bargain Car Loan?

You are buying a car and thinking of taking a one-year installment loan of $1,000 at an *APR* of 12% per year (1% per month) to be repaid in 12 equal monthly payments. The monthly payment is $88.85.

The salesperson trying to sell you the car makes the following pitch:

> Although the *APR* on this loan is 12% per year, in fact it really works out to be a much lower rate. Because the total interest payments over the year are only $66.19, and the loan is for $1,000, you will only be paying a "true" interest rate of 6.62%.

What is the fallacy in the salesperson's reasoning?

The fallacy is that with your first monthly payment (and each subsequent payment), you are paying not only interest on the outstanding balance, you are also repaying part of the principal. The interest payment due at the end of the first month is 1% of $1,000, or $10. Because your monthly payment is $88.85, the other $78.85 is repayment of principal. The full amortization schedule is presented in Table 4.7.

TABLE 4.7 **Amortization Schedule for a 12-Month Loan at 1% per Month**

Month	Beginning Balance	Total Payment	Interest Paid	Principal Paid	Remaining Balance
1	$1,000.00	$88.85	$10.00	$78.85	$921.15
2	$921.15	$88.85	$9.21	$79.64	$841.51
3	$841.51	$88.85	$8.42	$80.43	$761.08
4	$761.08	$88.85	$7.61	$81.24	$679.84
5	$679.84	$88.85	$6.80	$82.05	$597.79
6	$597.79	$88.85	$5.98	$82.87	$514.91
7	$514.91	$88.85	$5.15	$83.70	$431.21
8	$431.21	$88.85	$4.31	$84.54	$346.67
9	$346.67	$88.85	$3.47	$85.38	$261.29
10	$261.29	$88.85	$2.61	$86.24	$175.05
11	$175.05	$88.85	$1.75	$87.10	$87.96
12	$87.96	$88.85	$0.88	$87.97	$0.00
	Totals	$1,066.20	$66.20	$1,000.00	

4.9 Exchange Rates and Time Value of Money

Suppose you are considering investing $10,000 either in dollar-denominated bonds offering an interest rate of 10% per year or in yen-denominated bonds offering 3% per year. Which is the better investment for the next year and why?

The answer depends on how much the dollar/yen exchange rate will change during the year. Suppose that the exchange rate is now 100 yen per dollar and, therefore, your $10,000 is now worth 1 million yen. If you invest in yen-bonds, you will have 1,030,000 yen a year from now. If you invest in dollar-bonds, you will have $11,000 which will be worth more?

If the dollar falls in yen value by 8% per year, then the exchange rate a year from now will be 92 yen per dollar. The yen-bond will have a dollar value of $11,196 (i.e., 1,030,000/92), which is $196 more than the $11,000 you would have from the dollar-bond. If, on the other hand, the dollar falls in yen value by only 6% per year, then the exchange rate a year from now will be 94 yen per dollar. The yen-bond will have a dollar value of $10,957 (i.e., 1,030,000/94) which is $43 less than the $11,000 you would have from the dollar-bond.

At what future exchange rate would you be indifferent between the two bonds? To find the break-even exchange rate, divide 1,030,000 yen by $11,000. The result is 93.636 yen/dollar. Thus, we conclude that if the yen value of the dollar falls by more than 6.364% during the year, the yen-bond would be a better investment.[3]

Quick Check 4-8

If the exchange rate between the U.S. dollar and the British pound is $2 per pound, the dollar interest rate is 6% per year, and the pound interest rate is 4% per year, what is the "break-even" value of the future dollar/pound exchange rate one year from now?

4.9.1 Computing NPV in Different Currencies

To avoid confusion when making financial decisions with different currencies there is a simple rule that one must observe:

> In any time value of money calculation, the cash flows and the interest rate must be denominated in the same currency.

Thus, to compute the present value of cash flows denominated in *yen* you must discount using the *yen* interest rate, and to compute the present value of cash flows denominated in *dollars* you must discount using the *dollar* interest rate. If you compute the present value of payments denominated in yen using the dollar interest rate, you will get a misleading number.

For example, suppose that you are trying to decide whether you should invest in a Japanese project or an American project, both of which require an initial outlay of $10,000. The Japanese project will pay you ¥575,000 per year for five years, whereas the American one will pay $6,000 per year for five years. The dollar interest rate is 6% per year, the yen interest rate is 4% per year, and the current dollar price of a yen is $0.01 per yen. Which project has the higher *NPV*?

First, we compute the *NPV* of the American project using the dollar interest rate of 6%:

n	*i*	*PV*	*FV*	*PMT*	Result
5	6	?	0	$6,000	*PV* = $25,274

[3]Of course, you do not know in advance how much the exchange rate will change, so there is uncertainty in this investment. We deal with this uncertainty explicitly in later chapters.

Subtracting the $10,000 initial outlay, we find that *NPV* = $15,274.

Next we compute the *NPV* of the Japanese project using the yen interest rate to find:

n	*i*	*PV*	*FV*	*PMT*	Result
5	4	?	0	¥575,000	*PV* = ¥2,559,798

Next we convert the *PV* of the Japanese project from yen into dollars at the current exchange rate of $0.01 per yen to get a *PV* of $25,598. Subtracting the $10,000 initial outlay, we find that the *NPV* is $15,598. Thus, the Japanese project has a higher *NPV* and is the one that you should choose.

Note, however, that if you mistakenly computed the *PV* of the Japanese project using the dollar interest rate of 6% per year, you would get an *NPV* of only $14,221. You would, therefore, be led to choose the American project.

4.10 Inflation and Discounted Cash Flow Analysis

Dealing with inflation leads to a similar set of rules as dealing with different currencies. Let us consider the issue of saving for retirement. At age 20 you save $100 and invest it at a dollar interest rate of 8% per year. The good news is that at age 65 your $100 investment will have grown to $3,192. The bad news is that it will cost a lot more to buy the same things you buy today. For example, if the prices of all the goods and services you want to buy go up at 8% per year for the next 45 years, then your $3,192 will buy no more than your $100 will buy today. In a "real" sense, you will not have earned any interest at all. Thus, to make truly meaningful long-run savings decisions, you must take account of inflation as well as interest.

To take account of both interest and inflation we distinguish between nominal and real interest rates. The *nominal interest rate* is the rate denominated in dollars or in some other currency, and the *real interest rate* is denominated in units of consumer goods. This distinction between real and nominal interest rates was discussed in chapter 2 (see section 2.6.5).

The general formula relating the real rate of interest to the nominal rate of interest and the rate of inflation is:

$$1 + \text{Real Rate} = \frac{1 + \textit{Nominal Interest Rate}}{1 + \textit{Rate of Inflation}}$$

or equivalently,

$$\text{Real Rate of Interest} = \frac{\textit{Nominal Interest Rate} - \textit{Rate of Inflation}}{1 + \textit{Rate of Inflation}}$$

Using *APR*s with continuous compounding simplifies the algebraic relationship between real and nominal rates of return. With continuous compounding, the relation between *APR*s becomes:

$$\text{Real Rate of Interest} = \text{Nominal Rate} - \text{Inflation Rate}$$

So if we assume a nominal *APR* of 6% per year compounded continuously and an inflation rate of 4% per year compounded continuously, the real rate is exactly 2% per year compounded continuously.

4.10.1 Inflation and Future Values

From a financial planning perspective, there is a great advantage to knowing the real interest rate. This is because ultimately it is what you can buy with your accumulated savings in the future that you care about. Returning to our specific example of saving \$100 at age 20, not to be taken out until age 65, what we really want to know is how much you will have accumulated in the account when you reach age 65 in terms of real purchasing power. There are two alternative ways of calculating it—a short way and a long way. The short way is to compute the future value of the \$100 using the real interest rate of 2.857% per year for 45 years. We define this as the **real future value.**

$$\text{Real Future Value} = \$100 \times 1.02857^{45} = \$355$$

Alternatively, we can arrive at the same number in stages. First, we compute the **nominal future value** by using the nominal interest rate of 8% per year:

$$\text{Nominal } FV \text{ in 45 Years} = \$100 \times 1.08^{45} = \$3{,}192$$

Next, we figure out what the price level will be 45 years from now if the inflation rate is 5% per year:

$$\text{Price Level in 45 Years} = 1.05^{45} = 8.985$$

Finally, divide the nominal future value by the future price level to find the real future value:

$$\text{Real } FV = \frac{\textit{Nominal Future Value}}{\textit{Future Price Value}} = \frac{\$3{,}192}{8.985} = \$355$$

The end result is the same. We find that by saving \$100 today (age 20) and investing it for 45 years, we expect to have enough at age 65 to buy what would cost \$355 at today's prices.

Thus, we see that there are two equivalent ways of computing the real future value of \$355:

1. Compute the future value using the real rate of interest.
2. Compute the nominal future value using the nominal rate, and then deflate it to find the real future value.

Which of the two equivalent approaches one adopts depends on the particular context.

4.10.2 Saving for College: 1

Your daughter is 10 years old, and you are planning to open an account to provide for her college education. Tuition for a year of college is now \$15,000 and is expected to increase at the rate of 5% per year. If you put \$8,000 into an account paying an interest rate of 8% per year, will you have enough to pay for her first year's tuition eight years from now? If you compute the future value of the \$8,000 at an interest rate of 8% per year for eight years, you find:

$$FV = \$8{,}000 \times 1.08^{8} = \$14{,}807$$

Because \$14,807 is very close to \$15,000, it might appear that saving \$8,000 now is enough to provide for the first year of college tuition. But tuition level is a moving target. College tuition in the past increased at least at the general rate of inflation. For example, if inflation turns out to be 5% per year, the cost of the first year's college tuition will be \$15,000 $\times$ 1.05^{8} or \$22,162. So your \$14,807 will be short by about one-third.

4.10.3 Investing in Inflation-Proof CDs

You are investing \$10,000 for the next year. You face a choice between a conventional, one-year CD paying an interest rate of 8% or a CD that will pay you an interest rate of 3% per year plus the rate of inflation. We will call the former a *nominal CD* and the latter a *real CD*. Which will you choose?

Your choice depends on your forecast for inflation over the next year. If you are sure that the rate of inflation will be greater than 5%, you will prefer the real CD. Suppose, for example, that you think the rate of inflation will be 6%. Then your nominal rate of interest on the real CD will be 9%. If, however, you are sure that inflation will be 4% per year, then the nominal rate of interest on the real CD will be only 7%, so you are better off investing in the nominal CD.

Of course, because you do not know with certainty what the inflation rate will be, the decision is more complicated. We will return to this problem later when we discuss how to take account of uncertainty in investment decisions.

4.10.4 Why Debtors Gain from Unanticipated Inflation

Suppose you borrow \$1,000 at an interest rate of 8% per year and have to pay back principal and interest one year later. If the rate of inflation turns out to be 8% during the year, the real interest rate on the loan is zero. Although you must pay back \$1,080, its *real* value will be only \$1,000. The \$80 in interest just offsets the decline in the purchasing power of the \$1,000 principal. Another way to state this is that you are paying back the loan with "cheaper" dollars than the ones you borrowed. No wonder that when the interest rate on a loan is fixed in advance, debtors like unanticipated inflation and creditors do not.

4.10.5 Inflation and Present Values

In many financial problems in which present values are calculated, the future amount is not fixed in dollars. For example, suppose you plan to buy a car four years from now and want to invest enough money now to pay for it. Say the kind of car you have in mind now costs \$10,000, and the interest rate you can earn on your money is 8% per year.

In attempting to figure out the amount to invest now, it is natural to compute the present value of \$10,000 to be received in four years at 8%:

$$PV = \frac{\$10{,}000}{1.08^4} = \$7{,}350$$

So you might conclude that investing \$7,350 now is adequate to pay for the car four years from now.

But that would be a mistake. Almost surely, if the car you want costs \$10,000 today, a similar car will cost more four years from now. How much more? That depends on the rate of inflation. If inflation in car prices is 5% per year, then the car will cost $\$10{,}000 \times 1.05^4$ or \$12,155 in four years.

There are two equivalent ways to take account of inflation in problems such as this. The first is to compute the present value of the \$10,000 real future amount using the real discount rate. As we saw earlier in this chapter the real discount rate is:

$$\text{Real Rate of Interest} = \frac{\textit{Nominal Interest Rate} - \textit{Rate of Inflation}}{1 + \textit{Rate of Inflation}}$$

$$\text{Real Rate of Interest} = \frac{0.08 - 0.05}{1.05} = 0.02857 = 2.857\%$$

Using this real rate to compute the present value of the $10,000, we find:

$$PV = \frac{\$10{,}000}{1.02857^4} = \$8{,}934$$

The second way is to compute the present value of the $12,155 nominal future amount using the nominal discount rate of 8% per year:

$$PV = \frac{\$12{,}155}{1.08^4} = \$8{,}934$$

Either way, we get the same result: You must invest $8,934 now in order to pay the car's inflated price in four years. The reason we at first mistakenly computed the amount we needed to invest as only $7,350, was that we discounted a real future amount of $10,000 at a nominal discount rate of 8% per year.

4.10.6 Saving for College: 2

Recall that your daughter is 10 years old, and you are planning to open an account to provide for her college education. Tuition for a year of college is now $15,000. How much must you invest now in order to have enough to pay for her first year's tuition eight years from now, if you think you can earn a rate of interest that is 3% more than the inflation rate?

In this case you do not have an explicit estimate of the rate of inflation. But do you need one to answer the practical question before you? The answer is that you do not, provided you think that college tuition will rise at whatever the general inflation rate is. Under that assumption the real cost of college tuition eight years from now will be the same $15,000 it is today. By assuming that you can earn 3% per year more than the rate of inflation, you are, in effect, saying that the real discount rate is 3% per year. So you should calculate present value by discounting the $15,000 at 3% for eight years:

$$PV = \frac{\$15{,}000}{1.03^8} = \$11{,}841$$

If, by mistake, you were to discount the $15,000 using a nominal rate such as 8% per year, you would get a very different answer:

$$PV = \frac{\$15{,}000}{1.08^8} = \$8{,}104$$

The result is that you would not have enough to pay for tuition in eight years.

Beware: Never use a nominal interest rate when discounting real cash flows or a real interest rate when discounting nominal cash flows.

4.10.7 Inflation and Savings Plans

When considering a plan for long-run savings, it is essential to take account of inflation. The amount of money you can afford to save each year is likely to rise with the general cost of living because your income will probably also be going up. One easy way to take account of this without having to make an explicit forecast of the rate of inflation is to make your plans in terms of constant *real* payments and a *real* rate of interest.

4.10.8 Saving for College: 3

Recall that your daughter is 10 years old, and you are planning to open an account to provide for her college education. Tuition for a year of college is now $15,000. You want to save in equal real annual installments over the next eight years to have enough to pay for her first year's tuition eight years from now. If you think you can earn a real rate of interest of 3% per year, how much must you save each year? How much will you actually put into the account each year (in nominal terms) if the rate of inflation turns out to be 5% per year?

To find the annual real amount to save we first solve for *PMT:*

n	*i*	*PV*	*FV*	*PMT*	Result
8	3	0	\$15,000	?	*PMT* = \$1,686.85

So the amount to save each year must be the equivalent of \$1,686.85 of today's purchasing power. At an inflation rate of 5% per year, the actual amount of dollars that will have to be contributed to the plan each year are as shown in Table 4.8.

With this plan the nominal amount saved each year has to be adjusted upward in accordance with the actual rate of inflation. The result will be that the amount accumulated in the account in eight years will be enough to pay for tuition. Thus, if the rate of inflation turns out to be 5% per year, then the nominal amount in the account eight years from now will turn out to be \$22,162. The tuition required eight years from now is \$15,000 in real terms and \$22,162 in nominal terms.

To verify that the nominal future value of this saving plan will be \$22,162 if the inflation rate is 5% per year, we can compute the future value of the nominal cash flows in the last column of Table 4.9. First, note that if the real rate of interest is 3% per year, then the nominal rate of interest must be 8.15%:

$$1 + \text{Real Rate of Interest} = \frac{1 + \textit{Nominal Rate of Interest}}{1 + \textit{Rate of Inflation}}$$

$$1 + \text{Nominal Rate} = (1 + \text{Real Rate}) \times (1 + \text{Inflation})$$

$$\text{Nominal Rate} = \text{Real Rate} + \text{Inflation} + \text{Real Rate} \times \text{Inflation}$$

$$\text{Nominal Rate} = 0.03 + 0.05 + 0.03 \times 0.05 = 0.0815$$

Compounding each year's nominal payment forward at the nominal interest rate of 8.15%, as shown in Table 4.9, we find that the total nominal future value is indeed \$22,162.

Note that if your income goes up at 5% per year, then the nominal payment will remain a constant fraction of your income.

If the rate of inflation turns out to be 10% per year, and you increase your nominal payments into the plan at that rate, then the nominal amount in the account eight years from

TABLE 4.8 Nominal Dollar Amounts of a Real Annuity

Payment Number	Real Payment	Inflation Factor	Nominal Payment
1	\$1,686.85	1.05000	\$1,771.19
2	\$1,686.85	1.10250	\$1,859.75
3	\$1,686.85	1.15763	\$1,952.74
4	\$1,686.85	1.21551	\$2,050.38
5	\$1,686.85	1.27628	\$2,152.90
6	\$1,686.85	1.34010	\$2,260.54
7	\$1,686.85	1.40710	\$2,373.57
8	\$1,686.85	1.47746	\$2,492.25

TABLE 4.9 **Computing Nominal Future Value of a Real Annuity**

Payment Number	Real Payment	Inflation Factor	Nominal Payment	Future Value Factor	Nominal Future Value
1	$1,686.85	1.05000	$1,771.19	1.73056	$3,065.15
2	$1,686.85	1.10250	$1,859.75	1.60014	$2,975.87
3	$1,686.85	1.15763	$1,952.74	1.47956	$2,889.20
4	$1,686.85	1.21551	$2,050.38	1.36806	$2,805.04
5	$1,686.85	1.27628	$2,152.90	1.26497	$2,723.34
6	$1,686.85	1.34010	$2,260.54	1.16964	$2,644.02
7	$1,686.85	1.40710	$2,373.57	1.08150	$2,567.01
8	$1,686.85	1.47746	$2,492.25	1.00000	$2,492.25
			Total nominal future value		$22,161.89

now will turn out to be $15,000 × 1.1^8 or $32,154. This will have a real value in today's dollars of $15,000—just enough to pay the tuition.

4.10.9 Inflation and Investment Decisions

It is just as essential to take account of inflation in investment decisions as it is in saving decisions. When investing money in real assets such as real estate or plant and equipment, the future cash flows from the investment are likely to rise in nominal value because of inflation. If you fail to make the appropriate adjustments, you will tend to pass up worthwhile investment opportunities.

To see how important it is to take proper account of inflation, consider the following example. You currently heat your house with oil and your annual heating bill is $2,000. By converting to gas heat you estimate that this year you could cut your heating bill by $500, and you think that the cost differential between gas and oil is likely to remain the same for many years. The cost of installing a gas heating system is $10,000. If your alternative use of the money is to leave it in a bank account earning an interest rate of 8% per year, is the conversion worthwhile?

Note that there is no natural time horizon for this decision. We will, therefore, assume that the $500 cost differential will remain forever. We will also assume that the future outlays on replacement of heating equipment will be the same under both the oil and gas alternatives, so that we can ignore them for purposes of making this decision. Therefore, the investment is a perpetuity—you pay $10,000 now and get $500 per year forever. The internal rate of return on the investment in gas heat is 5% per year $\left(\text{i.e., } \frac{\$500}{\$10,000}\right)$.

Comparing this 5% per year rate of return to the 8% per year alternative, you might be inclined to reject the gas investment opportunity. But wait a minute. The 8% per year rate on the bank account is a nominal rate of interest. What about the 5% per year rate of return on the investment in gas heat?

If you think that the $500 cost differential between gas and oil will increase over time with the general rate of inflation, then the 5% rate of return on the investment is a *real* rate of return. You should, therefore, compare it to the expected *real* rate of interest on the bank account. If you expect the rate of inflation to be 5% per year, then the expected real interest rate on the bank account is 2.857% $\left(\text{i.e., } \frac{(0.08-0.05)}{1.05}\right)$. The 5% per year real yield on the investment in gas heat exceeds this, so perhaps the investment is worthwhile after all.

This example leads us to the following rule:

> When comparing investment alternatives, never compare a real rate of return to a nominal opportunity cost of money.

This rule is just a slightly different version of the caution we issued earlier in this chapter:

> Never use a nominal interest rate when discounting real cash flows or a real interest rate when discounting nominal cash flows.

4.11 Taxes and Investment Decisions

Up to this point our discussion has ignored income taxes. But what you have to spend in the future will be what is left after paying income taxes to the government. For example, suppose that you must pay 30% in taxes on any interest that you earn. You put $1,000 into a bank account offering an interest rate of 8% per year. This is the **before-tax interest rate.** Your **after-tax interest rate** is defined as what you earn after paying your income taxes.

Let us compute what it is. The interest income you will have to report on your income tax return is 0.08 × $1,000 or $80.[4] The tax on this interest income is 0.3 × $80 or $24. Thus, you will be left with $56 in interest income after taxes. Your after-tax interest rate is this $56 divided by your original investment of $1,000, or 5.6%. A shortcut way of computing your after-tax interest rate is to multiply the before-tax interest rate by 1 minus your tax rate:

$$\text{After-Tax Interest Rate} = (1 - \text{Tax Rate}) \times \text{Before-Tax Interest Rate}$$

In our example we get:

$$\text{After-Tax Interest Rate} = (1-0.3)\times 8\% = 0.7\times 8\% = 5.6\%$$

The rule for investing is:

> Invest so as to maximize the net present value of your after-tax cash flows.

Note that this is not necessarily the same as investing so as to minimize the taxes you pay. To see this, consider the following example.

4.11.1 Invest in Tax-Exempt Bonds?

In the United States, municipal bonds are exempt from income taxes. If you are in a high enough tax bracket, you might prefer to invest your money in municipal bonds. For example, if the interest rate on municipal bonds is 6% per year, and they are just as safe as the bank account paying an after-tax interest rate of 5.6% per year, then you would prefer to invest in the municipal bonds. The higher your tax bracket the bigger the advantage to you of investing in tax-exempt securities.

Suppose you are in a 20% tax bracket. Would it make sense for you to invest in municipal bonds paying 6% per year, if you can earn 8% per year from the bank? The answer is no, because even after paying income taxes on the interest from the bank, you would still have an after-tax interest rate that is higher than the tax-exempt rate on municipals:

$$\text{After-Tax Interest Rate on Bank Account} = (1-0.2)\times 8\% = 6.4\%$$

---

[4]You had better report it, too! In the United States, your bank directly informs the Internal Revenue Service how much it pays you in interest.

Therefore, if you followed the rule of minimizing your taxes, you would be led to make the wrong investment!

What is the personal tax bracket at which an individual would be exactly indifferent between investing in taxable and tax-exempt securities? The answer in our example is 25%. At a tax rate of 25%, the after-tax interest rate on the bank account is 6% (i.e., $0.75 \times 8\%$), the same as the rate on tax-exempt municipal bonds.

Summary

- Compounding is the process of going from present value (PV) to future value (FV). The future value of \$1 earning interest at rate i per period for n periods is $(1 + i)^n$.
- Discounting is finding the present value of some future amount. The present value of \$1 discounted at rate i per period for n periods is $\frac{1}{(1+i)^n}$.
- One can make financial decisions by comparing the present values of streams of expected future cash flows resulting from alternative courses of action. The present value of cash inflows less the present value of cash outflows is called net present value (NPV). If a course of action has a positive NPV, it is worth undertaking.
- In any time value of money calculation, the cash flows and the interest rate must be denominated in the same currency.
- Never use a nominal interest rate when discounting real cash flows or a real interest rate when discounting nominal cash flows.
- Always compare investment alternatives in terms of their returns net of income taxes.

Key Terms

- time value of money 108
- discounted cash flow 108
- compounding 108
- present value 108
- future value 108
- simple interest 108
- compound interest 108
- future value factor 110
- Rule of 72 111
- compound amount factor 111
- reinvestment rate 112
- annual percentage rate 113
- effective annual rate 113
- present value of \$1 115
- present value factor 116
- net present value 118
- opportunity cost of capital 118
- yield to maturity 120
- internal rate of return 120
- time line 123
- annuity 124
- immediate annuity 124
- ordinary annuity 124
- perpetuity 128
- growth perpetuity 128
- amortization 129
- amortization schedule 130
- real future value 133
- nominal future value 133
- before-tax interest rate 138
- after-tax interest rate 138

Answers to Quick Check Questions

Quick Check 4-1 If the interest rate is only 5% per year in the previous example, what is the future value? What are the simple interest and the compound interest?

Answer: $\$1{,}000 \times 1.05^5 = \$1{,}276.28$

Simple interest: $\$1{,}000 \times 0.05 \times 5 = \$250$

Compound interest: $\$276.28 - \$250 = \$26.28$

Quick Check 4-2 In 1626, Peter Minuit purchased Manhattan Island from the Native Americans for about $24 worth of trinkets. If the tribe had taken cash instead and invested it to earn 6% per year compounded annually, how much would they have had in 2006, 380 years later?

Answer: To answer this question, students can use the following formula (the answer is too large for most calculator displays):

$\$24 \times 1.06^{380} = \$99{,}183{,}639{,}918$ (99 billion, 183 million, 639 thousand and 918 dollars)

Quick Check 4-3 You take out a loan at an *APR* of 12% with monthly compounding. What is the effective annual rate on your loan?

Answer:

$$EFF = \left(1 + \frac{0.12}{12}\right)^{12} - 1\text{, hence, } EFF = 12.68\%$$

Quick Check 4-4 What is the present value of $100 to be received in four years at an interest rate of 6% per year?

Answer:

$$PV = \frac{\$100}{1.06^4} = \$79.21.$$

Quick Check 4-5 Suppose a $10,000 T-bill which will mature in 3 months is currently selling for $9,800. If you purchase and hold the T-bill to maturity what rate of return would you earn on this investment computed as a continuously compounding annual rate (over the 3-month period)?

Answer: Using $10,000 as the future value and the $9,800 selling price as the present value we have the following relationship: $PV = \$9{,}800 = \$10{,}000 \cdot e^{-i \cdot \frac{1}{4}}$. Solving for the unknown i we find

$$\frac{\ell n\left(\frac{PV}{FV}\right)}{-\frac{1}{4}} = \frac{\ell n\left(\frac{\$9{,}800}{\$10{,}000}\right)}{-0.25} = 0.0808108 = 8.081\% = i.$$

Quick Check 4-6 Show that the alternative decision criteria presented previously lead to the same result—that the investment is worthwhile.

Answer:

1. Invest if the future value of the investment is larger than the future value that can be obtained from the next best alternative.

   First, we compute the future value of the $10,000 if invested in the bank.

$$FV = \$10{,}000 \times 1.08^5 = \$14{,}693$$

Comparing the $14,693 computed future value to the $20,000 from the land, we conclude that investing in the land is worthwhile.

2. Invest if the *IRR* is greater than the opportunity cost of capital. Now we are ready to consider the investment's internal rate of return (*IRR*). By investing \$10,000 in the land today, you can get \$20,000 five years from now. What interest rate are you earning? In other words, we want to find i that solves the equation:

$$\$10,000 = \frac{\$20,000}{(1+i)^5}$$
$$i = 14.87\%$$

Thus, the internal rate of return on the investment in land is 14.87% per year. This should be compared to the 8% per year you could earn by putting your money in the bank. Clearly, you can earn a higher rate of return by investing in the land.

Note that because in this problem the \$10,000 investment in land is expected to double over the next five years, the Rule of 72 could be applied to get a "quick and dirty" approximation for the *IRR*. By manipulating the Rule of 72 we find that the *IRR* on an investment that doubles in n years is approximately equal to the number 72 divided by n:

$$\textit{Doubling Time} = \frac{72}{\textit{Interest Rate}}$$

hence

$$IRR = \frac{72}{\textit{Doubling Time}}$$

In our example, the approximate *IRR* would be:

$$IRR = \frac{72}{5} = 14.4\% \text{ per year}$$

This is close to the *IRR* of 14.87%. Even though the payback period rule is subject to many potential pitfalls, in this simple example it does work.

3. Choose the investment alternative with the fastest payback. We could ask how long it would take for our \$10,000 investment to grow to \$20,000 if we invested in the bank at 8% per year. To answer this question we are solving the equation for the number of periods, n:

$$\$10,000 = \frac{\$20,000}{1.08^n}$$

On the financial calculator we input *PV*, *FV*, and i and compute n. We find that n is 9.01 years. Because it takes only five years to double your money with the investment in land, clearly the land investment is better than putting your money in the bank. Note that using the Rule of 72 to find n we get:

$$\text{Doubling Time} = \frac{72}{8} = 9 \text{ Years}$$

Quick Check 4-7 Suppose you deposit \$1,000 now and then \$2,000 a year from now. How much will you have two years from now, if the interest rate is 10% per year?

Answer: Future Value of the Initial \$1,000 = \$1,000 × 1.1^2 = \$1,210
Future Value of the \$2,000 = \$2,000 × 1.1 = \$2,200
Total Future Value \$3,410

Quick Check 4-8 If the exchange rate between the U.S. dollar and the British pound is \$2 per pound, the dollar interest rate is 6% per year, and the pound interest rate is 4% per year, what is the "break-even" value of the future dollar/pound exchange rate one year from now?

Answer: You could invest \$1 today in dollar-denominated bonds and have \$1.06 one year from now. Or you could convert the dollar today into ½ pound and invest in pound-denominated bonds to have 0.52 pounds one year from now. For you to break even, the 0.52 pounds would have to be worth \$1.06 one year from now, so the break-even exchange rate is: $\frac{\$1.06}{£0.52}$, or \$2.03846 per pound.

Questions and Problems

1. If you invest \$1,000 today at an interest rate of 10% per year, how much will you have 20 years from now, assuming no withdrawals in the interim?
2. **a.** If you invest \$100 every year for the next 20 years starting one year from today and you earn interest of 10% per year, how much will you have at the end of the 20 years?
   b. How much must you invest each year if you want to have \$50,000 at the end of the 20 years?
3. What is the present value of the following cash flows at an interest rate of 10% per year?
   a. \$100 received five years from now.
   b. \$100 received 60 years from now.
   c. \$100 received each year beginning one year from now and ending 10 years from now.
   d. \$100 received each year for 10 years beginning now.
   e. \$100 each year beginning one year from now and continuing forever. (Hint: You do not need to use the financial keys of your calculator for this, just some common sense.)
4. You want to establish a "wasting" fund, which will provide you with \$1,000 per year for four years, at which time the fund will be exhausted. How much must you put in the fund now if you can earn 10% interest per year?
5. You take a one-year installment loan of \$1,000 at an interest rate of 12% per year (1% per month) to be repaid in 12 equal monthly payments.
   a. What is the monthly payment?
   b. What is the total amount of interest paid over the 12-month term of the loan?
6. You are taking out a \$100,000 mortgage loan to be repaid over 25 years in 300 monthly payments.
   a. If the interest rate is 16% per year, what is the amount of the monthly payment?
   b. If you can only afford to pay \$1,000 per month, how large a loan could you take?
   c. If you can afford to pay \$1,500 per month and need to borrow \$100,000, how many months would it take to pay off the mortgage?
   d. If you can pay \$1,500 per month, need to borrow \$100,000, and want a 25-year mortgage, what is the highest interest rate you can pay?
7. In 1626 Peter Minuit purchased Manhattan Island from the Native Americans for about \$24 worth of trinkets. If the tribe had taken cash instead and invested it to earn 8% per year compounded annually, how much would the Indians have had in 1986, 360 years later?
8. You win a \$1 million lottery, which pays you \$50,000 per year for 20 years. How much is your prize really worth, assuming an interest rate of 8% per year?
9. Your great-aunt left you \$20,000 when she died. You can invest the money to earn 12% per year. If you spend \$3,540 per year out of this inheritance, how long will the money last?

10. You borrow $100,000 from a bank for 30 years at an *APR* of 10.5%. What is the monthly payment? If you must pay two points up front, meaning that you only get $98,000 from the bank, what is the true *APR* on the mortgage loan?
11. Suppose that the mortgage loan described in question 10 is a one-year adjustable rate mortgage (ARM), which means that the 10.5% interest applies for only the first year. If the interest rate goes up to 12% in the second year of the loan, what will your new monthly payment be?
12. You just received a gift of $500 from your grandmother and you are thinking about saving this money for graduation, which is four years away. You have your choice between Bank A, which is paying 7% for one-year deposits, and Bank B, which is paying 6% on one-year deposits. Each bank compounds interest annually.
    a. What is the future value of your savings one year from today if you save your money in Bank A? Bank B? Which is the better decision?
    b. What savings decision will most individuals make? What likely reaction will Bank B have?
13. Sue Consultant has just been given a bonus of $2,500 by her employer. She is thinking about using the money to start saving for the future. She can invest to earn an annual rate of interest of 10%.
    a. According to the Rule of 72, approximately how long will it take for Sue to increase her wealth to $5,000?
    b. Exactly how long does it actually take?
14. Larry's bank account has a "floating" interest rate on certain deposits. Every year the interest rate is adjusted. Larry deposited $20,000 three years ago, when interest rates were 7% (annual compounding). Last year the rate was only 6%, and this year the rate fell again to 5%. How much will be in his account at the end of this year?
15. You have your choice between investing in a bank savings account, which pays 8% compounded annually (BankAnnual), and one that pays 7.5% compounded daily (BankDaily).
    a. Based on effective annual rates, which bank would you prefer?
    b. Suppose BankAnnual is only offering one-year certificates of deposit and if you withdraw your money early you lose all interest. How would you evaluate this additional piece of information when making your decision?
16. What are the effective annual rates of the following:
    a. 12% *APR* compounded monthly?
    b. 10% *APR* compounded annually?
    c. 6% *APR* compounded daily?
17. Harry promises that an investment in his firm will double in six years. Interest is assumed to be paid quarterly and reinvested. What effective annual yield does this represent?
18. Suppose you know that you will need $2,500 two years from now in order to make a down payment on a car.
    a. BankOne is offering 4% interest (compounded annually) for two-year accounts and BankTwo is offering 4.5% (compounded annually) for two-year accounts. If you know you need $2,500 two years from today, how much will you need to invest in BankOne to reach your goal? Alternatively, how much will you need to invest in BankTwo? Which bank account do you prefer?
    b. Now suppose you do not need the money for three years. How much will you need to deposit today in BankOne? BankTwo?
19. Lucky Lynn has a choice between receiving $1,000 from her great-uncle one year from today or $900 from her great-aunt today. She believes she could invest the $900 at a one-year return of 12%.

a. What is the future value of the gift from her great-uncle upon receipt? From her great-aunt?
b. Which gift should she choose?
c. How does your answer change if you believed she could invest the $900 from her great-aunt at only 10%? At what rate is she indifferent?

20. As manager of short-term projects, you are trying to decide whether or not to invest in a short-term project that pays one cash flow of $1,000 one year from today. The total cost of the project is $950. Your alternative investment is to deposit the money in a one-year bank certificate of deposit, which will pay 4% compounded annually.
a. Assuming the cash flow of $1,000 is guaranteed (there is no risk you will not receive it), what would be a logical discount rate to use to determine the present value of the cash flows of the project?
b. What is the present value of the project if you discount the cash flow at 4% per year? What is the net present value of that investment? Should you invest in the project?
c. What would you do if the bank increases its quoted rate on one-year CDs to 5.5%?
d. At what bank one-year CD rate would you be indifferent between the two investments?

21. Calculate the net present value of the following cash flows: You invest $2,000 today and receive $200 one year from now, $800 two years from now, and $1,000 a year for 10 years starting four years from now. Assume that the interest rate is 8%.

22. Your cousin has asked for your advice on whether or not to buy a bond for $995, which will make one payment of $1,200 five years from today, or invest in a local bank account.
a. What is the internal rate of return on the bond's cash flows? What additional information do you need to make a choice?
b. What advice would you give her if you learned the bank is paying 3.5% per year for five years (compounded annually)?
c. How would your advice change if the bank were paying 5% annually for five years? If the price of the bond were $900 and the bank pays 5% annually?

23. You and your sister have just inherited $300 and a savings bond from your great-grandfather who had left them in a safe deposit box. Because you are the oldest, you get to choose whether you want the cash or the bond. The bond has only four years left to maturity at which time it will pay the holder $500.
a. If you took the $300 today and invested it at an interest rate 6% per year, how long (in years) would it take for your $300 to grow to $500? (Hint: You want to solve for n or number of periods.) Given these circumstances, which are you going to choose?
b. Would your answer change if you could invest the $300 at 10% per year? At 15% per year? What other decision rules could you use to analyze this decision?

24. Suppose you have three personal loans outstanding to your friend Elizabeth. A payment of $1,000 is due today, a $500 payment is due one year from now, and a $250 payment is due two years from now. You would like to consolidate the three loans into one, with 36 equal monthly payments, beginning one month from today. Assume the agreed interest rate is 8% (effective annual rate) per year.
a. What is the annual percentage rate you will be paying?
b. How large will the new monthly payment be?

25. As CEO of ToysRFun, you are offered the chance to participate, without initial charge, in a project that produces cash flows of $5,000 at the end of the first period, $4,000 at the end of the next period, and a loss of $11,000 at the end of the third and final year.

a. What is the net present value if the relevant discount rate (the company's cost of capital) is 10%?
b. Would you accept the offer?
c. What is the internal rate of return? Can you explain why you would reject a project that has an internal rate of return greater than its cost of capital?

26. You must pay a creditor $6,000 one year from now, $5,000 two years from now, $4,000 three years from now, $2,000 four years from now, and a final $1,000 five years from now. You would like to restructure the loan into five equal annual payments due at the end of each year. If the agreed interest rate is 6% compounded annually, what is the payment?
27. Find the future value of the following ordinary annuities (payments begin one year from today and all interest rates compound annually):
    a. $100 per year for 10 years at 9%.
    b. $500 per year for 8 years at 15%.
    c. $800 per year for 20 years at 7%.
    d. $1,000 per year for 5 years at 0%.
    e. Now find the present values of the annuities in a–d.
    f. What is the relationship between present values and future values?
28. Suppose you will need $50,000 ten years from now. You plan to make seven equal annual deposits beginning three years from today in an account that yields 11% compounded annually. How large should the annual deposit be?
29. Suppose an investment offers $100 per year for five years at 5% beginning one year from today.
    a. What is the present value? How does the present value calculation change if one additional payment is added today?
    b. What is the future value of this ordinary annuity? How does the future value change if one additional payment is added today?
30. You are trying to decide whether to buy a car for 4.0% *APR* for the full $20,000 purchase price over three years or receive $1,500 cash back and finance the rest at a bank rate of 9.5%. Both loans have monthly payments over three years. Which should you choose?
31. You are looking to buy a sports car costing $23,000. One dealer is offering a special reduced financing rate of 2.9% *APR* on new car purchases for three-year loans, with monthly payments. A second dealer is offering a cash rebate. Any customer taking the cash rebate would, of course, be ineligible for the special loan rate and would have to borrow the balance of the purchase price from the local bank at the 9% annual rate. How large must the cash rebate be on this $23,000 car to entice a customer away from the dealer who is offering the special 2.9% financing?
32. Show proof that investing $475.48 today at 10% allows you to withdraw $150 at the end of each of the next four years and have nothing remaining.
33. As pension manager, you are considering investing in a preferred stock, which pays $5,000,000 per year *forever* beginning one year from now. If your alternative investment choice is yielding 10% per year, what is the present value of this investment? What is the highest price you would be willing to pay for this investment? If you paid this price, what would be the dividend yield on this investment?
34. A new lottery game offers a choice for the grand prize winner. You can either receive a lump sum of $1,000,000 immediately or an annuity of $100,000 per year forever, with the first payment *today.* (If you die, your estate will still continue to receive payments.) If the relevant interest rate is 9.5% compounded annually, what is the difference in value between the two prizes?

35. Find the future value of a $1,000 lump-sum investment under the following compounding periods: (Hint: Either figure out effective annual rate or change number of periods and interest rate as compounding period shortens.)
    a. 7% compounded annually for 10 years.
    b. 7% compounded semiannually for 10 years.
    c. 7% compounded monthly for 10 years.
    d. 7% compounded daily for 10 years.
    e. 7% compounded continuously for 10 years.
36. Sammy Jo charged $1,000 worth of merchandise one year ago on her MasterCard, which has a stated interest rate of 18% *APR* compounded monthly. She made 12 regular monthly payments of $50, at the end of each month, and refrained from using the card for the past year. How much does she still owe?
37. Suppose you are considering borrowing $120,000 to finance your dream house. The annual percentage rate is 9% and payments are made monthly.
    a. If the mortgage has a 30-year amortization schedule, what are the monthly payments?
    b. What effective annual rate would you be paying?
    c. How do your answers to parts a and b change if the loan amortizes over 15 years rather than 30?
38. Suppose last year you took out the loan described in problem 37a. Now interest rates have declined to 8% per year. Assume there will be no refinancing fees.
    a. What is the remaining balance of your current mortgage after 12 payments? (Hint: Look for future value.)
    b. What would be your payment if you refinanced your mortgage at the lower rate for 29 years?

Exchange Rates and the Time Value of Money

39. The exchange rate between the pound sterling and the dollar is currently $1.50 per pound, the dollar interest rate is 7% per year, and the pound interest rate is 9% per year. You have $100,000 in a one-year account that allows you to choose between either currency, and it pays the corresponding interest rate.
    a. If you expect the dollar/pound exchange rate to be $1.40 per pound a year from now and are indifferent to risk, which currency should you choose?
    b. What is the break-even value of the dollar/pound exchange rate one year from now?

Real versus Nominal Interest Rates

40. The interest rate on conventional 10-year Treasury bonds is 7% per year and the interest rate on 10-year TIPS (Treasury inflation-protected securities) is 3.5% per year. You have $10,000 to invest in one of them.
    a. If you expect the average inflation rate to be 4% per year, which bond offers the higher expected rate of return?
    b. Which would you prefer to invest in?
41. You are 20 years from retirement, and expect to live another 20 years after retirement. If you start saving now, how much will you be able to withdraw *each year* for every dollar *per year* that you save, assuming an effective annual interest rate of:
    a. 0, 1%, 2%, 3%, 3.5%, 4%, 6%, 8%, and 10%?
    b. How would your answer change if you expect the rate of inflation to be 4% per year?

APPENDIX

Adjusting a Mortgage for Points

Many banks offer mortgages that include *points.* Points are essentially an extra fee paid to the bank up front. Thus, if you take out a three-year $10,000 mortgage with two points, you have to pay 2% of the mortgage amount to the bank at inception. In other words, instead of getting $10,000 at the beginning from the bank, you really only get $9,800. Let us see what points do to the actual interest rate on a mortgage. Suppose you take out the three-year, $10,000 (two points) mortgage from the bank at a stated *APR* of 12% with monthly payments. This corresponds to a monthly interest rate of 1%.

The first step is to compute the actual payment that the bank requires each month. This is done based on the total amount of the mortgage, $10,000.

n	*i*	*PV*	*FV*	*PMT*	Result
36	1	$10,000	0	?	*PMT* = $332.14

The *PV* of the mortgage is not really $10,000, but only $9,800. Thus, together with the monthly payments of $332.14, we can compute the monthly interest rate:

n	*i*	*PV*	*FV*	*PMT*	Result
36	?	$9,800	0	−$332.14	*i* = 1.11757%

This monthly interest rate corresponds to an *APR* of 12 × 1.11757% = 13.41%

Thus, when one bank offers you an *APR* of 13% on the preceding three-year mortgage and charges no points and a second bank offers you an *APR* of 12% with two points, you now know which bank offers the better deal. (Hint: It is not the second bank.)

CHAPTER 5

Household Saving and Investment Decisions

OBJECTIVES

- Analyze how much to save for retirement.
- Determine whether to defer taxes or pay them now.
- Determine whether to get a professional degree.
- Determine whether to buy or rent a house?

CONTENTS

In chapter 4 we explained how to use discounted cash flow analysis in making financial decisions. In this chapter we apply those discounted cash flow concepts to the major financial decisions we all must make at different stages of our lives. Starting with the decision about how much to save for retirement, we develop a life-cycle model for comprehensive financial planning. We then analyze whether you should defer taxes or pay them immediately, whether you should invest in a professional education, and whether you should buy or rent a house.

5.1 A Life-Cycle Model of Saving

Consider the following example. You are currently 35 years old, expect to retire in 30 years at age 65, and then to live for 15 more years until age 80. Your current labor income is \$30,000 per year, and you have not yet accumulated any assets.

We simplify the example by ignoring taxes. Also let us assume that your *real* labor income adjusted for inflation remains at \$30,000 per year until age 65. In other words, we assume that your income will keep pace with inflation, but not beat it.

How much should you spend for consumption now and how much should you save for retirement?

Every dollar you save will earn interest until you take it out. Of course, the cost of living will be going up, too. We will assume that the interest rate you earn will exceed the rate of inflation by 3% per year. In other words, the real rate of interest is 3% per year.

There are two approaches that you could take to computing how much you should save for your retirement: (1) Aim for a target replacement rate of preretirement income, and (2) aim for maintaining the same level of consumption spending before and after retirement. We will examine both approaches next.

5.1.1 Approach 1: Target Replacement Rate of Preretirement Income

Many experts recommend that in making a savings plan, you should aim for a replacement rate equal to 75% of your preretirement income. Let us apply this rule to our situation. With a real income before retirement of \$30,000, the target level of retirement income is $0.75 \times 30{,}000$ or \$22,500 per year.

The method for computing how much saving is needed to reach the desired target consists of two steps:

- First compute the amount you need to have accumulated in your personal retirement account when you reach retirement age.
- Then compute the annual amount of saving needed to reach that future value.

So, first we compute the amount that you have to have in your retirement fund at age 65 to be able to withdraw \$22,500 per year for 15 years:

Using the *Annuity Present Value Factor:*

$$PV_{PMT}(PMT, i, n) = PMT \cdot \frac{1-(1+i)^{-n}}{i} \qquad PV_{PMT}(\$22,500,\ 3\%,\ 15) = \$268,603.54$$

n	15
i	3%
PMT	\$22,500.00
PV	\$268,603.54

Next we compute how much you need to save each year to have \$268,603.54 accumulated 30 years from now. Using the *Sinking Fund Factor:*

$$PMT_{FV}(FV, i, n) = FV \cdot \frac{i}{(1+i)^n - 1} \qquad PMT_{FV}(\$268,603.54, 3\%, 30) = \$5,645.85$$

n	30
i	3%
FV	\$268,603.54
PMT	\$5,645.85

So the conclusion from this procedure is that in order to be able to take out a retirement benefit of \$22,500 per year for 15 years, you would need to save \$5,645.85 per year in each of the next 30 years.

Now, let us consider a problem that arises when you use this approach. The solution does not necessarily result in your having the same consumption level after retirement as you did during your working years. In the preceding example, your consumption spending during the working years when you are saving \$5,645.85 of your \$30,000 annual income will be \$24,354.15 per year, but then in retirement you will have only \$22,500 to spend each year.

One way to deal with this problem is to redo the calculations using a higher replacement rate than 75%. If that replacement rate turns out to be too high, then try a lower one. You could continue applying this trial-and-error procedure until you find a replacement rate that results in the same consumption spending before and after retirement. Approach 2 addresses the problem directly without resorting to a trial-and-error search.

Box 5.1 Demographic Pressures on European Pension Systems

A growing number of state pension systems in Europe have become unsustainable because of early retirement, increased life expectancy, and low birth rates. European pension systems operate in a pay-as-you-go fashion, in which current workers finance the pensions of retirees. This system operates on the assumption that current workers greatly outnumber retired workers, but their ratio has been steadily shrinking. Many current European governments have acknowledged this problem but have not done much besides postponing the problem for future administrations to address. The failure to address the fundamental underlying issues and potential solutions is primarily due to resistance from many workers, who are generally unhappy about the proposed changes to public pension schemes. However, European governments must greatly reduce the scope of the pay-as-you-go system in order to ensure that today's workers will be able to count on a secure retirement system.

Employees can be encouraged to put more savings in private retirement accounts, either through their employers or with fund-management firms. Such actions would force workers to take more responsibility for their own retirement. State retirement ages are expected to be restructured or eliminated, and people are expected to be encouraged to retire later as life expectancies continue to increase. An increase in immigration, although controversial, would also ease the burden of younger workers. Finally, birth rates, which have been in rapid decline throughout Europe, could increase—ensuring that Europe's current workers would continue to greatly outnumber retirees. This can be accomplished by removing structural obstacles that make it difficult for women in Europe to simultaneously have a career and a family, possibly through revisions in the tax system and employment law. Unless governments take action, the pay-as-you-go state pensions in Europe could fail as a growing number of workers live longer and retire earlier.

Source: Adapted from "Work Longer, Have More Babies," *The Economist,* September 25, 2003.

Quick Check 5-1

Recompute the saving needed in the example if the target replacement rate is 80%. What does the new saving level imply about consumption spending before and after retirement?

5.1.2 Approach 2: Maintain the Same Level of Consumption Spending

Let us now consider how much you need to save if your goal is to spend the same amount on consumption before and after retirement. This implies a constant stream of the same amount in each of the next 45 years, denoted by C. The amount saved each year from age 35 to 65 is \$30,000 minus C. At age 65, the total accumulation will be \$47.58(\$30,000 − C).[1] The amount withdrawn from the retirement account each year after age 65 will be C. Its present value at age 65 is \$11.94C.[2]

To find C we set the two amounts equal to each other.

$$\$47.58(\$30{,}000 - C) = \$11.94C$$
$$C = \$23{,}982$$

So consumption spending is \$23,982 per year. Annual savings during the working years must, therefore, be \$6,018 per year (i.e., \$30,000 – \$23,982). The total accumulation at age 65 will be \$286,298.

Columns 1 through 4 in Table 5.1 and Figure 5.1 show the time profiles of income, consumption, and saving derived in this example. They demonstrate that income is \$30,000 until age 65, and then it drops off to zero. Consumption stays level at \$23,982 per year from age 35 until age 80.

TABLE 5.1 Salary, Consumption, and Saving over the Life Cycle

Age	Salary	Consumption	Saving	Human Capital	Retirement Fund
(1)	(2)	(3)	(4)	(5)	(6)
35	\$30,000	\$23,982	\$6,018	\$588,013	0
45	30,000	23,982	6,018	446,324	\$68,987
55	30,000	23,982	6,018	255,906	161,700
65	30,000	23,982	(23,982)	0	286,298
66	0	23,982	(23,982)	0	270,905
70	0	23,982	(23,982)	0	204,573
75	0	23,982	(23,982)	0	109,832
80	0	23,982	(23,982)	0	0

[1]The computation uses the *Annuity Compound Amount Factor:* $FV_{PMT}(PMT, i, n) = PMT \cdot \frac{(1+i)^n - 1}{i}$ or FV_{PMT}(\$1, 3%, 30) = \$47.58.

[2]The computation is based on the *Annuity Present Value Factor:* $PV_{PMT}(PMT, i, n) = PMT \cdot \frac{1-(1+i)^{-n}}{i}$ or PV_{PMT}(\$1, 3%, 15) = \$11.94.

FIGURE 5.1

Salary, Consumption, and Saving over the Life Cycle

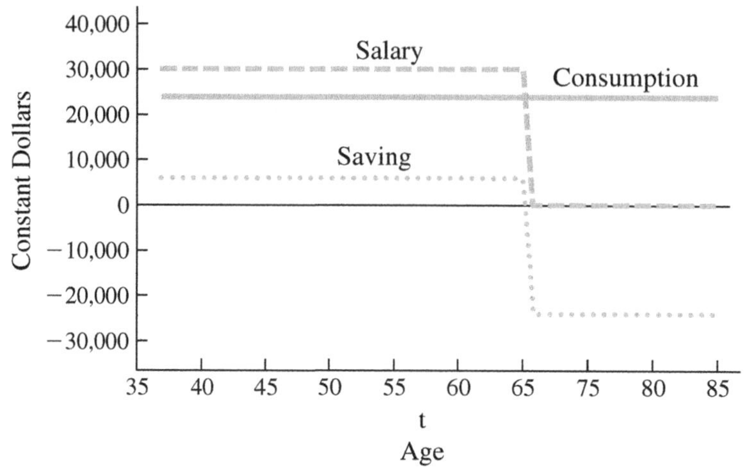

The equation that we have solved in order to find C can be written in a slightly different and more general way:

$$\sum_{t=1}^{45} \frac{C}{(1+i)^t} = \sum_{t=1}^{30} \frac{Y_t}{(1+i)^t} \tag{5.1}$$

where i is the interest rate and Y_t is labor income in year t.

Equation 5.1 says that the present value of consumption spending over the next 45 years equals the present value of labor income over the next 30 years. Economists call the present value of one's future labor income **human capital,** and they call the constant level of consumption spending that has a present value equal to one's human capital **permanent income.** (See Box 5.2 about the economists who were awarded Nobel Prizes for their contributions to the theory of human capital and consumption spending.)

In our example, with labor income of $30,000 per year for 30 years, your human capital is $588,013 at age 35, and your permanent income is $23,982 per year.[3] As you get older, the *PV* of your remaining labor income declines, so your human capital falls steadily until it reaches zero at age 65.

Figure 5.2 and columns 5 and 6 in Table 5.1 show the time profiles of human capital and the accumulated amount in the retirement fund implied by the pattern of income and saving in Figure 5.1 and columns 2 and 4 of Table 5.1. The retirement fund starts out at zero

FIGURE 5.2

Human Capital, Retirement Assets, and Total Wealth over the Life Cycle

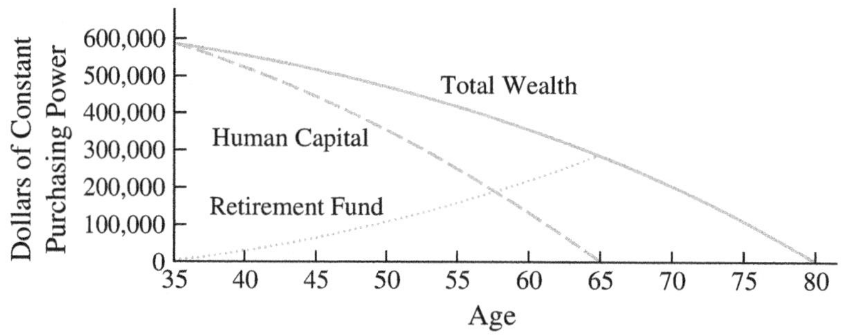

[3]Using the *Annuity Present Value Factor* we solve for the value of human capital at age 35: $PV_{PMT}(PMT, i, n) = PMT \cdot \frac{1-(1+i)^{-n}}{i}$ or PV_{PMT}($30,000, 3%, 30) = $588,013. Then using the *Capital Recovery Factor* we can compute the value of permanent income: $PMT_{PV}(PV, i, n) = PV \cdot \frac{i}{1-(1+i)^{-n}}$ or PMT_{PV}($588,013, 3%, 45) = $23,982.

Box 5.2 Nobel Prizes for the Theory of Permanent Income, Life-Cycle Savings and Human Capital

Milton Friedman was awarded the Nobel Prize in economic science in 1976. A contribution cited by the prize committee as being of primary importance was his theory that permanent income and not year-to-year income is the determining factor when assessing total consumption outlays. Friedman demonstrated that a much greater proportion of the former type of income is saved than the latter. (Adapted from http://nobelprize.org/nobel-prizes/economics/laureates/1976/press.html.)

Franco Modigliani received the Nobel Prize in 1985 in part for the construction and development of the life-cycle hypothesis of household saving. The underlying idea of the life-cycle hypothesis—that people save for their old age—is, of course, not new; nor is it Modigliani's own. His achievement lies primarily in the rationalization of the idea into a formal model, which he developed in different directions and integrated within a well-defined and established economic theory. The life-cycle model is today the basis of most dynamic models used for the study of consumption and saving. (Adapted from http://nobelprize.org/nobel-prizes/economics/laureates/1985/press.html.)

Gary Becker received the Nobel Prize in 1992 for having extended the domain of microeconomic analysis to a wide range of human behavior. His most noteworthy contribution is in the area of human capital. The theory of human capital is considerably older than Becker's work, but his achievement was to have formulated and formalized the microeconomic foundations of the theory. The theory of human capital has created a uniform analytical framework for studying the return on education and on-the-job training. The human capital approach also helps explain trade patterns across countries; in fact, differences in the supply of human capital among countries have been shown to have more explanatory power than differences in the supply of real capital. (Adapted from http://nobelprize.org/nobel-prizes/economics/laureates/1992/press.html.)

at age 35, and it gradually grows to a high of $285,298 at age 65. It then declines to zero at age 80. The individual's total wealth, defined as human capital plus retirement assets, declines continuously between ages 35 and 80.

Quick Check 5-2

Georgette is currently 30 years old, plans to retire at age 65, and expects to live to age 85. Her salary is $25,000 per year, and she intends to maintain a constant level of real consumption spending over the next 55 years. Assume no taxes, no growth in real labor income, and a real interest rate of 3% per year.

A. What is the value of Georgette's human capital?
B. What is her permanent income?

Let us consider what effect a different interest rate would have on both permanent income and human capital. Table 5.2 shows that the higher the interest rate, the lower the value of human capital, but the higher the level of permanent income. Because you save throughout your work years, you are better off with a higher real interest rate, even though the value of your human capital is lower.

Quick Check 5-3

In Table 5.2, what would human capital and permanent income be at a real interest rate of 3.5% per year?

TABLE 5.2 Human Capital and Permanent Income as Functions of the Real Interest Rate (i%)

i =	Human Capital (i) =	Permanent Income (i) =	Saving (i) =
0	900000	20000	10000
1	774231	21450	8550
2	671894	22784	7216
3	588013	23982	6018
4	518761	25037	4963
5	461174	25946	4054
6	412945	26718	3282
7	372271	27362	2638
8	337734	27892	2108
9	308210	28325	1675
10	282807	28674	1326

Assumptions: You are currently 35 years old, expect to retire in 30 years at age 65, and then live for 15 more years until age 80. Your real salary is $30,000 per year, and you have not yet accumulated any assets.

Now suppose that instead of starting out at age 35 with no accumulated assets, you have $10,000 in a savings account. How does that affect the amount you can consume over your lifetime? The answer is that it enables you to increase consumption spending in each of the next 45 years by $407.85, assuming the interest rate is 3% per year.

On the other hand, suppose you wanted to leave a bequest of $10,000 to your children after you die at age 80. With unchanged lifetime income, how does the intended bequest affect your lifetime consumption stream? Answer: It would reduce your consumption by $107.85 in each of the next 45 years.

The general formula that expresses the lifetime consumption possibilities open to you as a function of your income, initial wealth, and bequests is:

$$\sum_{t=1}^{T}\left[\frac{C_t}{(1+i)^t}+\frac{B_t}{(1+i)^t}\right]=W_0+\sum_{t=1}^{R}\frac{Y_t}{(1+i)^t} \tag{5.2}$$

Where:

C_t = consumption spending in year t
Y_t = labor income in year t
i = interest rate
R = number of year until retirement
T = number of year of life
W_0 = value of initial wealth
B_t = bequest made in year t

Equation 5.2 says that the present value of your lifetime consumption spending and bequests equals the present value of your lifetime resources—initial wealth and future labor income. This is the **intertemporal budget constraint** that you face in deciding on a lifetime consumption spending plan.

Quick Check 5-4

What effect would a $1 million inheritance that you expect to receive 30 years from now have on your permanent income?

Note that any lifetime consumption spending plan that satisfies your budget constraint (i.e., equation 5.2) is a **feasible plan.** There are many possible feasible plans. To choose among them you must specify a criterion for quantitatively assessing the welfare or satisfaction (economists use the term *utility*) that you receive from each feasible plan. A quantitative model that enables you to choose the best among all feasible plans is called an **optimization model.** Developing optimization models for lifetime financial planning is beyond the scope of this text.[4]

Now let us consider the effect of changes in real income over the life cycle. For example, Dr. Omar Ben Holim has just graduated from medical school at age 30 and has started training to be a surgeon at Mount Heaven Hospital. Omar's real salary for the next five years will be $25,000 per year. After completing his residency, however, Omar expects to earn $300,000 per year in real terms until he retires at age 65. Given his future expectations, he decides to start enjoying a high standard of living immediately. If he wants to maintain the same level of real consumption spending for the rest of his life and his life expectancy is 85 years, how much should he plan to save now and in the future? Assume that the real interest rate is 3% per year, and that Omar can either borrow or lend at that same rate.

TABLE 5.3 **Omar's Life-Cycle Saving Plan**

Age	Salary	Consumption	Saving	Human Capital	Other Assets or Liabilities
30	0	0	0	5,186,747	0
31	25,000	193,720	(168,720)	5,317,349	(168,720)
32	25,000	193,720	(168,720)	5,451,869	(342,502)
33	25,000	193,720	(168,720)	5,590,425	(521,497)
34	25,000	193,720	(168,720)	5,733,138	(705,862)
35	25,000	193,720	(168,720)	5,880,132	(895,758)
36	300,000	193,720	106,280	5,756,536	(816,351)
37	300,000	193,720	106,280	5,629,232	(734,562)
38	300,000	193,720	106,280	5,498,109	(650,319)
39	300,000	193,720	106,280	5,363,053	(563,549)
40	300,000	193,720	106,280	5,223,944	(474,175)
44	300,000	193,720	106,280	4,624,507	(89,053)
45	300,000	193,720	106,280	4,463,242	14,555
65	300,000	193,720	106,280	0	2,882,067
66	0	193,720	(193,720)	0	2,774,809
84	0	193,720	(193,720)	0	188,078
85	0	193,720	(193,720)	0	0

[4]For a review of life-cycle optimization models see R. C. Merton, *Continuous-Time Finance,* chapters 4–6.

FIGURE 5.3

Omar's Life-Cycle Savings Plan

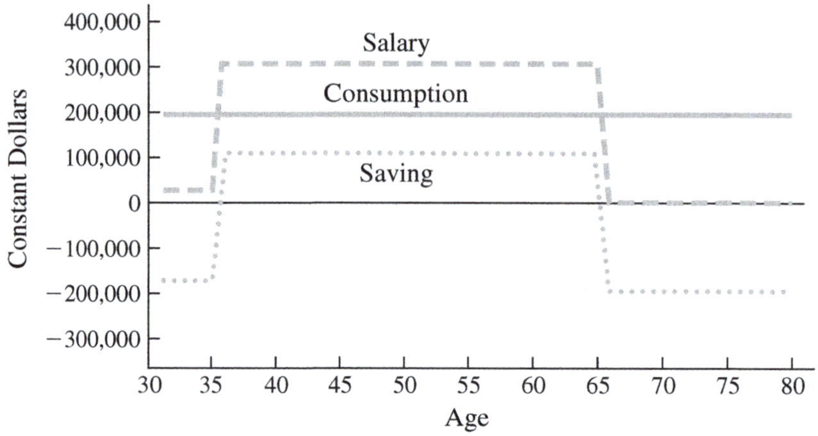

Table 5.3 and Figure 5.3 show Omar's expected pattern of salary and planned consumption spending and saving on the assumption that he wants to have the same real consumption every year. His human capital initially is \$5,186,747, and his permanent income is \$193,720. In order to spend \$193,720 per year during the five years of his residency, he will have to borrow ("dissave") \$168,720 each year to supplement his \$25,000 salary. His total indebtedness will grow to a maximum of \$895,758 at age 35, and then decline thereafter as a result of his saving \$106,280 every year from age 36 until he retires at age 65. Note that he will not have paid off his debt until age 45. One is never too young to start learning finance (see Box 5.3).

Quick Check 5-5

Suppose that Omar is credit constrained and cannot borrow during the next five years. How does that affect his lifetime saving and consumption plan?

Box 5.3 Financial Literacy and Retirement Savings

There is a rising trend in the United States and Europe for people to take on more responsibility for their investments, specifically their retirement funds. However, many people face obstacles in their own lack of financial understanding.

Most of us tend to think that we know more than we actually do about basic financial concepts, such as inflation, risk diversification, and compound interest. The low personal savings rates and frequent bankruptcy in the United States and Great Britain attest to the lack of financial literacy among many citizens. Governments can suffer by taking responsibility for citizens who have not saved enough for their retirement, and therefore many private firms and government agencies have put programs in place to teach younger workers about basic financial concepts—such as saving and keeping track of their investments.

However, it is important to distinguish between financial education and financial advice—which can be offered by firms and fund managers, and can be less objective. Nevertheless, people with a greater understanding of financial concepts have been shown to save more and make higher returns on their long-term investments.

Source: Adapted from "Caveat Investor," *The Economist*, January 12, 2006.

5.2 Taking Account of Social Security

In many countries the government obliges citizens to participate in a mandatory retirement income system called social security.[5] Under such systems, people pay a tax during their working years and in return qualify for a lifetime annuity in their old age. Such a system of mandatory saving should influence the amount of voluntary saving that we do for retirement. Let us use our life-cycle planning model to examine the right way to take account of social security.

To address this question in the context of our life-cycle discounted cash flow planning model, we first recognize that social security alters the profile of our lifetime net cash inflows. We return to our first example in which you are 35 years old, and your salary will be $30,000 per year for the next 30 years. Your human capital is $588,013—the *PV* of labor income at an interest rate of 3% per year. Suppose the optimal level of consumption spending is a constant $23,982 per year (equal to your permanent income). Annual savings in the preretirement years, must, therefore be $6,018 per year. The total accumulation at age 65 will be $286,309, which is enough to support a retirement income of $23,982 per year for 15 years.

Suppose that social security benefits are equal to what you would have if you had saved each year an amount equal to the amount you pay in social security taxes and earned a real interest rate of 3% per year. Thus, if you pay $2,000 per year in social security taxes for 30 years, you will receive in benefits $7,970 per year for 15 years starting at age 66.[6] What impact will social security have on your savings and your welfare under these circumstances?

The answer is that you will simply reduce your personal voluntary savings by the amount of social security taxes. So your savings will fall from $6,018 per year to $4,018. The difference of $2,000 is the amount you will pay in social security taxes. Thus, you reduce your private saving by an amount equal to the "savings" imposed on you by the social security system. Your pool of private savings will suffice to provide a life annuity of $16,012, which when added to your social security benefit of $7,970 will give you a total retirement income of $23,982 per year.

Thus, if social security pays you the same rate of return you could earn on your private saving, your lifetime consumption plan will not be affected by the existence of social security. There will only be a substitution of forced saving for voluntary private saving.

But what happens if social security pays an implied real interest rate that differs from 3%? If it pays a rate higher than 3%, you will be able to afford a higher lifetime consumption stream than $23,982; if it pays less than 3% per year, your consumption stream will be lower.

In many countries, the social security system offers a higher rate of return to people in the lower end of the income distribution than to those in the upper end. But the fact that benefits are paid in the form of a lifetime annuity implies that no matter how rich or poor you are, the longer you live, the higher your actual rate of return. The effective rate of return earned in the social security system is an important issue (see Box 5.4).

Quick Check 5-6

Suppose that social security offers a 3% real rate of return to someone who pays a 10% tax on a salary of $30,000 per year for 40 years. How large must the annual benefit payment be if it is calculated to last for 20 years?

---

[5] In the United States, the social security system is called OASDI, which stands for old age, survivors, and disability insurance. As the name implies, it provides not only old age benefits, but also benefits for dependent family members of workers who die during their working years, and benefits to those who can no longer work due to disability.

[6] Using the *Annuity Compound Amount Factor* we find the retirement fund in 30 years to be: $FV_{PMT}(PMT, i, n) = PMT \cdot \frac{(1+i)^n - 1}{i}$ or $FV_{PMT}(\$2{,}000, 3\%, 30) = \$95{,}151$. Then taking the *Capital Recovery Factor* we can calculate the yearly retirement benefit as: $PMT_{PV}(PV, i, n) = PV \cdot \frac{i}{1-(1+i)^{-n}}$ or $PMT_{PV}(\$95{,}151, 3\%, 15) = \$7{,}970$.

Box 5.4 Financial Innovation to Combat Longevity Risks

As life expectancies around the world continue to rise, insurance companies and corporate pension schemes must find a way to accommodate the consequences of this significant demographic trend. Many annuity providers and pension schemes have few or no risk management tools to deal with increased life expectancy. This can pose a serious problem for organizations that must pay individuals an income from retirement until death.

Several institutions have posed solutions for this dilemma, for instance, the longevity bonds issued by the European Investment Bank. This bond issue is tied to an index of the survivorship of Welsh and English men who were 65 years old at the time of the placement. The bonds are structured so that the payments decline over the bond's life depending on the realization of this longevity index.

Insurance companies in the United Kingdom have expressed interest in buying pension promises from firms that don't want to assume such risks. Hedging these risks would minimize the impact of the rising demographic trend of early retirees living longer and collecting more pension money. Such longevity trading has emerged, and will continue to expand as more people live longer and enjoy lengthier retirements.

Source: Adapted from "When Old Age Becomes a Risk Factor," *Financial Times*, December 12, 2005.

5.3 Deferring Taxes Through Voluntary Retirement Plans

In many countries governments encourage voluntary saving for retirement through provisions of the tax code. In the United States, people are permitted to establish tax-advantaged accounts, known as individual retirement accounts (IRAs), to which contributions are deductible from current income for tax purposes, and interest on these contributions is not taxed until the money is withdrawn. These plans are called *tax deferred* rather than *tax exempt* because any amounts withdrawn from the plan are taxed at the time of withdrawal.

Some people believe that there is an advantage to such tax deferral only if you will be in a lower tax bracket when you withdraw the money. But that is not correct. Tax deferral is quite advantageous even for people who remain in the same tax bracket after retirement.

To see why, consider the following example, summarized in Figure 5.4. Suppose that you face a tax rate of 20% both before and after retirement. The interest rate is 8% per year. You are 30 years before your retirement date and contribute \$1,000 to the plan. Your total before-tax amount accumulated at retirement will be $\$1{,}000 \cdot 1.08^{30} = \$10{,}062.65$. You will have to pay taxes at the rate of 20% on the entire amount, if you choose to withdraw it at that time. Thus, your taxes will be $0.20 \cdot \$10{,}062.65 = \$2{,}012.53$ and you will be left with \$8,050.12 after taxes.

If, instead, you choose not to participate in the retirement plan and invest in an ordinary savings plan, you have to pay 20% of the \$1,000 or \$200 immediately in additional taxes. The remaining \$800 will go into the ordinary savings plan, and interest earnings on the \$800 will be taxed each year. The after-tax interest rate earned is, therefore, $(1 - 0.20) \cdot 8\%$ or 6.4%. The amount accumulated at retirement from this ordinary savings plan is $\$800 \cdot 1.064^{30} = \$5{,}144.45$. Because you have paid the taxes on the original contribution and on the interest along the way, the amount accumulated is not subject to further tax.

Clearly, the tax-deferred savings plan provides a larger after-tax benefit because \$8,050.12 is greater than \$5,144.45. Thus, even though you remain in the same 20% tax bracket both before and after retirement, the amount you have to spend in the future is almost twice as much under the tax-deferred savings plan.

FIGURE 5.4

The Advantage of Tax-Deferred Saving

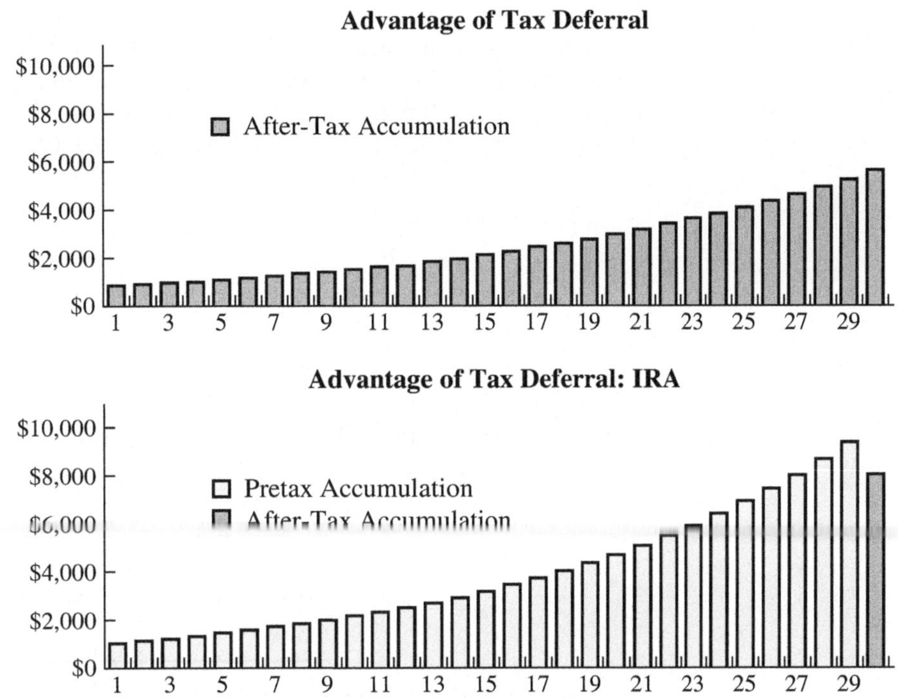

When your tax rate remains unchanged, the benefit of deferral can be summarized in the rule: *Deferral earns you the pretax rate of return after tax.* That is, if you paid the initial tax and invested $800 at the pretax rate of 8%, you would have $\$800 \cdot 1.08^{30} = \$8,050.12$.

Quick Check 5-7

Suppose that the investor's tax rate is 30% instead of 20%. How large would be the advantage of tax deferral compared to our example with a 20% tax rate?

5.4 Should You Invest in a Professional Degree?

Education and training can be viewed as an investment in human capital. Although there may be many reasons for acquiring additional schooling, one purpose is to increase people's earning power, that is, increase their human capital.

Let us consider the costs and benefits of additional education. The economic costs consist of *explicit* costs such as tuition and the *implicit* costs of forgone earnings during the time spent in school. The economic benefits consist of the value of the increased stream of earnings attributable to the additional years of education. Like other investment decisions, the investment is worthwhile if the present value of the expected incremental benefits exceeds the present value of the expected incremental costs.

For example, consider Joe Grad who has just graduated from college and is deciding whether to go on for his master's degree. Joe figures that if he takes a job immediately, he can earn $30,000 per year in real terms for the remainder of his working years. If he goes on for two more years of graduate study, however, he can increase his earnings to $35,000 per year. The cost of tuition is $15,000 per year in real terms. Is this a worthwhile investment if the real interest rate is 3% per year?

Ignoring uncertainty, Joe must give up $45,000 (tuition plus forgone earnings) in each of the next two years in order to increase his earnings by $5,000 per year over his remaining career.

Suppose Joe is now 20 years old and expects to retire at age 65. The relevant cash flows for this investment are incremental outflows of $45,000 in each of the next two years and then incremental inflows of $5,000 in each of the succeeding 43 years. The present value of the outflows is $86,106; the present value of the inflows is $113,026. The net present value of the investment in human capital is, therefore, $26,920, and it is worthwhile.[7]

Quick Check 5-8

Suppose that Joe is 30 years old instead of 20. If all the other assumptions remain the same, does the investment in the graduate degree still have a positive *NPV*?

5.5 Should You Buy or Rent?

You are currently renting a house for $10,000 per year and have an option to buy it for $200,000. Property taxes are deductible for income tax purposes, and your tax rate is 30%. The maintenance and property taxes are estimated to be:

Maintenance	$1,200
Property Taxes	$2,400
Total	$3,600

These costs are currently included in the rent.

Let us assume that your objective is to provide yourself with housing at the lowest present value of cost. Should you buy or continue to rent?

The present value of cost equals the discounted value of the after-tax outflows discounted at the after-tax rate of interest. Because property taxes can be deducted from income for federal income tax purposes, the after-tax outflow for property taxes each year is 0.7 · $2,400, or $1,680. Because no date for eventually selling the house has been specified, we will assume for simplicity an infinite horizon.

If you buy the house, then you will have to pay $200,000 immediately, and the expected after-tax cash outflow will consist of the maintenance expenses and property taxes net of the income tax savings from deductibility of the property taxes:

$$\text{Cash Outflow in Year } t = \$1,200 + \$1,680 = \$2,880$$

Letting *i* be the before-tax discount rate, the present value cost of owning the house is:

$$PV \text{ Cost of Owning} = \$200,000 + \frac{\$2,880}{0.7i}$$

where we have assumed that the properly maintained house continues in perpetuity and have applied the annuity formula. Similarly, the present value cost of renting the house can be written as:

$$PV \text{ Cost of Renting} = \frac{\$10,000}{0.7i}$$

If *PV* Cost of Renting > *PV* Cost of Owning, then it is better to own rather than rent.

---

[7]We first compute the present value of the outflows using the *Annuity Present Value Factor*: $PV_{PMT}(PMT, i, n) = PMT \cdot \frac{1-(1+i)^{-n}}{i}$ or in this case PV_{PMT}($45,000, 3%, 2) = $86,106. Next we compute the present value of the inflow using both the *Annuity Present Value Factor* and the *Present Value Factors:* PV_{PMT}($5,000, 3%, 43) = $119,910 and PV_{FV} ($119,910, 3%, 2) = $113,026.

Because we are assuming that the maintenance costs and property taxes are fixed in *real* terms, i should be a *real* interest rate. Let us assume no inflation so that the real and nominal before-tax discount rate is 3% per year. Then the real after-tax rate is 2.1% per year.[8] Computing the present value costs under each alternative, we find:

$$PV \text{ Cost of Owning} = \$200{,}000 + \frac{\$2{,}880}{0.021} = \$337{,}143$$

and

$$PV \text{ Cost of Renting} = \frac{\$10{,}000}{0.021} = \$476{,}190$$

Therefore, you would be better off buying the house.

The buy-or-rent decision is really an investment decision. In effect you are laying out \$200,000 today in order to receive future cash benefits equal to the after-tax savings in rental costs. In present value terms, you save \$139,047 (i.e., \$476,190 − \$337,143). This is the *NPV* of the investment in the house.

Of course, the relation between *PV* Cost of Renting and *PV* Cost of Owning depends on the rent charged. At what rent would you be indifferent between buying and renting?

This break-even rent (i.e., the annual rental costs at which you would be indifferent between owning or renting) is found by setting *PV* Cost of Owning equal to *PV* Cost of Renting and solving for X:

$$\frac{X}{0.021} = \$200{,}000 + \frac{\$2{,}880}{0.021}$$
$$X = 0.021 \cdot \$200{,}000 + \$2{,}880$$
$$X = \$4{,}200 + \$2{,}880 = \$7{,}080$$

Thus, if the rent is less than \$7,080 per year, you would prefer to keep on renting rather than to buy.

Quick Check 5-9

Suppose that the real interest rate before taxes was 4% instead of 3%. What would be the break-even rent?

Summary

- In making lifetime saving/consumption decisions: (1) Do the analysis in real terms (constant dollars) to simplify the calculations and to avoid having to forecast inflation. (2) Start by computing the present value of your lifetime resources. The present value of your lifetime spending cannot exceed this amount.
- Social security or any other forced saving program will offset voluntary saving. It may have a positive or a negative effect on the present value of your total lifetime resources.
- Tax-deferred retirement accounts are advantageous because they allow you to earn a before-tax rate of return until money is withdrawn from the account. They are advantageous if you are in the same tax bracket before and after you retire, and even more so if your tax bracket is lower after you retire.

[8]With no inflation the real after-tax rate equal (1 − tax rate) times the before-tax rate. In this case: $(1 - 0.3) \cdot 3\% = 0.7 \cdot 3\% = 2.1\%$.

- Getting a professional degree or other training can be evaluated as an investment in human capital. As such, it should be undertaken if the present value of the benefits (such as increase in your earnings) exceeds the present value of the costs (such as tuition and forgone salary.)
- In deciding whether to buy or rent an apartment or a consumer durable, choose the alternative with the lower present value of costs.

Key Terms

- human capital 152
- permanent income 152
- intertemporal budget constraint 154
- feasible plan 155
- optimization model 155

Internet Reference Materials

Insurance and Pensions, Organization for Economic Co-operation and Development (OECD): http://www.oecd.org/about/0,2337.en_2649_37411_1_1_1_1_37411,00.html
Savings Calculator, MSN Money: http://moneycentral.msn.com/Investor/calcs/n_savapp/main.asp

Answers to Quick Check Questions

Quick Check 5-1 Recompute the saving needed in the example if the target replacement rate is 80%. What does the new saving level imply about consumption spending before and after retirement?

Answer: The target level of spending in retirement is 0.8 · \$30,000, or \$24,000 per year. First, we compute the amount that you have to have in your retirement fund at age 65 to be able to withdraw \$24,000 per year for 15 years:

Using the *Annuity Present Value Factor* we have:

n	15
i	3%
PMT	\$24,000.00
PV	\$286,510.44

$$PV_{PMT}(PMT, i, n) = PMT \cdot \frac{1-(1+i)^{-n}}{i} \text{ or}$$

$$PV_{PMT}(\$24{,}000, 3\%, 15) = \$286{,}510.44.$$

Next we compute how much we need to save each year to have \$286,510.44 accumulated 30 years from now using the *Sinking Fund Factor*:

n	30
i	3%
FV	\$286,510.44
PMT	\$6,022.24

$$PMT_{FV}(FV, i, n) = FV \cdot \frac{i}{(1+i)^n - 1} \text{ or}$$

$$PMT_{FV}(\$286{,}510, 3\%, 30) = \$6{,}022.24.$$

Your consumption spending before retirement will be \$23,977.76 per year, which is very close to the level of \$24,000 you will have after retirement. So in this case, aiming for a replacement rate of 80% results in almost the same consumption spending before and after retirement.

Quick Check 5-2 Georgette is currently 30 years old, plans to retire at age 65 and to live to age 85. Her labor income is \$25,000 per year, and she intends to maintain a constant level of real consumption spending over the next 55 years. Assume no taxes, no growth in real salary, and a real interest rate of 3% per year.

- What is the value of Georgette's human capital?
- What is her permanent income?

Answer:

n	35
i	3%
PMT	\$25,000.00
PV	\$537,180.50

Using the *Annuity Present Value Factor* we solve for the current level of human capital as: $PV_{PMT}(\$25{,}000, 3\%, 35) = \$537{,}180.50$.

n	55
i	3%
PV	\$537,180.50
PMT	\$20,063.19

Using the *Capital Recovery Factor* we can calculate permanent income as: $PMT_{PV}(PV, i, n) = PV \cdot \dfrac{i}{1-(1+i)^{-n}}$ or $PMT_{PV}(\$537{,}180.50, 3\%, 55) = \$20{,}063.19$.

Quick Check 5-3 In Table 5.2, what would be human capital and permanent income at a real interest rate of 3.5% per year?

Answer:

n	30
i	3.5%
PMT	\$30,000.00
PV	\$551,761.36

Using the *Annuity Present Value Factor* we solve for the current level of human capital as: $PV_{PMT}(\$30{,}000, 3.5\%, 30) = \$551{,}761.36$.

n	45
i	3.5%
PV	\$551,761.36
PMT	\$24,527.69

Using the *Capital Recovery Factor* we can calculate permanent income as: $PMT_{PV}(\$551{,}761.36, 3.5\%, 45) = \$24{,}527.69$.

Quick Check 5-4 What effect would a \$1 million inheritance that you expect to receive 30 years from now have on your permanent income?

Answer: The present value of your lifetime resources would increase by the *PV* of the expected inheritance and permanent income would increase by the annuitized value of that increase in lifetime resource. Assuming a real interest rate of 3% per year and assuming that the \$1 million inheritance is in constant dollars:

n	30
i	3%
FV	\$1,000,000.00
PV	\$411,986.76

Using the *Present Value Factor* we compute the increase in the present value of your lifetime resources: $PV_{FV}(FV, i, n) = FV \cdot \dfrac{1}{(1+i)^n}$ or $PV_{FV}(\$1{,}000{,}000, 3\%, 30) = \$411{,}986.76$.

n	45
i	3%
PV	\$411,986.76
PMT	\$16,802.95

Then compute the increase in permanent income using the *Capital Recovery Factor:* $PMT_{PV}(\$411{,}986.76, 3\%, 45) = \$16{,}802.95$.

Quick Check 5-5 Suppose that Omar cannot borrow during the next five years. How does that affect his lifetime saving and consumption plan?

Answer: If he cannot borrow, he will only be able to consume what he earns, namely \$25,000 per year for five years. At the end of that time he will increase his consumption to equal his permanent income. Let us figure out what his human capital and permanent income will be in another five years.

n	30
i	3%
PMT	\$300,000.00
PV	\$5,880,132.40

Using the *Annuity Present Value Factor* we can solve for the level of Omar's human capital after five years as: $PV_{PMT}(\$300{,}000, 3\%, 30) = \$5{,}880{,}132.40$.

n	50
i	3%
PV	\$5,880,132.40
PMT	\$228,534.25

Using the *Capital Recovery Factor* we can recalculate permanent income as:

$PMT_{PV}(\$5{,}880{,}132.40, 3\%, 50) = \$228{,}534.25$. So starting at age 35, Omar can consume \$228,534.25 per year for the remainder of his life.

Quick Check 5-6 Suppose that social security offers a 3% real rate of return to someone who pays a 10% tax on a salary of \$30,000 per year for 40 years. How large must the annual benefit payment be if it is calculated to last for 20 years?

Answer: The future value of the taxes paid over 40 years should equal the present value of the benefits received over the following 20 years when both streams are discounted at 3% per year.

n	40
i	3%
PMT	\$3,000.00
FV	\$226,203.78

First calculate the future value of the taxes using the *Annuity Compound Amount Factor:*

$FV_{PMT}(PMT, i, n) = PMT \cdot \frac{(1+i)^n - 1}{i}$ or

$FV_{PMT}(\$3{,}000, 3\%, 20) = \$226{,}203.78$.

n	20
i	3%
PV	\$226,203.78
PMT	\$15,204.45

Then compute the annual retirement benefit using the *Capital Recovery Factor:*
$PMT_{PV}(\$226{,}203.78, 3\%, 20) = \$15{,}204.45$.

So the annual benefit payment should be \$15,204.45 in real terms, which is a replacement rate of preretirement income of about 50%.

Quick Check 5-7 Suppose that the investor's tax rate is 30% instead of 20%. How large would be the advantage of tax deferral compared to our example with a 20% tax rate?

Answer: As in the example in the text, your total before-tax amount accumulated at retirement will still be $\$1{,}000 \cdot 1.08^{30} = \$10{,}062.65$. You will have to pay taxes at the rate of 30% on the entire amount so your taxes will be $0.3 \cdot \$10{,}062.65 = \$3{,}018.80$, and you will be left with $7,043.85 after taxes. If, instead, you choose not to participate in the retirement plan and invest in an ordinary savings plan, you have to pay 30% of the $1,000 or $300 immediately in additional taxes. The remaining $700 will go into the ordinary savings plan, and interest earnings on the $700 will be taxed each year. The after-tax interest rate earned is, therefore, $(1 - 0.3) \cdot 8\%$, or 5.6%. The amount accumulated at retirement from this ordinary savings plan is $\$700 \cdot 1.056^{30} = \$3{,}589.35$.

Quick Check 5-8 Suppose that Joe is 30 years old instead of 20. If all the other assumptions remain the same, does the investment in the graduate degree still have a positive *NPV?*

Answer: As in the example in the text, Joe must give up $45,000 (tuition plus forgone earnings) in each of the next two years in order to increase his earnings by $5,000 per year over his remaining career. Joe is now 30 years old and expects to retire at age 65. The relevant cash flows for this investment are incremental outflows of $45,000 in each of the next two years and then incremental inflows of $5,000 in each of the succeeding 33 years. The present value of the outflows is $86,106; the present value of the inflows is $97,869. The net present value of the investment in human capital is, therefore, $11,763, and it is still worthwhile.

Quick Check 5-9 Suppose that the real interest rate before taxes was 4% instead of 3%. What would be the break-even rent?

Answer: The after-tax real discount rate is now $0.7 \cdot 4\% = 2.8\%$ per year. The annual rental costs at which you would be indifferent between owning or renting, is found by setting *PV* Cost of Owning equal to *PV* Cost of Renting and solving for *X*:

$$\frac{X}{0.028} = \$200{,}000 + \frac{\$2{,}880}{0.028}$$

$$X = 0.028 \cdot \$200{,}000 + \$2{,}880 = \$5{,}600 + \$2{,}880 = \$8{,}480$$

Questions and Problems

1. Fred's company has a defined-benefit pension plan. Suppose the plan pays a benefit equal to 1% of final salary per year of service. Fred is 40 years old and has worked for the company for 15 years. His last year's salary was $50,000 and is expected to remain so in real terms until retirement. The expected rate of inflation is 4%.
   a. If normal retirement age is 65, the interest rate is 8%, and Fred's life expectancy is 80, what is the present value of his accrued pension benefit?
   b. What effect should his pension benefit have on Fred's planned saving, assuming he has a 75% target replacement rate?
2. Analyze the "expert's" responses to the following questions:

   Question: How early do you recommend people begin saving for retirement? Would it be too early for my 14-year-old to start saving?

   Expert: It's never too early.

   Question: For a college student, what would you suggest for a savings plan?

   Expert: I'd suggest deciding on a specific amount to set aside each month, then making sure you do it, no matter the temptations not to.
3. Analyze the following newspaper column:

   Many of us who started families late share a nightmare image: having to pay huge college bills just as we're giving up paychecks and shouldering the steep costs of retirement. In fact, the double whammy might not be so bad, assuming the parents have prepared properly. On the plus side, older parents are likely to have enjoyed their best earnings years before the college costs begin, allowing them to put aside more than younger parents can. They've also had more years for investments to compound. In the ideal situation, older parents can avoid borrowing to meet college costs, taking the preferred route of earning interest on investments rather than paying it on student loans.

(Excerpted from Jeff Brown's Personal Finance column in the *Philadelphia Inquirer*, May 11, 1998.)

4. Assume that you are 40 years old and wish to retire at age 65. You expect to be able to average a 6% annual rate of interest on your savings over your lifetime (both prior to retirement and after retirement). You would like to save enough money to provide $8,000 per year beginning at age 66 in retirement income to supplement other sources (social security, pension plans, etc.). Suppose you decide that the extra income needs to be provided for only 15 years (up to age 80). Assume that your first contribution to the savings plan will take place one year from now.
   a. How much must you save each year between now and retirement to achieve your goal?
   b. If the rate of inflation turns out to be 6% per year between now and retirement, how much will your first $8,000 withdrawal be worth in terms of today's purchasing power?
5. You are saving for retirement and you come across the following table. It shows the percentage of your current salary that you should save for your retirement in order to retire with an annuity equal to 70% of your salary if you have not yet saved anything. It assumes that your annual salary will remain constant in real terms until retirement, and that you will live for 25 years after retiring. For instance, if you have 35 years left before you retire and earn 3.5% per year on your investments, then you should save 17.3% of your current salary.

TABLE A Saving Rate Needed to Achieve 70% Replacement Rate

Real Interest Rate	Years to Retirement		
	15	25	35
3.5% per annum	?	?	17.30%
4.5% per annum	?	?	?

Fill in the missing numbers in Table A.

6. Continuing the previous problem, now fill in Table B. It assumes that instead of targeting a 70% replacement rate of preretirement income, your goal is to maintain the same level of consumption spending both before and after retirement.

TABLE B Saving to Maintain Lifetime Consumption Spending

Real Interest Rate	Years to Retirement		
	15	25	35
3.5% per annum	?	?	19.82%
4.5% per annum	?	?	?

7. Willie is 35 years old, plans to retire at 50, and to live to the ripe old age of 100. His labor income as a plumber is $150,000 per year, and he expects to maintain a constant level of real consumption spending for the remainder of his life. Assuming a steady real salary, the complete absence of taxes, and a real interest rate of 2% per annum:
   a. What is the value of Willie's human capital?
   b. What is the level of his permanent income?
8. You are saving for retirement and you come across the following table. It shows the increase in the annual benefit you can receive in retirement per dollar that you increase your annual retirement saving in the years before retirement. It assumes that you will live for 20 years after retiring. For instance, if you have 30 years left before you retire and earn an interest rate of 3% per year, then you will obtain an increase of $3.20 in your annual retirement benefit for every $1 per year increase in annual saving. Fill in the missing table values.

	Years to Retirement		
Interest Rate	20	25	30
0.0%	$1.00	$1.25	$1.50
0.5%	$1.10	$1.40	$1.70
1.0%	$1.22	$1.57	?
1.5%	$1.35	$1.75	$2.19
2.0%	$1.49	$1.96	$2.48
3.0%	$1.81	?	$3.20
3.5%	?	$2.74	$3.63
4.0%	$2.19	$3.06	$4.13
4.5%	$2.41	$3.43	$4.69
5.0%	$2.65	$3.83	?

9. Analyze the following newspaper column:

   What's the best age for a person to start collecting Social Security benefits? According to conventional wisdom, retirement starts at age 65. It's true that full benefits don't start until age 65, but 62-year-olds can retire and collect 80% of their benefits.

   Take the hypothetical cases of John and Mary, who have the same birthday and who are both slated to start drawing $1,000 a month in Social Security benefits at age 65. On his 62nd birthday, John decides to go ahead and start claiming his benefits of $800 a month (80% of $1,000). Mary decides to wait until she's 65, when she can claim the full $1,000. Three years later, Mary turns 65 and begins receiving $1,000 a month from the Social Security Administration. John continues to receive $800 a month. But he has already been paid $28,800 whereas Mary received nothing.

   Five years go by, with Mary drawing $1,000 a month and John $800 a month. At 70, John has received $76,800, compared to Mary's $60,000. When they reach 77, Mary will pull ahead. So, it seems if a person doesn't live past 76, it would better to start collecting Social Security benefits at 62. For those who reach their upper 70's, it pays to wait until they are 65 to collect Social Security.

   (Adapted from © 1998, *Atlanta Business Chronicle,* Gary Summer, contributing writer, June 29, 1998.)

10. *Challenge Question:* George Thriftless is 45 years old, earns $50,000 per year, and expects that his future earnings will keep pace with inflation, but will not exceed inflation. He has not yet saved anything toward his retirement. His company does not offer any pension plan. George pays Social Security taxes equal to 7.5% of his salary, and he assumes that when he retires at age 65, he will receive $12,000 per year in inflation-adjusted Social Security benefits for the rest of his life. His life expectancy is age 85.

    George buys a book on retirement planning that recommends saving enough so that when private savings and Social Security are combined, he can replace 80% of his preretirement salary. George buys a financial calculator and goes through the following calculations:

    First, he computes the amount he will need to receive in each year of retirement to replace 80% of his salary: 0.8 × $50,000 = $40,000.

    Since he expects to receive $12,000 per year in Social Security benefits, he calculates that he will have to provide the other $28,000 per year from his own retirement fund.

    Using the 8% interest rate on long-term default-free bonds, George computes the amount he will need to have at age 65 as $274,908 (the present value of $28,000 for 20 years at 8% per year). Then he computes the amount he will have to save in each of the next 20 years to reach that future accumulation as $6,007 (the annual payment that will produce a future value of $274,908 at an interest rate of 8% per year). George feels pretty confident that he can save 12% of his salary (i.e., $6,007/$50,000) in order to ensure a comfortable retirement.

    a. If the expected long-term *real* interest rate is 3% per year, approximately what is the long-term expected rate of inflation?

    b. Has George correctly taken account of inflation in his calculations? If not, how would you correct him?

    c. How much should George save in each of the next 20 years (until age 65) if he wants to maintain a constant level of consumption over the remaining 40 years of his life (from age 45 to age 85)? Ignore income taxes.

11. You are 30 years old and are considering full-time study for an MBA degree. Tuition and other direct costs will be $15,000 per year for two years. In addition you will have to give up a job with a salary of $30,000 per year. Assume tuition is paid and salary received at the *end* of the year. By how much does your salary have to increase (in real terms) as a result of getting your MBA degree to justify the investment? Assume a real interest rate of 3% per year and ignore taxes. Also assume that the salary increase is a constant real amount that starts after you complete your degree (at the end of the year following graduation) and lasts until retirement at age 65.

12. Suppose you currently rent an apartment and have an option to buy it for $200,000. Property taxes are $2,000 per year and are deductible for income tax purposes. Annual maintenance costs on the property are $1,500 per year and are *not* tax deductible. You expect property taxes and maintenance costs to increase at the rate of inflation. Your income tax rate is 40%, you can earn an *after-tax* real interest rate of 2% per year, and you plan to keep the apartment forever. What is the "break-even" annual rent such that you would buy it if the rent exceeds this amount?

13. You have decided to acquire a new car that costs $30,000. You are considering whether to lease it for 3 years or to purchase it and finance the purchase with a 3-year installment loan. The lease requires no down payment and lasts for 3 years. Lease payments are $400 monthly starting *immediately,* whereas the installment loan will require monthly payments starting a month from now at an annual percentage rate (*APR*) of 8%.

a. If you expect the resale value of the car to be $20,000 3 years from now, should you buy or lease it?
b. What is the break-even resale price of the car 3 years from now, such that you would be indifferent between buying leasing it?

14. Using the finance concepts presented in this chapter, construct a personal balance sheet showing your assets, liabilities, and net worth.
    a. Did you value your assets at cost or at current market value? Why?
    b. Did you include your human capital as an asset? Why?
    c. Did you include deferred taxes as a liability? Why?
15. *Challenge Question:* Suppose you buy a house for $200,000 when you are 35 years old. You make a 20% down payment and borrow the other 80% from a mortgage lender. The mortgage loan is at a fixed interest rate of 8% per year for 30 years and requires level annual payments. At age 65, you plan to take out a "reverse mortgage" loan that will allow you to borrow a constant annual amount for the rest of your life to be paid off by the sale of your house when you die. Your life expectancy is age 85. The interest rate on both the original mortgage loan and the reverse mortgage will be 8% per year.
    a. Suppose that you expect the inflation rate to be 3% per year and you can rent an equivalent house for $10,000 per year. Is it worth buying the house?
    b. Show how buying the house will affect your assets, liabilities, and cash flow over the next 50 years.
    c. In *Making the Most of Your Money,* J. B. Quinn has written:

    Over the long run, the value of homes should follow the inflation rate. But over the time that you own your particular house, its value might rise or fall or stall. You can't predict. But there are reasons other than profit for owning a house.

    - Mortgage payments force to save, while rental payments don't.
    - You get tax deductions, and can tax-shelter your capital gains.
    - You're landlord free.
    - You know the deep contentment of holding a spot of ground that others can enter by invitation only.
    - You won't lose your lease.
    - You can renovate to suit.
    - A house is collateral for a loan.

    Please comment on Ms. Quinn's analysis.

CHAPTER 6

The Analysis of Investment Projects

OBJECTIVES

- To show how to use discounted cash flow analysis to make investment decisions such as whether to enter a new line of business.
- Analyze how to decide whether to invest in equipment to reduce operating costs.

CONTENTS

In the previous chapter we discussed how to apply discounted cash flow analysis to some of the major financial decisions that people face in their personal lives. In this chapter we apply those same techniques to the analysis of investment decisions by business firms, such as whether to launch a new product or to invest in research laboratories, factories, machinery, warehouses, showrooms, marketing campaigns, and training of employees. The process of analyzing such decisions is called *capital budgeting.*

This chapter discusses how businesses handle the capital budgeting process. Although the details vary from firm to firm, any capital budgeting process consists of three elements:

- coming up with proposals for investment projects
- evaluating them
- deciding which ones to accept and which to reject

What criteria should management use in deciding which investment projects to undertake? In chapter 1 we showed that in order to maximize the welfare of its shareholders, the objective of a firm's management is to only undertake those projects that increase—or at least do not decrease the market value of shareholders' equity. For this, management needs a theory of how the decisions it makes affect the market value of the firm's equity shares. Such a theory was provided in chapter 4: Management should compute the discounted present value of the future expected cash flows from a project and undertake only those projects with positive net present value (*NPV*).

6.1 The Nature of Project Analysis

The basic unit of analysis in the capital budgeting process is the individual investment project. Investment projects start with an idea for increasing shareholder wealth by producing a new product or improving the way an existing product is produced. Investment projects are analyzed as a sequence of decisions and possible events over time starting with the original concept, gathering information relevant to assessing the costs and benefits of implementing it, and devising an optimal strategy for implementing the project over time.

To illustrate the sequence of stages involved in investment project analysis, suppose you are a film industry executive whose job is to come up with proposals for new movies and to analyze their potential value to your company's shareholders. Typically, producing a movie for the mass market involves major outlays of cash over several years before there are any cash inflows from customers who pay to see it. Roughly speaking, the movie will increase shareholder wealth only if the present value of the cash inflows exceeds the present value of the outlays.

Forecasting the likely cash outlays and inflows from the movie is a complicated task. The cash flows will depend on a sequence of decisions and actions that are under your control and on a sequence of events that are not entirely under your control. At each stage in the project's life, from conceiving the idea for the movie's theme to the distribution of the final product to movie theaters and video stores, unpredictable events will occur that affect the stream of cash flows. At each stage you will have to decide whether to continue the project, to discontinue it, to delay it, or to accelerate it. You will also have to decide whether to reduce the level of spending (e.g., by eliminating some costly scenes) or to increase it (e.g., by launching a television advertising campaign).

It is not simply forecasting a project's cash flows that is difficult. Evaluating their likely effect on the market value of shareholders' equity is also complicated. To simplify our exposition of the complicated nature of project analysis in this chapter, we will proceed in stages. In this chapter we will analyze projects as if the future cash flows are known with certainty and use a discounted cash flow valuation procedure similar to the one discussed in chapter 4. Then later in chapter 17 we will consider ways to take account of uncertainty and of the value of managerial options.

6.2 Where Do Investment Ideas Come From?

Most investment projects requiring capital expenditures fall into three categories: new products, cost reduction, and replacement of existing assets. Here are some examples:

- Should the firm start a new-product line that requires investment in plant, equipment, and inventories?
- Should the firm invest in automated equipment that will allow it to reduce its labor costs?
- Should the firm replace an existing plant in order to expand capacity or lower operating costs?

A common source of ideas for investment projects is the firm's existing customers. Surveys of customers, both formal and informal, can suggest new demands that can be met by producing new products and services or by improving existing ones. A firm that manufactures computer equipment, for example, may discover from surveying its customers that providing a repair service for computers might be a profitable new line of business.

Many firms establish a research and development (R&D) department to identify potential new products that are technologically feasible to produce and that seem to satisfy a perceived customer demand. In the pharmaceutical industry, for example, the R&D activity is the source of virtually all new-product ideas.

Another source of project ideas is the competition. For example, if the XYZ software company, which produces a financial planning package for personal computers, knows that a competitor, ABC software company, is working on a new upgrade in its competing product, XYZ may want to consider upgrading its own product. XYZ may want to consider acquiring ABC. Acquisitions of one company by another are capital budgeting projects.

Ideas for capital projects to improve products or reduce costs often come from the production divisions of corporations. For example, engineers, production managers, or other employees who are in close contact with the production process may spot ways to cut costs by reorganizing an assembly line or by replacing labor-intensive operations with automated equipment requiring a capital outlay.

In corporations with incentive systems that encourage managers and other employees to think about opportunities for profitable growth and operating improvements, there is generally a regular flow of proposals for investment projects. The rest of this chapter discusses techniques for evaluating projects and deciding which ones are likely to enhance shareholder value.

Quick Check 6-1

Where do you think new project ideas come from in the movie business?

6.3 The Net Present Value Investment Rule

Chapter 4 developed the investment criterion that is most obviously related to the goal of maximizing shareholder wealth—the *net present value rule.* A project's **net present value** (*NPV*) is the amount by which it is expected to increase the wealth of the firm's current shareholders. Stated as an investment criterion for the firm's managers, the *NPV* rule is: *Invest if the proposed project's NPV is positive.*

FIGURE 6.1

Cash Flow Forecasts for the Protojean Project

Year (t)	Cash Flows (CF_t) (in thousands of dollars)
0	−\$100
1	\$50
2	\$40
3	\$30

Year	0	1	2	3
Net cash flow	−100	50	40	30

To illustrate how to calculate a project's *NPV* we present the following example. Generic Jeans Company, a manufacturer of casual clothing, is considering whether to produce a new line of jeans called Protojeans. It requires an initial outlay of \$100,000 for new specialized equipment, and the firm's marketing department forecasts that given the nature of consumer preferences for jeans the product will have an economic life of three years. The cash flow forecasts for the Protojean project are shown in Figure 6.1.

A negative sign in front of a cash flow forecast for a particular year means a cash outflow. In the case of the Protojean project, there is only one negative cash flow, and that is at the start of the project (time zero). Subsequent cash flows are all positive: \$50,000 at the end of the first year, \$40,000 at the end of year 2, and \$30,000 at the end of year 3.

To calculate the project's *NPV* we need to specify the capitalization rate (k) to use to discount the cash flows. This is called the project's **cost of capital.**

$$NPV(k) = \sum_{t=0}^{n} \frac{CF_t}{(1+k)^t}$$

Table 6.1 shows the calculation of the net present value of the Protojean project. Each year's cash flow is discounted at a rate of 8% per year, and the resulting present value is shown in column 3. Thus, the present value of the \$50,000 to be received at the end of the first year is \$46,296.30, and so on. Column 4 shows the cumulative sum of the present values of all of the cash flows.

The project's *NPV* is the last entry in column 4 of Table 6.1. To the nearest penny it is \$4,404.82. This means that by going forward with the Protojean project, management expects to increase the wealth of the shareholders of the Generic Jeans Company by \$4,404.82.

TABLE 6.1 Calculation of *NPV* of the Protojean Project

Year (1)	Cash Flows (thousands of dollars) (2)	Present Value of Cash Flow at 8% per Year (3)	Cumulative Present Value (4)
0	−100	−100.00000	−100.00000
1	50	46.29630	−53.70370
2	40	34.29355	−19.41015
3	30	23.81497	4.40482

$$NPV(k = 8\%) = \sum_{t=0}^{3} \frac{CF_t}{(1+8\%)^t}$$

Quick Check 6-2

Suppose that the Protojean project is expected to have a third-year cash flow of only $10,000 instead of $30,000. If all other cash flows are the same and the discount rate is still 8% per year, what is its *NPV*?

6.4 Estimating a Project's Cash Flows

Calculating a project's *NPV* once one has the cash flow forecasts is the easy part of capital budgeting. Much more difficult is estimating a project's expected cash flows. Project cash flow forecasts are built up from estimates of the incremental revenues and costs associated with the project. Let us illustrate how cash flow estimates can be derived from estimates of a project's sales volume, selling price, and fixed and variable costs.

Suppose you are a manager in the personal computer division of Compusell Corporation, a large firm that manufactures many different types of computers. You come up with an idea for a new type of personal computer, which you call the PC1000. You may be able to develop a prototype of the PC1000 and even test market it for relatively little money and, therefore, you do not bother doing a full-fledged discounted cash flow analysis in the early phases of the project.

If your project idea gets to the point at which a large sum of cash must be expended, then you must prepare a capital appropriation request that details the amount of capital required and the projected benefits to the corporation from undertaking the project. Table 6.2 shows the estimated annual sales revenue, operating costs, and profit for the PC1000. It also shows the estimated capital outlay required.

Your estimates assume that sales will be 4,000 units per year at a price of $5,000 per unit. A new production facility will be leased for $1.5 million per year and production equipment will have to be purchased at a cost of about $2.8 million. The equipment will be depreciated over seven years using the straight-line method. In addition, you estimate a need for $2.2 million for working capital—primarily to finance inventories—thus bringing the total initial outlay required to $5 million.

Now consider the project's expected cash flows in the future. First, over how long a period will the project generate cash flows? The natural planning horizon to use in the analysis is the seven-year life of the equipment because at that time presumably a new decision would have to be made about whether to renew the investment.

In years 1 through 7 the net cash inflow from operations can be computed in two equivalent ways:

$$\text{(1)}\quad \text{Cash Flow} = \text{Revenue} - \text{Cash Expenses} - \text{Taxes}$$

$$\text{(2)}\quad \text{Cash Flow} = \text{Revenue} - \text{Total Expenses} - \text{Taxes} + \text{Noncash Expenses}$$
$$= \text{Net Income} + \text{Noncash Expenses}$$

The two approaches (if done properly) will always result in precisely the same estimates of net cash flow from operations.

The only noncash operating expense in the case of the PC1000 is depreciation, and the relevant numbers are (in $ millions):

Revenue	Cash Expenses	Depreciation	Total Expenses	Taxes	Net Income	Cash Flow
$20	$18.1	$0.4	$18.5	$0.6	$0.9	$1.3

TABLE 6.2 **Forecasting Cash Flows for the PC1000 Project**

Sales:	
4,000 units at a price of $5,000	$20,000,000 per year
Fixed Costs:	
Lease payments	$1,500,000 per year
Property taxes	200,000
Administration	600,000
Advertising	500,000
Depreciation	400,000
Other	300,000
Total Fixed Costs	$3,500,000 per year
Variable Costs:	
Direct labor	$2,000 per unit
Materials	1,000
Selling expenses	500
Other	250
Variable Cost Per Unit	$3,750 per unit
Total Variable Costs for 4,000 Units	$15,000,000 per year
Total Annual Operating Costs	$18,500,000 per year
Annual Operating Profit	$1,500,000 per year
Corporate Income Taxes at 40%	$600,000 per year
After-Tax Operating Profit	$900,000 per year
Forecast of Initial Capital Outlay for PC1000	
Purchase of Equipment	$2,800,000
Working Capital	$2,200,000
Total Capital Outlay	$5,000,000

Using approach 1, we get:

$$\text{Cash Flow} = \$20 - \$18.1 - \$0.6 = \$1.3 \text{ million} \tag{1}$$

Using approach 2, we get:

$$\text{Cash Flow} = \$0.9 + \$0.4 = \$1.3 \text{ million} \tag{2}$$

To complete the estimation of project cash flows we need to estimate the cash flow in the final year (year 7) of the planning horizon. The natural assumption to make in this case is that the equipment will have no residual value at the end of the seven years, but that the working capital will still be intact and, therefore, be worth $2.2 million. This does not mean that the project will be liquidated at the end of seven years. It only means that were Compusell to liquidate it, it could probably get back the full $2.2 million in working capital it had to invest initially.

To summarize the project's cash flows, there is an initial outlay of $5 million, cash inflows of $1.3 million at the end of years 1 through 7, and an additional $2.2 million cash inflow at the end of the project's life in year 7. The cash flow diagram for the investment, therefore, looks as follows:

Year	0	1	2	3	4	5	6	7
Cash flow	−5	1.3	1.3	1.3	1.3	1.3	1.3	1.3 2.2

Notice that the cash flow pattern from this project looks like a seven-year coupon bond with an annual coupon payment of \$1.3 million, a face value of \$2.2 million, and a price of \$5 million. This similarity makes the calculation of the project's *NPV* and *IRR* very simple using the standard time-value-of-money keys on a financial calculator.

The next step is to figure out what rate (k) to use to discount these cash flows and compute the project's net present value (*NPV*). Suppose that k is 15%. Then using the financial calculator to compute *NPV* we find:

$$\begin{aligned} NPV(k = 15\%) &= \sum_{t=0}^{7} \frac{CF_t}{(1+15\%)^t} \\ &= -\$5 \text{ million} + PV_{PMT}(\$1.3 \text{ million}, 15\%, 7) \\ &\quad + PV_{FV}(\$2.2 \text{ million}, 15\%, 7) \\ &= -\$5 \text{ million} + \$5.409 \text{ million} + \$0.827 \text{ million} \\ &= \$1.236 \text{ million.} \end{aligned}$$

Quick Check 6-3

What would be the *NPV* of the PC1000 project if the variable costs are \$4,000 per unit instead of \$3,750?

6.5 Cost of Capital

Cost of capital is the risk-adjusted discount rate (k) to use in computing a project's net present value. The standard way of dealing with uncertainty about future cash flows is to use a larger discount rate. We develop the ways for determining what risk premium to use in chapter 16. There are, however, three important points to keep in mind when figuring out a project's cost of capital:

- The risk of a particular project may be different from the risk of the firm's existing assets.
- The cost of capital should reflect only the market-related risk of the project (its beta as defined in chapter 13).
- The risk that is relevant in computing a project's cost of capital is the risk of the project's cash flows and not the risk of the financing instruments (stocks, bonds, etc.) the firm issues to finance the project.

Let us explain each of these three points.

The first point to keep in mind is that the discount rate relevant to a particular project may be different from the rate that is relevant to the firm's existing assets. Consider a firm whose *average* cost of capital for its existing assets is 16% per year. In evaluating a project, does this mean that the firm should use a 16% discount rate? If the project happens to be a "mini-replica" of the assets currently held by the firm, then the answer is yes.

However, in general, using the firm's average cost of capital to evaluate specific new projects will not be correct.

To see why, take an extreme example. Assume the project under consideration is nothing more than the purchase of riskless U.S. government securities in which the firm has the opportunity to buy these securities at below-market prices. That is, suppose that 25-year U.S. Treasury bonds paying \$100 per year are selling in the market at \$1,000, but the firm has the opportunity to buy \$1 million worth of these bonds for \$950 each. If these cash flows are discounted at the firm's cost of capital (16% per year), the present value of each bond is \$634 and, hence, the *NPV* of the project appears to be −\$315,830!*

Common sense tells us if the firm can buy for \$950 something that can be immediately sold for \$1,000, then the firm should do so. The problem is not the *NPV* method itself, but its improper use. The risk class of this project is not the same as that of the overall firm. The proper discount rate for this project is 10% not 16%, and when the *NPV* is computed using this proper rate, we find that the *NPV* = \$50,000.

Having made the point in the extreme, consider a more practical example of an all-equity-financed firm with three divisions: (1) an electronics division, which is 30% of the market value of the firm's assets and has a cost of capital of 22%, (2) a chemical division, which is 40% of the market value of the firm with a cost of capital of 17%; and (3) a natural gas transmission division, which is 30% of the firm's value and has a cost of capital of 14%. The cost of capital for the firm is the weighted average of the costs of capital of each of its divisions or $0.3 \times 22\% + 0.4 \times 17\% + 0.3 \times 14\% = 17.6\%$.

If the firm adopts the capital budgeting rule of using 17.6% as the cost of capital for all projects, then it is likely to accept projects in the electronics division that have significantly negative *NPV* and to pass up profitable natural gas transmission projects with positive *NPV*. The fact that 17.6% is close to the correct discount rate for chemical projects is simply lucky. In this case, the firm should adopt a policy of using different costs of capital, at least at the divisional level.

Sometimes it may be necessary to use a cost of capital that is totally unrelated to the cost of capital of the firm's current operations. For example, imagine an all-equity-financed steel company that is considering the acquisition of an integrated oil company that is 60% crude oil reserves and 40% refining. Suppose that the market capitalization rate on crude oil investments is 18.6% and on refining projects is 17.6%. The market capitalization rate on the oil company shares is, therefore, $0.6 \times 18.6\% + 0.4 \times 17.6\% = 18.2\%$.

Suppose further that the market price of the oil company's shares is "fair" in the sense that at the current price of \$100 per share, the expected return on the shares is 18.2%. Suppose that the market capitalization rate for steel projects is 15.3%. An analysis of the expected cash flows of the oil company shows that the present value computed using the *steel company's cost of capital* of 15.3% is \$119.

An investment banker further reports that all the shares could be acquired for a tender offer bid of \$110 per share. It would appear, therefore, that to undertake this acquisition will provide a positive *NPV* of −110 + \$119 = \$9 per share. In fact, the correct *NPV* is −110 + \$100 = −\$10 per share! If undertaken, we would expect to observe the oil company's shares rise and the steel company's shares fall in value to reflect this negative *NPV* decision.

To return to the PC1000 project, it should now be clear that the relevant discount rate to use in calculating the project's *NPV* must reflect the risk of the PC business and not Compusell's existing mix of businesses.

The second point to keep in mind is that *the risk that is relevant in computing a project's cost of capital is the risk of the project's cash flows and not the risk of the financing instruments used to fund the project.*

---

*Per bond $PV = PV_{PMT}(\$100, 16\%, 25) + PV_{FV}(\$1{,}000, 16\%, 25) = \$634.17$
On a per bond basis, the *NPV* is: $NPV = PV - \$950 = -\$315.83$

For example, suppose that Compusell Corporation is planning to finance the $5 million outlay required to undertake the PC1000 project by issuing bonds. Suppose Compusell has a high credit rating because it has almost no debt outstanding and, therefore, can issue $5 million worth of bonds at an interest rate of 6% per year.

It would be a mistake to use 6% per year as the cost of capital in computing the *NPV* of the PC1000 project. As we will see in chapter 16, the way a project is financed can have an effect on its *NPV*, but that effect is not measured correctly by discounting the project's expected future cash flows using the interest rate on the debt that is issued to finance the project.

The third point to make about the project's cost of capital is that it should reflect only the systematic or market-related risk of the project, not the project's unsystematic risk. We will discuss this point at length in chapter 13.

Quick Check 6-4

Suppose that the average cost of capital for Compusell's existing mix of businesses is 12% per year. Why might this not be the right discount rate to use in computing the *NPV* of the PC1000 project?

6.6 Sensitivity Analysis Using Spreadsheets

Sensitivity analysis in capital budgeting consists of testing whether the project will still be worthwhile even if some of the underlying variables turn out to be different from our assumptions. A convenient and ubiquitous tool for doing sensitivity analysis is a computerized spreadsheet program such as Excel, which is illustrated in Table 6.3.

Table 6.3 lays out the estimation of the net cash flows for the PC1000 project in a spreadsheet format similar to the ones explored in chapter 3. Rows 1 through 5 state the input assumptions behind the forecast values in the spreadsheet. The formulas in each of the cells are written in terms of the variables in cells B2 through B5, so that when these inputs are changed, the entire table is recalculated. Thus, the input in cell B3 is unit sales. Initially this is set at 4,000 units.

Rows 8 through 15 are forecasts of the project's income statements over the next seven years. Row 16 contains the forecasts of operating cash flows in each year, calculated by adding together the contents of row 15 (net profit) and row 12 (depreciation). Rows 17 through 20 show the calculation of the investment cash flows—investment in working capital and plant and equipment. Row 17 contains the forecast of the working capital required each year, and row 18 calculates the change in this amount from year to year (i.e., the additional cash invested in working capital during that year). Note that the only nonzero entries in row 18 are a cash inflow of $2,200,000 in cell B18 and a cash outflow of $2,200,000 in year 7. Row 19 contains the forecasts of new investment in plant and equipment in each year. Row 20 is the total investment cash flow in each year, the sum of rows 18 and 19. Finally, row 21 shows the net cash flow in each year, which is the sum of the operating cash flow (row 16) and the investment cash flow (row 20). The *NPV* is computed in cell B22.

Table 6.4 and Figure 6.2 show the sensitivity of the project's *NPV* to this assumed value for unit sales. It was produced by changing the entry in cell B3 of Table 6.3 and tracing the corresponding changes in net cash flow from operations and in *NPV*.

6.6.1 Break-Even Point

A particularly interesting question to ask is at what sales volume the *NPV* of the project would be zero. This is the project's **break-even point,** which means the point of indifference between accepting and rejecting the project.

TABLE 6.3 Spreadsheet Analysis of the PC1000 Project

	A	B	C	D	E	F	G	H	I
1	***Assumptions:***								
2	*Cost of capital*	15%							
3	*Unit sales in year 1*	4,000							
4	*Sales growth rate*	0%							
5	*Price*	$5,000							
6	***Cash Flow Forecasts***				YEAR				
7		0	1	2	3	4	5	6	7
8	Sales revenue		$20,000,000	$20,000,000	$20,000,000	$20,000,000	$20,000,000	$20,000,000	$ 20,000,000
9	Expenses								
10	Cash fixed costs		$3,100,000	$3,100,000	$3,100,000	$3,100,000	$3,100,000	$3,100,000	$3,100,000
11	Variable costs		$15,000,000	$15,000,000	$15,000,000	$15,000,000	$15,000,000	$15,000,000	$15,000,000
12	Depreciation		$400,000	$400,000	$400,000	$400,000	$400,000	$400,000	$400,000
13	Operating profit		$1,500,000	$1,500,000	$1,500,000	$1,500,000	$1,500,000	$1,500,000	$1,500,000
14	Taxes		$600,000	$600,000	$600,000	$600,000	$600,000	$600,000	$600,000
15	Net profit		$900,000	$900,000	$900,000	$900,000	$900,000	$900,000	$900,000
16	**Operating Cash Flow**		$1,300,000	$1,300,000	$1,300,000	$1,300,000	$1,300,000	$1,300,000	$1,300,000
17	Working capital	$2,200,000	$2,200,000	$2,200,000	$2,200,000	$2,200,000	$2,200,000	$2,200,000	–
18	Change in working capital	$2,200,000	–	–	–	–	–	–	$(2,200,000)
19	Investment in plant and equipment	$2,800,000	–	–	–	–	–	–	–
20	**Investment Cash Flows**	$(5,000,000.00)							$2,200,000
21	**Net cash flow**	$(5,000,000.00)	$1,300,000	$1,300,000	$1,300,000	$1,300,000	$1,300,000	$1,300,000	$3,500,000
22	***NPV***	$1,235,607							

TABLE 6.4 **Sensitivity of the PC1000's *NPV* to Sales Volume**

Sales Volume (units per year)	Net Cash Flow from Operations	Net Present Value of Project
2,000	−\$200,000	−\$5,005,022
3,000	\$550,000	−\$1,884,708
3,604*	\$1,003,009	0
4,000	\$1,300,000	\$1,235,607
5,000	\$2,050,000	\$4,355,922
6,000	\$2,800,000	\$7,476,237

* *NPV* break-even point.
Assumptions: The investment in working capital is fixed at \$2,200,000 for all levels of sales and is received back as a cash inflow in year 7.

From Figure 6.2 we can see that the break-even point is approximately 3,600 units per year. A little algebra shows that its exact value is 3,604 units per year. Thus, as long as the sales volume exceeds 3,604 units per year over the seven-year life of the equipment, the project shows a positive *NPV*.

The algebraic solution for the break-even volume is as follows. In order for the *NPV* to be 0, cash flow from operations must be \$1,003,009. To find this break-even value for the cash flow from operations we do the following calculation:

Find the *PMT* that satisfies:

$$PV_{PMT}(PMT,\ 15\%,\ 7) + PV_{FV}(\$2.2\text{ million},\ 15\%,\ 7) - \$5\text{ million} = 0$$

or:

$$PV_{PMT}(PMT,\ 15\%,\ 7) = \$5\text{ million} - PV_{FV}(\$2.2\text{ million},\ 15\%,\ 7) = \$4{,}172{,}939$$
$$PMT_{PV}(\$4{,}172{,}939,\ 15\%,\ 7) = \$1{,}003{,}009$$

Now we must find the number of units per year (Q) that corresponds to an operating cash flow of this amount. A little algebra reveals that the break-even level of Q is 3,604 units per year:

$$\text{Cash Flow} = \text{Net Profit} + \text{Depreciation}$$
$$= 0.6(1{,}250Q - 3{,}500{,}000) + 400{,}000 = 1{,}003{,}009$$
$$Q = \frac{4{,}505{,}015}{1{,}250} = 3{,}604 \text{ units per year}$$

FIGURE 6.2

Sensitivity of the PC1000's *NPV* to Sales Volume

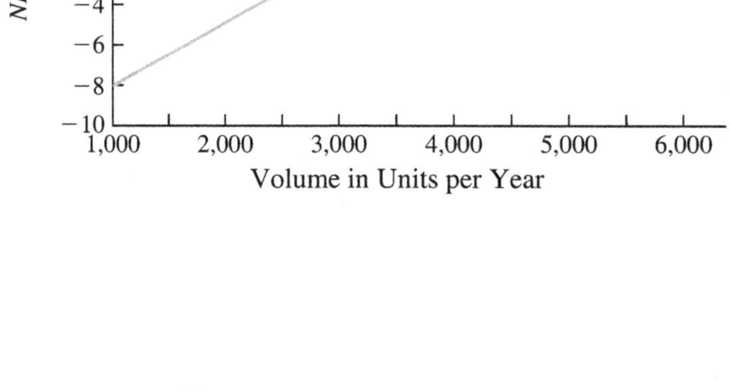

Quick Check 6-5

What would be the break-even volume for the PC1000 project if the cost of capital is 25% per year instead of 15% per year?

6.6.2 Sensitivity of *NPV* to Sales Growth

What happens if we change the assumed sales growth rate from zero to 5% per year? The answer is found in Table 6.5. Operating cash flow (row 16) grows by more than 5% per year because many of the production costs are fixed. Working capital (row 17), which is a fixed proportion of sales, grows at 5% per year. The increase in working capital (row 18) is a cash outflow each year and is recouped as a cash inflow in year 7. The net result is that the *NPV* of the project increases from $1,235,607 to $2,703,489.

6.7 Analyzing Cost-Reducing Projects

Our analysis of the PC1000 project was an example of a decision about whether to launch a new product. Another major category of capital budgeting projects is cost saving.

For example, suppose a firm is considering an investment proposal to automate its production process to save on labor costs. It can invest $2 million now in equipment and thereby save $700,000 per year in pretax labor costs. If the equipment has an expected life of five years and if the firm pays income tax at the rate of $33\frac{1}{3}\%$, is this a worthwhile investment?

To answer this question we must compute the *incremental* cash flows due to the investment. Table 6.6 shows the cash inflows and outflows associated with this project. Column 1 shows the firm's revenues, costs, and cash flow *without* the investment; column 2 shows them *with* the investment. Column 3, the difference between columns 1 and 2, is the increment due to the investment.

There is an initial cash outflow of $2 million to purchase the equipment. In each of the five subsequent years, there is a cash inflow of $600,000, which is the increased net profit of $200,000 plus the $400,000 in annual depreciation charges. The depreciation charges, although an expense for accounting purposes, are not a cash outflow. The cash flow diagram for this project is:

Year	0	1	2	3	4	5
Cash flow (in $ millions)	−2	.6	.6	.6	.6	.6

Now let us consider the impact of the project on the firm's value. How much will the firm be worth if it undertakes the project as compared to not undertaking it?

The firm must give up $2 million now, but in return it will receive an incremental after-tax cash flow of $600,000 at the end of each of the next five years. To compute the *NPV* of the project, we need to know the project's cost of capital, *k*. Let us assume that it is 10% per year.

Discounting the $600,000 per year for five years at 10% per year, we find that the present value of the after-tax cash flows is $2,274,472:

$$NPV = PV_{PMT}(\$0.6\text{million}, 10\%, 5) - \$2 \text{ million} = \$2{,}274{,}472 - \$2{,}000{,}000 = \$274{,}472$$

Thus, the labor cost savings are worth $274,472 more than the $2 million cost of acquiring them by undertaking the project. The wealth of current shareholders of the firm is expected to increase by this amount if the project is undertaken.

TABLE 6.5 **PC1000 Project with 5% Growth**

	A	B	C	D	E	F	G	H	I
1	***Assumptions:***								
2	*Cost of capital*	15%							
3	*Unit sales in year 1*	4,000							
4	*Sales growth rate*	5%							
5	*Price*	$5,000							
6	***Cash Flow Forecasts***					YEAR			
7		0	1	2	3	4	5	6	7
8	Sales		$20,000,000	$21,000,000	$22,050,000	$23,152,500	$24,310,125	$25,525,631	$26,801,913
9	Expenses								
10	Cash fixed costs		$ 3,100,000	$ 3,100,000	$ 3,100,000	$ 3,100,000	$ 3,100,000	$ 3,100,000	$ 3,100,000
11	Variable costs		$15,000,000	$15,750,000	$16,537,500	$17,364,375	$18,232,594	$19,144,223	$20,101,435
12	Depreciation		$ 400,000	$ 400,000	$ 400,000	$ 400,000	$ 400,000	$ 400,000	$ 400,000
13	Operating profit		$ 1,500,000	$ 1,750,000	$ 2,012,500	$ 2,288,125	$ 2,577,531	$ 2,881,408	$ 3,200,478
14	Taxes		$ 600,000	$ 700,000	$ 805,000	$ 915,250	$ 1,031,013	$ 1,152,563	$ 1,280,191
15	Net profit		$ 900,000	$ 1,050,000	$ 1,207,500	$ 1,372,875	$ 1,546,519	$ 1,728,845	$ 1,920,287
16	**Operating Cash Flow**		$ 1,300,000	$ 1,450,000	$ 1,607,500	$ 1,772,875	$ 1,946,519	$ 2,128,845	$ 2,320,287
17	Working capital	$ 2,200,000	$ 2,310,000	$ 2,425,500	$ 2,546,775	$ 2,674,114	$ 2,807,819	$ 2,948,210	$ –
18	Change in working capital	$ 2,200,000	$ 110,000	$ 115,500	$ 121,275	$ 127,339	$ 133,706	$ 140,391	$(2,948,210)
19	Investment in plant and equipment	$ 2,800,000	–	–	–	–	–	–	–
20	**Investment Cash Flow**	$ (5,000,000)	$ (110,000)	$ (115,500)	$ (121,275)	$ (127,339)	$ (133,706)	$ (140,391)	$ 2,948,210
21	**Net Cash Flow**	$ (5,000,000)	$ 1,190,000	$ 1,334,500	$ 1,486,225	$ 1,645,536	$ 1,812,813	$ 1,988,454	$ 5,268,497
22	***NPV***	$ 2,703,489							

TABLE 6.6 **Cash Flows With and Without Investment in Labor Saving Equipment**

	Without Investment (1)	With Investment (2)	Difference Due to Investment (3)
Revenue	\$5,000,000	\$5,000,000	0
Labor costs	1,000,000	300,000	−700,000
Other cash expenses	2,000,000	2,000,000	0
Depreciation	1,000,000	1,400,000	400,000
Pretax profit	1,000,000	1,300,000	300,000
Income taxes (at $33\frac{1}{3}\%$)	333,333	433,333	100,000
After-tax profit	666,667	866,667	200,000
Net cash flow (after-tax profit + depreciation)	1,666,667	2,266,667	600,000

Quick Check 6-6

Suppose that investing in the equipment would reduce labor costs by \$650,000 per year instead of \$700,000. Would the investment still be worthwhile?

6.8 Projects with Different Lives

Suppose in the previous example of labor-saving equipment that there are two different types of equipment with different economic lives. The longer-lived equipment requires twice the initial outlay but lasts twice as long. A difficulty that arises in this situation is how to make the two investments comparable given that they last for different periods of time.

One approach is to assume that the shorter-lived equipment will be replaced at the end of five years with the same type of equipment that will last for another five years. Both alternatives will then have the same expected life of 10 years, and their *NPV*s can be computed and compared.

An easier approach is to employ a concept called **annualized capital cost.** It is defined as the annual cash payment that has a present value equal to the initial outlay. The alternative with the lowest annualized capital cost is the preferred alternative.

In our example, when we convert the \$2 million initial capital outlay into an equivalent five-year annuity at a discount rate of 10% per year, we find that the *PMT* is \$527,595.

Or we solve for the *PMT*

$$PMT_{PV}(\$2 \text{ million}, 10\%, 5) = \$527{,}595$$

The longer-lived machine will last for 10 years but costs \$4 million. What is its annualized capital cost?

We solve for the *PMT* such that

$$PMT_{PV}(\$4 \text{ million}, 10\%, 10) = \$650{,}982$$

So the machine that lasts for only five years and costs \$2 million is the preferred alternative because it has the lower annualized capital cost.

Quick Check 6-7

What would have to be the economic life of the machine that costs \$4 million for it to be preferred over the machine that costs \$2 million?

6.9 Ranking Mutually Exclusive Projects

Sometimes two or more projects are mutually exclusive, meaning that the firm will take at most only one of them. An example is a project that requires exclusive use of the same unique resource such as a particular parcel of land. In all such cases, a firm should choose the project with the highest *NPV*. Some firms, however, rank projects according to their *IRR*, and this ranking system may be inconsistent with the objective of maximizing shareholder value.

For example, suppose that you own a parcel of land and have two alternatives for developing it. You can construct an office building on it, requiring an initial outlay of \$20 million, or you can make a parking lot out of it, requiring an initial outlay of \$10,000. If you build an office building, you estimate that you will be able to sell it in one year for \$24 million and your *IRR* is, therefore, 20% (\$24 million minus \$20 million divided by \$20 million). If you make it into a parking lot, you estimate that you will have a cash inflow of \$10,000 per year forever. Your *IRR* on the parking lot is, therefore, 100% per year. Which project should you choose?

The parking lot has the higher *IRR*, but you would not necessarily want to choose it because at any cost of capital below 20% per year, the *NPV* of the office building is greater. For example, at a cost of capital of 15%, the *NPV* of the office building is \$869,565 whereas the *NPV* of the parking lot is \$56,667. Therefore, at a cost of capital of 15%, the shareholders of the corporation are better off if the office building project is taken.

Figure 6.3 shows the *NPV* profiles of both projects, *NPV* plotted as a function of the cost of capital. The discount rate used to compute the project's *NPV* (the project's cost of capital) is measured along the horizontal axis and the *NPV* is measured along the vertical axis. The figure shows clearly that a discount rate of 20% per year is the critical "switch-over point" for the two mutually exclusive projects. At any discount rate above 20% per year the parking lot has a higher *NPV*, and at rates below 20% the office building has a higher *NPV*.

To understand better why *IRR* is not a good measure for ranking mutually exclusive projects, note that a project's *IRR* is independent of its *scale*. In our example, the parking lot has a very high *IRR*, but its scale is small compared to the office building. If the parking lot were on a larger scale, it might offer a higher *NPV* than the office building.

Thus, suppose that the parking lot project requires an initial outlay of \$200,000 to build a multistory facility and that the annual net cash flow will then be \$200,000 per year forever. The *NPV* of the parking lot project would now be 20 times greater than before.

Quick Check 6-8

At what scale would the *NPV* of the parking lot project be equal to that of the office building project?

6.10 Inflation and Capital Budgeting

Now let us consider how to take account of inflation in evaluating capital projects. Consider an investment that requires an initial outlay of \$2 million. In the absence of inflation it is expected to produce an annual after-tax cash flow of \$600,000 for five years and the cost of capital is 10% per year. Under these assumptions we found that the project has an *NPV* of \$274,472.

FIGURE 6.3

***NPV* as a Function of the Discount Rate**

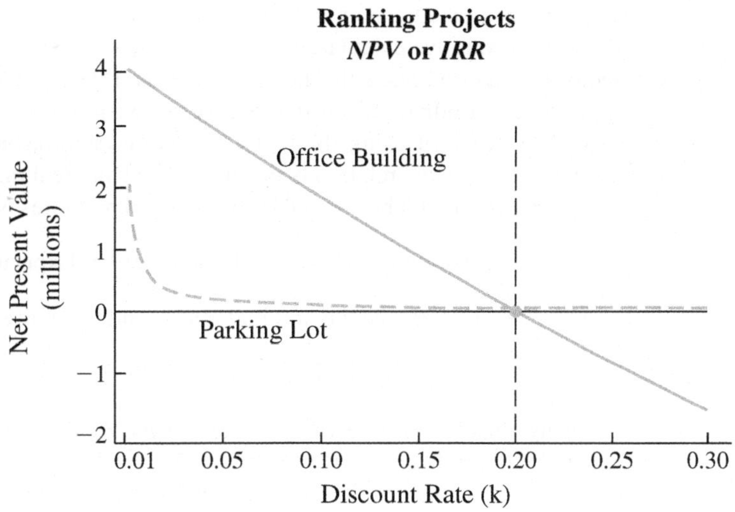

Now let us assume an inflation rate of 6% per year. The expected cash flows are presented in Table 6.7.

The *nominal* cash flow projections are inflated at the rate of 6% per year to reflect our expectations in terms of "then-year dollars." The *real* cash flow projections are in terms of "today's dollars."

Just as we distinguish between real and nominal cash flow projections, so too we distinguish between the real and nominal cost of capital. The real rate is the rate that would prevail in a zero-inflation scenario. The nominal rate is the rate that we actually observe.

Even if a firm does not explicitly set its cost of capital in real terms, setting one in nominal terms implies a certain real rate. For example, if the nominal cost of capital is 14% per year, and the expected rate of inflation is 6% per year, then the implied real cost of capital is approximately 8% per year.

RULE: There are two correct ways of computing *NPV:*
1. Use the nominal cost of capital to discount nominal cash flows.
2. Use the real cost of capital to discount real cash flows.

Let us illustrate the correct way of adjusting for inflation in our numerical example. We have already computed the *NPV* and *IRR* using the second approach that uses real cash flow estimates and a real cost of capital of 10% per year:

$$NPV = \$274,472$$

Because the *NPV* is positive, this project is worthwhile.

TABLE 6.7 **Investment under 6% Inflation**

Year	Real Cash Flow	Nominal Cash Flow (6% inflation)
1	$600,000	$636,000
2	600,000	674,160
3	600,000	714,610
4	600,000	757,486
5	600,000	802,935

Now let us take the nominal approach. Before doing so, we must make a slight modification in the way we calculate the nominal rate. For most purposes it would be perfectly adequate to approximate the nominal rate as 16%—the real rate of 10% plus the 6% expected rate of inflation. But in this case we want to be exact in order to demonstrate the exact equivalence of using the real and nominal approaches to capital budgeting, so we must present the exact relation between nominal and real rates.

The exact relation between the nominal and real rates is:

$$\text{Nominal Rate} = (1 + \text{Real Rate})(1 + \text{Expected Inflation}) - 1$$

Therefore, in our example the nominal rate would be 16.6% rather than 16% per year:

$$\text{Nominal Rate} = 1.1 \times 1.06 - 1 = 0.166 \text{ or } 16.6\%$$

Using this 16.6% rate to compute the *NPV* of the nominal cash flow estimates in Table 6.7 will produce an *NPV* of $274,472, exactly the same result as we obtain using the real approach. This is logical because the increase in the current wealth of shareholders from undertaking the project should not be affected by the unit of account chosen to compute the project's *NPV* (i.e., whether we use inflated dollars or dollars of constant purchasing power).

$$NPV(k = 16.6\%) = \sum_{t=1}^{5} \frac{\$600{,}000(1 + 6\%)^t}{(1 + 16.6\%)^t} - \$2{,}000{,}000 = \$274{,}472$$

Beware: Never compare the *IRR* computed using real cash flow estimates to a nominal cost of capital.

Quick Check 6-9

Analyze the same project assuming an expected rate of inflation of 8% per year instead of 6%.

Summary

- The unit of analysis in capital budgeting is the investment project. From a finance perspective, investment projects are best thought of as consisting of a series of contingent cash flows over time, whose amount and timing are partially under the control of management.
- The objective of capital budgeting procedures is to assure that only projects that increase shareholder value (or at least do not reduce it) are undertaken.
- Most investment projects requiring capital expenditures fall into three categories: new products, cost reduction, and replacement. Ideas for investment projects can come from customers and competitors, or from within the firm's own R&D or production departments.
- Projects are often evaluated using a discounted cash flow procedure wherein the incremental cash flows associated with the project are estimated and their *NPV* is calculated using a risk-adjusted discount rate, which should reflect the risk of the project.
- If the project happens to be a "mini-replica" of the assets currently held by the firm, then management should use the firm's cost of capital in computing the project's net

present value. However, sometimes it may be necessary to use a discount rate that is totally unrelated to the cost of capital of the firm's current operations. The correct cost of capital is the one applicable to firms in the same industry as the new project.

- It is always important to check whether cash flow forecasts have been properly adjusted to take account of inflation over a project's life. There are two correct ways to make the adjustment: (1) Use the nominal cost of capital to discount nominal cash flows, and (2) use the real cost of capital to discount real cash flows.

Key Terms

- net present value 172
- cost of capital 173
- sensitivity analysis 178
- break-even point 178
- annualized capital cost 183

Answers to Quick Check Questions

Quick Check 6-1 Where do you think new project ideas come from in the movie business?

Answer: Sources of new project ideas in the movie business are:

- sequels to successful movies (e.g., *The Godfather II, III, IV,* etc.).
- best-selling novels.

Quick Check 6-2 Suppose that the Protojean project is expected to have a third-year cash flow of only $10,000 instead of $30,000. If all other cash flows are the same and the discount rate is still 8% per year, what is its *NPV*?

Answer: The new cash flow diagram for the Protojean project is:

Year	0	1	2	3
Net cash flow	−100	50	40	10

$$NPV@8\% \text{ per year} = -\$11{,}471.83$$

Quick Check 6-3 What would be the *NPV* of the PC1000 project if the variable costs are $4,000 per unit instead of $3,750?

Answer: If the variable costs for the PC1000 were $4,000 per unit instead of $3,750 we would have the following profit and cash flow projections:

Sales Revenue (4,000 units at a price of $5,000)	$20,000,000 per year
Total Fixed Costs	$3,500,000 per year
Total Variable Costs (4,000 units at $4,000 per unit)	$16,000,000 per year
Total Annual Operating Costs	$19,500,000 per year
Annual Operating Profit	$500,000 per year
Corporate Income Taxes at 40%	$200,000 per year
After-Tax Operating Profit	$300,000 per year
Net Cash Flow from Operations	$700,000 per year

In other words, the net cash flow from operations in years 1 through 7 would fall by \$600,000. This is because before-tax costs are higher by \$1 million per year (4,000 units × \$250 per unit). Because the tax rate is 0.4, after-tax profits and cash flow are lower by 0.6 × \$1 million or \$600,000.

Using a financial calculator to find the new *NPV*, we find:

$$PV_{PMT}(\$0.7 \text{ million}, 15\%, 7) + PV_{FV}(\$2.2 \text{ million}, 15\%, 7) - \$5 \text{ million}$$
$$= \$2,912,294 + \$827,061 - \$5,000,000 = -\$1,260,645$$

So the project would not be worthwhile if the variable costs were \$4,000 per unit.

Quick Check 6-4 Suppose that the average cost of capital for Compusell's existing mix of businesses is 12% per year. Why might this not be the right discount rate to use in computing the *NPV* of the PC1000 project?

Answer: Compusell's existing lines of business may have a different risk than the risk of the PC business.

Quick Check 6-5 What would be the break-even volume for the PC1000 project if the cost of capital is 25% per year instead of 15% per year?

Answer: In order for the *NPV* to be 0 when the cost of capital is 25% per year, cash flow from operations must be \$1,435,757. To find this break-even value for the cash flow from operations we do the following calculation: Solve for *PMT* that makes $NPV = 0$

$PV_{PMT}(PMT, 25\%, 7) + PV_{FV}(\$2.2 \text{ million}, 25\%, 7) - \$5 \text{ million} = 0$ or $PV_{PMT}(PMT, 25\%, 7) = \$4,538,627$. Solving for the payment:

$$PMT_{PV}(\$4,538,627, 25\%, 7) = \$1,435,757$$

Now we must find the number of units per year (Q) that corresponds to an operating cash flow of this amount. A little algebra reveals that the break-even level of Q is 4,181 units per year:

$$\text{Cash Flow} = \text{Net Profit} + \text{Depreciation}$$
$$= 0.6(1,250Q - 3,500,000) + 400,000 = 1,435,757$$
$$Q = \frac{5,226,262}{1,250} = 4,181 \text{ units per year}$$

Quick Check 6-6 Suppose that investing in the equipment would reduce labor costs by \$650,000 per year instead of \$700,000. Would the investment still be worthwhile?

Answer: Let us first show what the incremental after-tax cash flow is:

	Without Investment	With Investment	Difference Due to Investment
Revenue	\$5,000,000	\$5,000,000	0
Labor costs	1,000,000	350,000	−650,000
Other cash expenses	2,000,000	2,000,000	0
Depreciation	1,000,000	1,400,000	400,000
Pretax profit	1,000,000	1,250,000	250,000
Income taxes (at $33\frac{1}{3}\%$)	333,333	416,667	83,334
After-tax profit	666,667	833,333	166,666
Net cash flow (after-tax profit + depreciation)	1,666,667	2,233,333	566,666

Thus, if the labor cost saving is only \$650,000 per year, the incremental net cash flow in years 1–5 is only \$566,666 instead of \$600,000. In other words, the incremental net cash flow falls by \$33,333, which is (1 − tax rate) × the change in before-tax labor cost savings. The project's *NPV* falls but still remains positive.

$$PV_{PMT}(\$566{,}666,\ 10\%,\ 5) = \$2{,}148{,}110$$

$$NPV = \$2{,}148{,}110 - \$2{,}000{,}000 = \$148{,}110$$

Quick Check 6-7 What would have to be the economic life of the machine that costs \$4 million for it to be preferred over the machine that costs \$2 million?

Answer: To match the annualized capital cost of \$527,595 per year for the first machine, the second machine would have to last 14.89 years. We find this number using a financial calculator as follows:

n	*i*	*PV*	*FV*	*PMT*	Result
?	10	−4,000,000	0	527,595	$n = 14.89$ years

Or *n* which solves

$$PV_{PMT}(\$527{,}595,\ 10\%,\ n) = \$4{,}000{,}000$$

Therefore, to be preferred to the first machine, the second machine would have to have an economic life longer than 14.89 years. Rounding to the nearest year, we get 15 years.

Quick Check 6-8 At what scale would the *NPV* of the parking lot project be equal to that of the office building project?

Answer: The parking facility project has an *NPV* of \$56,667 for an investment of \$10,000, and the office building project has an *NPV* of \$869,565. To find the scale at which the parking facility has an *NPV* of \$869,565 we solve:

$$\text{Scale} = \$869{,}565/\$56{,}667 = 15.345$$

Thus, at a cost of capital of 15% per year, the scale of the parking facility project has to increase by a factor exceeding 15 to make its *NPV* greater than that of the office building project.

Quick Check 6-9 Analyze the same project assuming an expected rate of inflation of 8% per year instead of 6%.

Answer:

Year	Real Cash Flow	Nominal Cash Flow (8% inflation)
1	\$600,000	\$648,000
2	600,000	699,840
3	600,000	755,827
4	600,000	816,293
5	600,000	881,597

$$NPV(k = 18.8\%) = \sum_{t=1}^{5} \frac{\$600{,}000(1.08)^t}{(1.188)^t} - \$2{,}000{,}000 = \$274{,}472$$

$$\text{Nominal cost of capital} = 1.1 \times 1.08 - 1 = 0.188 \text{ or } 18.8\%$$

Questions and Problems

The Net Present Value Investment Rule

1. Your firm is considering two investment projects with the following patterns of expected future net after-tax cash flows:

Year	Project A	Project B
1	\$1 million	\$5 million
2	2 million	4 million
3	3 million	3 million
4	4 million	2 million
5	5 million	1 million

   The appropriate cost of capital for both projects is 10%.
   If both projects require an initial outlay of \$10 million, which is the better project?
2. Consider the previous problem. Given the patterns of the two cash flow series is the ranking of the projects dependent on the cost of capital? Explain.
3. You have taken a product management position within a major consumer goods firm after graduation. The contract is for four years and your compensation package is as follows:
   - \$5,000 relocation expense
   - \$55,000 annual salary
   - \$10,000 bonus if annual goals are met
   - \$15,000 additional bonus at the end of four years if your team achieves a given market share

   You are confident in your abilities and assume there is a 65% chance in receiving each annual bonus and a 75% chance in receiving the fourth year additional bonus. The effective annual interest rate is 8.5%. What is the net present value of your compensation package?
4. A. Fung Fashion, Inc. anticipates real net cash flows to be \$100,000 this year. The real discount rate is 15% per year.
   a. What is the present value of these cash flows if they are expected to continue forever?
   b. What is the present value of these cash flows if the real net cash flows are expected to grow at 5% per year forever?
   c. What is the present value of these cash flows if the expected growth rate is −5% per year?

Estimating a Project's Cash Flows

5. A firm is considering investing \$10 million in equipment which is expected to have a useful life of four years and is expected to reduce the firm's labor costs by \$4 million per year. Assume the firm pays a 40% tax rate on accounting profits and uses the straight-line depreciation method. What is the after-tax cash flow from the investment in years 1 through 4? If the firm's discount rate for this investment is 15% per year, is it worthwhile? What are the investment's *IRR* and *NPV*?
6. Hu's Software Design, Inc. is considering the purchase of a computer that has an economic life of 4 years and it is expected to have no salvage value. It will cost \$80,000 and it will be depreciated using the straight-line depreciation method. It will save the company \$35,000 the first year and it is assumed that the savings after that

will have a growth rate of −5%. It will also reduce net working capital requirements by $7,000. The corporate tax rate is 35% and the appropriate discount rate is 14%. What is the value that the purchase will add to the firm?

7. Leather Goods Inc. wants to expand its product line into wallets. It is considering producing 50,000 units per year. The price will be $15 per wallet the first year and the price will increase 3% per year. The variable cost is expected to be $10 per wallet and will increase by 5% per year. The machine will cost $400,000, and will have an economic life of 5 years. It will be fully depreciated using the straight line method. The discount rate is 15% and the corporate tax is 34%. What is the *NPV* of the investment?
8. Steiness Danish Ham, Inc. is contemplating buying a new machine that has an economic life of 5 years. The cost of the machine is 1,242,000 krone and will be fully depreciated using the straight-line depreciation method over the 5 years. At the end of 5 years, it will have a market value of 138,000 krone. It is estimated that the new machine will save the company 345,000 krone per year due to reduced labor costs. Moreover, it will lead to a reduction in net working capital of 172,500 krone because of the higher yield from raw materials inventory. The net working capital will be recovered by the end of the 5 years. If the corporate tax rate is 34% and the discount rate is 12% what is the *NPV* of the project?

Cost of Capital

9. Capital budgeting is the formalized analytical approach to deciding what new investment projects a firm should be engaged in undertaking. As such the appropriate cost of capital must consider:

   . . . the risk of the project's cash flows and not the risk of the financing instruments, e.g., stocks, bonds, etc., the firm issues to finance the project.

   Discuss this statement in terms of the firm's balance sheet.

Sensitivity Analysis

10. Tax-Less Software Corporation is considering an investment of $400,000 in equipment for producing a new tax preparation software package. The equipment has an expected life of 4 years. Sales are expected to be 60,000 units per year at a price of $20 per unit. Fixed costs excluding depreciation of the equipment are $200,000 per year, and variable costs are $12 per unit. The equipment will be depreciated over 4 years using the straight-line method with a zero salvage value. Working capital requirements are assumed to be 1/12 of annual sales. The market capitalization rate for the project is 15% per year, and the corporation pays income tax at the rate of 34%. What is the project's *NPV*? What is the break-even volume?
11. Pepe's Ski Shop is contemplating replacing its ski boot foam injection equipment with a new machine. The old machine has been completely depreciated but has a current market value of $2,000. The new machine will cost $25,000 and have a life of ten years and have no value after this time. The new machine will be depreciated on a straight-line basis assuming no salvage value. The new machine will increase annual revenues by $10,000 and increase annual nondepreciation expenses by $3,000.
    - **a.** What is the additional after-tax net cash flow realized by replacing the old machine with the new machine? (Assume a 50% tax rate for all income, i.e., the capital gains tax rate on the sale of the old machine is also 50%. Draw a time line.)
    - **b.** What is the *IRR* of this project?
    - **c.** At a cost of capital of 12%, what is the net present value of this cash flow stream?
    - **d.** At a cost of capital of 12%, is this project worthwhile?

12. Saunders' Sportswear, Inc. is planning on expanding its line of sweatshirts. This will require an initial investment of $8 million. This investment will be depreciated on a straight-line method over 4 years and will have no salvage value. The firm is in the 35% tax bracket. The price of the sweatshirts will be $30 the first year and will increase in price by 4% per year in nominal terms thereafter. The unit cost of production will be $5 the first year and will increase by 3% per year in nominal terms thereafter. Labor costs will be $10 per hour the first year and will increase by 3.5% in nominal terms each subsequent year. Revenues and costs are paid at year-end. The nominal discount rate is 12%. Calculate the *NPV* of the project using the following additional data.

	Year 1	Year 2	Year 3	Year 4
Unit sales	50,000	100,000	125,000	100,000
Labor hours	20,800	20,800	20,800	20,800

13. PCs Forever is a company that produces personal computers. It has been in operation for two years and is at capacity. It is considering an investment project to expand its production capacity. The project requires an initial outlay of $1,000,000: $800,000 for new equipment with an expected life of four years and $200,000 for additional working capital. The selling price of its PCs is $1,800 per unit, and annual sales are expected to increase by 1,000 units as a result of the proposed expansion. Annual fixed costs (excluding depreciation of the new equipment) will increase by $100,000, and variable costs are $1,400 per unit. The new equipment will be depreciated over four years using the straight-line method with a zero salvage value. The hurdle rate for the project is 12% per year, and the company pays income tax at the rate of 40%.
   a. What is the accounting break-even point for this project?
   b. What is the project's *NPV*?
   c. At what volume of sales would the *NPV* be zero?
14. Healthy Hopes Hospital Supply Corporation is considering an investment of $500,000 in a new plant for producing disposable diapers. The plant has an expected life of 4 years. Sales are expected to be 600,000 units per year at a price of $2 per unit. Fixed costs excluding depreciation of the plant are $200,000 per year, and variable costs are $1.20 per unit. The plant will be depreciated over 4 years using the straight-line method with a zero salvage value. The discount rate for the project is 15% per year, and the corporation pays income tax at the rate of 34%.
   Find:
   a. The level of sales that would give a zero accounting profit.
   b. The level of sales that would give a 15% after-tax accounting rate of return on the $500,000 investment.
   c. The *IRR*, *NPV*, and payback period (both conventional and discounted) if expected sales are 600,000 units per year.
   d. The level of sales that would give an *NPV* of zero.

Analyzing Cost-Reducing Projects

15. Determine which of the following cash flows are incremental cash flows that should be incorporated into a *NPV* calculation.
   a. The sale of an old machine, when a company is replacing property, plant, and equipment for a new product launch.
   b. The cost of research and development for a new product concept that was conducted over the past year that is now being put into production.

c. A dividend payment partially funded by a given project's contribution to the net income for that year.
d. New equipment purchased for a project.
e. The annual depreciation expense on new equipment purchased for a project.
f. Net working capital expenditures of $10 million in year 0, $12 million in year 1, and $5 million in year 2.
g. Potential rental income that was forgone from a previously unused warehouse owned by the company, which is now being used as part of a new product launch.

16. Real Estate, Inc. has purchased a building for $1 million dollars. The economic life of the building is thirty years and it will be fully depreciated over the thirty years using the straight-line depreciation method. The discount rate is 14% and the corporate tax rate is 35%. Assume there is no inflation. What is the minimum lease payment the company should ask for? Assume that the lease payment is due immediately.
17. You are in the finance department of a firm and you are evaluating a project proposal. You have developed the following financial projections and you are calculating:
   a. The incremental cash flows of the project.
   b. The net present value of the project given a discount rate of 13%.

The corporate tax rate is 34% and the financial projections are in thousands.

	Year 0	Year 1	Year 2	Year 3	Year 4	Year 5
Sales revenue		10,000	10,000	10,000	10,000	10,000
Operating costs		3,000	3,000	3,000	3,000	3,000
Investment	17,500					
Depreciation		3,500	3,500	3,500	3,500	3,500
Net working capital	300	350	400	300	200	0

Projects with Different Lives

18. Suppose you are considering replacing the pin setters in your bowling alley. The manufacturer offers you the regular model costing $12,000 or the heavy-duty model costing $15,000. The regular model has an economic life of 10 years. Assuming the models have identical operating characteristics and maintenance costs what does the economic life of the deluxe model have to be for it to be preferred? Assume a 10% cost of capital.
19. Suppose Hu's Software Design, Inc. from problem 6 has a choice between two computer systems. The first one will cost $80,000 and will have an economic life of 4 years. Annual maintenance costs would be $10,000. The other alternative would cost $135,000 and would have an economic life of 6 years. The annual maintenance would cost $13,000. Both alternatives would be fully depreciated using the straight-line method. Neither computer system will have a salvage value. The cost savings generated on an annual basis are assumed to be the same and the company expects to generate sufficient profits to realize the depreciation tax shield. The discount rate is 11% and the corporate tax rate is 35%. Which computer should be chosen?
20. Electricity, Inc. is choosing between two pieces of equipment. The first choice costs $500,000 and will last five years. It will be depreciated using the straight-line depreciation method and will have no salvage value. It will have an annual maintenance cost of $50,000. The second choice will cost $600,000 and will last eight years. It will also be depreciated using the straight-line depreciation method and will have no salvage value. It will have an annual maintenance cost of $55,000. The discount

rate is 11% and the tax rate is 35%. Which machine should be chosen and what assumptions underlie that choice?

21. Refer to the previous problem. Electricity, Inc. is faced with the same choices; however, it now expects that a new technology will be introduced into the industry in year nine. This will force the company to replace the choice made today at the end of year nine, because the new technology will be so cost effective. All the other necessary information is the same as explained in problem 20. Which choice should be made?
22. Kitchen Supplies, Inc. must replace a machine in its manufacturing plant that will have no salvage value. It has a choice between two models. The first machine will last 5 years and will cost $300,000. It will generate an annual cost savings of $50,000. Annual maintenance costs will be $20,000. The machine will be fully depreciated using the straight-line depreciation method and will have no salvage value. The second machine will last 7 years and will cost $600,000. It will generate an annual cost savings of $70,000. This machine will also be fully depreciated using the straight-line depreciation method, but is expected to have a salvage value of $60,000 at the end of the seventh year. The annual maintenance cost is $15,000. Revenues in each case are expected to be the same. The annual tax rate is 35% and the cost of capital is 10%. Which machine should the company purchase?

Ranking Mutually Exclusive Projects

23. Assume the following three mutually exclusive projects, each requiring an initial outlay of $10,000, have the following after-tax cash flow streams:

Year	Project 1	Project 2	Project 3
1	$0	$2,000	$4,000
2	$2,500	$2,000	$4,000
3	$10,000	$8,000	$4,000

Which project should be undertaken if the cost of capital is 8%? What if the cost of capital is 10%?

24. *Challenge Question:* Your firm is considering two investment projects with the following patterns of expected future net after-tax cash flows:

Year	Project A	Project B
1	$0	$2,000
2	$2,500	$200

Suppose both projects require an initial outlay of $2,000 and have identical costs of capital. Determine a complete decision rule conditional on the cost of capital for undertaking the projects if they are independent projects. Repeat the decision rule if they are mutually exclusive. Hint: Calculate the project *IRR*s and *NPV*s of the two projects at alternative costs of capital equal to 0%, 5%, 10%, and 15%.

Inflation and Capital Budgeting

25. Finnerty's Brew Pub is considering buying more machinery that will allow the pub to increase its portfolio of beers on tap. The new machinery will cost $65,000 and will be

depreciated on a 10-year basis. It is expected to have no value after 10 years. The improved selection is anticipated to increase sales by $30,000 for the first year and increase at the rate of inflation of 3% for each year after that. Production costs are expected to be $15,000 for the first year and are also expected to increase at the rate of inflation. The real discount rate is 12% and the nominal risk-free interest rate is 6%. The corporate tax rate is 34%. Should Mr. Finnerty buy the machinery?

26. You are a financial analyst at Wigit, Inc. and you are considering two mutually exclusive projects. Unfortunately, the figures for project 1 are in nominal terms and the figures for project 2 are in real terms. The nominal discount rate for both projects is 17%, and inflation is projected to be 3%.

a. Determine which project to choose.

b. You are troubled about the cash flows in real terms. You are concerned that there may be a problem in determining the total cash flow in real terms and the depreciation tax shield. What is it that has you concerned?

	Project 1	Project 2
0	−$100,000	−$90,000
1	30,000	25,000
2	60,000	55,000
3	75,000	80,000

27. *Challenge Problem:* Your next assignment at Wigit, Inc. also entails determining the *NPV* of a project that is expected to last four years. There is an initial investment of $400,000, which will be depreciated at the straight-line method over four years. At the end of four years, it is assumed that you will be able to sell some of the equipment that is part of the initial investment for $35,000 (a nominal figure). Revenues for the first year are expected to be $225,000 in real terms. The costs involved in the project for the first year are as follows: (1) parts will be $25,000 in real terms the first year; (2) labor will be $60,000 in real terms for the first year and (3) other costs will be $30,000 in real terms for the first year. The growth rates of revenues and costs are as follows: (1) revenue will have a real growth rate of 5%; (2) the cost of parts will have a 0% real growth rate; (3) cost of labor will have a 2% real growth rate; and (4) other costs will have a 1% real growth rate from year 2 to year 3 and a −1% growth rate the last two years. The real changes in net working capital for the year 0 to year 4 are as follows: (1) −$20,000; (2) −$30,000; (3) −$10,000; (4) $20,000; (5) $40,000. The real discount rate is 9.5% and the inflation rate is 3%. The tax rate is 35%.

28. Patriots Foundry (PF) is considering getting into a new line of business: producing souvenir statues of Paul Revere. This will require purchasing a machine for $40,000. The new machine will have a life of two years (both actual and for tax purposes) and will have no value after two years. PF will depreciate the machine on a straight-line basis. The firm thinks it will sell 3,000 statues per year at a price of $10 each, variable costs will be $1 per statue and fixed expenses (not including depreciation) will be $2,000 per year. PF's cost of capital is 10%. All of the foregoing figures assume that there will be no inflation. The tax rate is 40%.

a. What is the series of expected future cash flows?

b. What is the expected net present value of this project? Is the project worth undertaking?

c. What is the *NPV* break-even quantity?

Now assume instead that there will be inflation of 6% per year during each of the next two years and that both revenues and nondepreciation expenses increase at that rate. Assume that the real cost of capital remains at 10%.

d. What is the series of expected nominal cash flows?

e. What is the net present value of this project, and is this project worth undertaking now?

f. Why does the *NPV* of the investment project go down when the inflation rate goes up?

29. Mr. Salles is considering a business venture that would offer guided tours of the romantic Greek isles and the Italian countryside. After four years, Mr. Salles intends to retire. The initial investment would be $50,000 in a computer and phone system. This investment would be depreciated on the straight-line method, and is expected to have no salvage value. The corporate tax rate is 35%. The price of each tour will be $5,000 per customer and the price will remain constant in real terms. Mr. Salles will pay himself $50 per hour and anticipates an annual increase in salary of 5% in real terms. The cost of each customer during the tours is $3,500, and this cost is expected to increase by 3% in real terms. Assume that all revenues and costs occur at year end. The inflation rate is 3.5%. The risk-free nominal rate is 6% and the real discount rate for costs and revenues is 9%. Using the additional following data, calculate the *NPV* of the project.

	Year 1	Year 2	Year 3	Year 4
Number of customers	100	115	130	140
Hours worked	2,080	2,080	2,080	2,080

30. Camile, the owner of the Germanos Tree farm has contracted with the government of his native land to provide cedar tree saplings to aid in that government's efforts to reforest part of the country and return the cedar tree to its past glory. The project is expected to continue in perpetuity. At the end of the first year, the following nominal and incremental cash flows are expected:

Revenues	$125,000
Labor Costs	$65,000
Other Costs	$45,000

Camille has contracted with an air freight shipping company to transport the saplings. The contract is for a fixed payment of $35,000 in nominal terms per year. The first payment is due at the end of the first year. Revenues are expected to grow at 4% in real terms. Labor costs are expected to grow at 3% per year. Other costs are expected to decrease at 0.5% per year. The real discount rate for revenues and costs is 8% and inflation is expected to be 3.5%. There are no taxes and all cash flows occur at year-end. What is the *NPV* of the contract?

Suggested Readings

Chapter 2

Crane, D., K. Froot, S. Mason, R. C. Merton, A. Perold, Z. Bodie, E. Sirri, and P. Tufano. *The Global Financial System: A Functional Perspective.* Boston: Harvard Business School Press, 1995.

Kohn, M. *Financial Institutions and Markets.* 2nd Ed. Oxford University Press, 2004.

Merton, R. C., and Z. Bodie. "Design of Financial Systems: Toward a Synthesis of Function and Structure." *Journal of Investment Management* 3, 1st Quarter 2005.

Miller, M. *Financial Innovations & Market Volatility.* Cambridge: Blackwell, 1991.

Chapter 3

Fraser, L., and A. Ormiston. *Understanding Financial Statements,* 8th ed. Upper Saddle River, NJ: Pearson Prentice Hall, 2007.

Hutton, A., "Beyond Financial Reporting: An Integrated Approach to Corporate Disclosure." *Journal of Applied Corporate Finance* 16, Fall 2004.

Penman. S. *Financial Statement Analysis and Security Valuation,* 3rd ed. New York, NY: McGraw-Hill Irwin, 2007.

Wild, J., K. R. Subramanyam, and R. Halsey. *Financial Statement Analysis,* 9th ed. New York: McGraw-Hill Irwin, 2007.

Chapter 4

Fisher, I. *The Theory of Interest: As Determined by Impatience to Spend Income and Opportunity to Invest It.* 1930. New York: Augustus M. Kelley, 1965.

Chapter 5

Bodie, Z. "Thoughts on the Future: Life-Cycle Investing in Theory and Practice." *Financial Analysts Journal* 59, January–February 2003.

———. D. McLeavey, and L. Siegel, ed. *The Future of Life-Cycle Saving and Investing.* Charlottesville, VA: Research Foundation of CFA Institute, 2007.

Merton, R. C. "Thoughts on the Future: Theory and Practice in Investment Management." *Financial Analysts Journal* 59, January–February 2003.

Modigliani, F., and R. Brumberg. "Utility Analysis and the Consumption Function: An Interpretation of Cross-Section Data." *Post Keynesian Economics.* Ed. K. Kurihara. New Brunswick, N. J.: Rutgers University Press, 1954.

Chapter 6

Berk, J., and P. DeMarzo. *Corporate Finance.* Boston, MA: Pearson Addison Wesley, 2007.

Brealey, R., S. Myers, and F. Allen. *Principles of Corporate Finance,* 8th ed. New York: McGraw-Hill Irwin, 2006.

Hishleifer, J. "On the Theory of Optimal Investment Decision." *Journal of Political Economy* 66, August 1958.

Ross, S., R. Westerfield, and J. Jaffe. *Corporate Finance,* 8th ed. New York: McGraw-Hill Irwin, 2008.

Glossary

acquisition The acquiring by one firm of a controlling interest in another.

actuaries Professionals trained in mathematics and statistics who gather and analyze data and estimate the probabilities of illness, accidents, and other such risks.

adjusted present value A method of calculating a project's net present value that takes into account the value that is created by the project's debt financing.

adverse selection A type of incentive problem in which those who purchase insurance against risk are more likely to be at risk than the general population.

after-tax interest rate The interest rate earned after paying income taxes.

alpha The difference between the average rate of return on a security or portfolio of securities and the rate predicted by the Capital Asset Pricing Model.

amortization The process of paying off a loan's principal gradually over time.

amortization schedule A table that shows the portions of loan payments that go toward principal and interest over the period of the loan.

annual percentage rate The annualized rate of interest on loans and savings accounts, with a certain frequency of compounding (contrast with effective annual rate).

annualized capital cost The annual cash payment that has a present value equal to the initial outlay.

arbitrage The purchase and immediate sale of equivalent assets in order to earn a sure profit from a difference in their prices.

asset Anything that has economic value.

asset allocation Choosing how much to invest in major asset classes such as stocks, bonds, and cash.

at-the-money The state of an option whose exercise price is equal to the current price of the underlying security.

before-tax interest rate The interest rate earned without taking into account income taxes.

beta A measure of a security's market-related risk, showing how much a security's rate of return tends to change when the return on the market portfolio changes; risk as measured in the CAPM.

binomial option pricing model A widely used model for pricing options that assumes that in each period the underlying security can take only one of two possible values.

Black-Scholes formula The most widely used option pricing model, named for its developers, Fischer Black and Myron Scholes. It assumes a lognormal distribution and continuous adjustment of the replicating portfolio.

book value The value of an asset as listed on its company's officially recognized balance sheet.

break-even point The sales volume at which either net profit or the net present value of a project is zero.

call option An instrument that gives its holder the right to buy some asset at a specified price on or before some specified expiration date. Sometimes shortened to *call.*

capital asset pricing model An equilibrium theory based on the mean-variance theory of portfolio selection.

capital gain The gain in the market price of an asset over the period it is held.

capital loss The loss in the market price of an asset over the period it is held.

CAPM The capital asset pricing model.

capital market The market for long-term debt and equity securities.

capital market line In the capital asset pricing model, the risk–return trade-off line between standard deviation and expected return which represents the best risk–reward combinations available to all investors.

caps Upper limits placed on compensation under an insurance contract.

cash budget A short-term plan to forecast cash outflows and inflows.

cash cycle time The number of days between the date a firm must start to pay cash to its suppliers and the date it begins to receive cash from its customers.

cash dividend A distribution of cash to the shareholders of a corporation.

cash settlement The settlement of a forward or option contract in cash rather than by delivery of the underlying commodity or security.

collateral The asset pledged as security for a debt.

collateralization Giving the lender the right to seize specific business assets in the event of default. It is widely used to reduce the incentive problems associated with lending.

commercial banks Financial intermediaries that perform two functions: taking deposits and making loans.

commercial loan rate The rate charged by banks on loans made to businesses.

compound interest Interest paid on interest earned in previous periods.

compounding The process of going from present value to future value.

confidence interval A certain range of values for a random variable with a specified probability of occurrence.

continuous probability distribution A random variable has such a distribution when it can take any numerical value within its range.

copayments A fraction of a loss that an insured party must cover from his or her own resources.

corporation A firm that is a legal entity distinct from its owners.

correlation A statistical measure of the degree to which two random variables tend to move together.

cost of capital The capitalization rate used to discount a project's cash flows in computing its net present value.

counterparty Also called *counterpart*. The party on the other side of a contract.

coupon bond A bond that obligates the issuer to make periodic payments of interest (called *coupon payments*) to the bondholder for the life of the bond.

credit risk The risk that the counterparty to a contract will default.

current yield A bond's annual coupon divided by its price.

decision tree A graphic representation of the sequence of decisions and possible consequences involved in making a strategic decision.

deductible An amount of money that the insured party must pay out of his or her own resources before receiving any compensation from the insurer.

default risk The possibility that some portion of the interest or the principal on a fixed-income instrument will not be paid in full.

defined-benefit pension plan A type of pension plan in which the employee's pension benefit is determined by a formula that takes into account years of service and, in most cases, wages or salary.

defined-contribution pension plan A type of pension plan in which the employer and usually the employee too make regular contributions and the beneficiary receives the value of the assets plus the accumulated earnings.

derivatives Financial instruments whose payoffs are defined in terms of the prices of other assets.

discounted cash flow analysis Making decisions based on the calculation of net present value of future cash flows.

discounted dividend model Any model that computes the value of a share of stock as the present value of its expected future cash dividends.

diversifiable risk The part of a security's risk that can be eliminated by combining it with other risky assets.

diversification principle The theory that by diversifying across risky assets investors can sometimes achieve a reduction in their overall risk exposure with no reduction in their expected return.

diversifying A method of reducing risk by holding small amounts of many risky assets instead of concentrating in only one or a few risky assets.

dividend policy A corporation's policy regarding paying out cash to its shareholders.

dividend yield A stock's annualized dollar dividend divided by its price, expressed as a percentage.

effective annual rate An equivalent interest rate on a loan or savings account if interest were compounded only once per year (contrast with APR).

efficient markets hypothesis The proposition that an asset's current price fully reflects all publicly available information about future economic fundamentals affecting the asset's value.

efficient portfolio A portfolio that offers the investor the highest possible expected rate of return at a specified level of risk.

efficient portfolio frontier A graph showing the best combinations of portfolio risk and return than an investor can attain by diversifying. See also *capital market line.*

exchange rate The price of one currency in terms of another.

exclusions Losses that might seem to meet the conditions for coverage under the insurance contract but are specifically excluded.

exercise price The price that must be paid for the underlying asset in an option contract. Also called *strike price.*

expectations hypothesis The theory that the forward price of an asset equals its expected future spot price.

expected rate of return The sum over all possible outcomes of each possible rate of return multiplied by its probability.

expiration date The last date by which an option can be exercised.

external financing Funding that originates from outside a firm, usually from lenders or investors.

face value The promised cash payment on a bond's maturity date.

feasible consumption plan A life-cycle spending plan that has a present value less than or equal to the present value of the household's lifetime resources.

finance The study of how people allocate resources over time in an uncertain environment.

financial futures Futures contracts in which the underlying asset is a stock, bond, or other financial asset.

financial guarantees Insurance against credit risk.

financial system The set of markets and other institutions used for financial contracting and the exchange of assets and risks.

fixed-income instruments Also called *debt instruments.* They promise to pay fixed sums of cash in the future.

flow of funds The flows of saving, investment, and external financing among different economic sectors over a period of time.

forward contract An agreement between two parties to exchange some item in the future at a prearranged price.

forward price The delivery price of an item specified at the time a forward contract is entered into that makes the value of the contract equal to zero.

fundamental value The price well-informed investors would pay for an asset in a free and competitive market.

future value The amount of money an investment will grow to at some date in the future by earning interest at a compound rate.

futures contract A standardized forward contract that is traded on some organized exchange.

growth annuity An annuity in which the cash flows from an investment grow at a constant rate.

growth stocks Stocks that have relatively high price/earnings ratios because their future investments are expected to earn rates of return in excess of the market capitalization rate.

hedge ratio The fraction of one unit of an asset needed in a portfolio designed to replicate the payoffs from a derivative security (such as a call option) on that asset.

hedgers Parties who reduce their exposure to risk by giving up part of the potential for gain.

hedging A method of transferring risk in which an action taken to reduce one's exposure to loss also causes one to give up possible gains.

human capital The present value of one's future labor income.

immediate annuity A periodic cash flow that starts immediately, as in a savings plan or a lease.

implied dividend A dividend that can be inferred from the futures price of a stock index.

implied volatility The value of volatility that makes the observed market price of the option equal to the value computed using the option pricing formula.

index options Calls and puts on a stock index or any other economic index.

indexing An investment strategy of matching the performance of some index.

index-linked bonds Bonds whose interest and principal are denominated in terms of the basket of goods and services used to compute the cost of living in a particular country.

insuring Paying some amount for sure to avoid the possibility of incurring larger losses.

intangible assets Assets whose physical embodiment is irrelevant to their value.

interest-rate arbitrage Borrowing at a lower rate and lending at a higher rate when default risk is held constant.

interest-rate cap An interest-rate insurance policy in which the maximum interest rate is guaranteed.

interest-rate floor A guarantee of a minimum interest rate on a loan.

internal financing Funding that originates within a firm, including retained earnings, accrued wages, and accounts payable.

intertemporal budget constraint The restriction that the present value of one's lifetime consumption spending cannot exceed present value of one's lifetime resources.

in-the-money The state of an option that would have positive value if the current time were its expiration date.

intrinsic value Also called *tangible value.* The hypothetical value of an option if it were exercised immediately.

investment banks Firms whose primary function is to help businesses, governments, and other entities raise funds to finance their activities.

Law of One Price The idea that, in a competitive market, if two assets are equivalent, they will have the same market price.

liability Any claim on the assets of an entity other than owner's equity.

life annuities Contracts that promise periodic payments for as long as the purchaser lives.

limited liability A feature of common stock whereby if a firm is liquidated and the proceeds from the sale are insufficient to pay off all the firm's debts, the creditors cannot assess the common stockholders for more money to meet this shortfall.

liquidity The relative ease and speed with which an asset can be converted into cash.

long position In a financial contract, the term used to describe the position of the buyer.

margin call A demand from a broker or a counterparty for an investor to add more collateral.

market capitalization rate Also called *risk-adjusted discount rate.* The expected rate of return that anonymous investors require in order to be willing to invest in the specified risky asset.

market portfolio A portfolio that holds all assets in proportion to their outstanding total market values.

market-weighted stock indexes A type of index that represents the price performance of a portfolio that holds each stock in proportion to its total market value.

maturity For fixed-income instruments, the length of time until the repayment of the entire amount borrowed.

mean In probability distribution, the sum over all possible outcomes of each possible rate of return multiplied by its probability.

merger The joining of two firms into a single firm.

minimum-variance portfolio The portfolio of risky assets with the lowest possible variance.

money market The market for short-term debt (less than one year).

moral hazard A situation in which having insurance against some risk causes the insured party to take greater risk or to take less care in preventing the event that gives rise to the loss.

mortgage rate The interest rate that home buyers pay on the loans they take to finance their homes.

mutual fund A portfolio of stocks, bonds, or other assets purchased in the name of a group of investors and managed by a professional investment company or other financial institution.

net present value The amount by which a project is expected to increase the wealth of a firm's current shareholders.

net worth The value of an entity's assets minus liabilities.

nominal future value The future value of a sum not adjusted for inflation.

nominal interest rate An interest rate not adjusted for inflation (contrast with real interest rate).

nominal prices Prices in terms of some currency not adjusted for inflation.

nondiversifiable risk The portion of a portfolio's risk that cannot be eliminated by diversification.

normal distribution The most widely used continuous probability distribution, typified by its bell-shaped curve.

opportunity cost of capital The rate that could be earned on capital if it were invested elsewhere in assets of the same risk.

optimal combination of risky assets The portfolio of risky assets that is mixed with a riskless asset to achieve the most efficient portfolio.

option The right to purchase or sell something at a fixed price in the future.

ordinary annuity An annuity in which the cash flows start at the end of the current period rather than immediately.

out-of-the-money The state of an option that would be worthless if the current time were its expiration date.

over-the-counter markets Also called *off-exchange markets.* Networks for trading assets that have no central location.

par bonds Coupon bonds with a market price equal to their face value.

partnership An unincorporated firm with two or more owners who share the equity in the business.

payoff diagram A chart that shows the relation between the value of a derivative at expiration and the price of its underlying asset.

percent-of-sales method A planning forecast that assumes that most of the items on a company's income statement and balance sheet will maintain the same ratio to sales in the next year as in the previous year.

permanent income The constant level of consumption spending that has a present value equal to one's human capital.

perpetuity A stream of cash flows that lasts forever.

portfolio selection The process of making choices about how to invest one's wealth.

portfolio theory Quantitative analysis for risk management.

precautionary saving Saving that is motivated by the desire to have enough wealth to cover unanticipated expenses in the future.

premium bond A bond whose market price is higher than its face value.

present value The sum in hand today that would be equivalent in value to some specified future payments.

price/earnings multiple The ratio of a firm's stock price to its earnings per share.

principal-agent problem A situation arising when agents do not make the same decisions that the principals would have made if the principals knew what the agents knew and were making the decisions themselves.

probability distributions The statistical term for a random variable's set of possible values and associated probabilities.

purchasing-power parity The theory that exchange rates adjust so as to maintain the same inflation-adjusted price of a representative basket of goods and services in different currency areas.

pure discount bonds Also called *zero-coupon bonds.* Bonds that promise a single payment of cash at some date in the future, called the maturity date.

put The option to sell a specified item at a fixed price.

put option An instrument that gives its holder the right to sell some asset at a specified price on or before some specified expiration date.

put-call parity relation The price relation among the price of the put, the price of the call, the price of the underlying security, and the present value of the exercise price.

rate of return on capital Capital's productivity expressed as a percentage per year.

real future value The future value adjusted for inflation.

real interest rate The interest rate corrected for inflation.

real interest-rate parity The theory that the expected real interest rate on riskless loans is the same all over the world.

real prices Prices corrected for inflation.

reinvestment rate The interest rate at which funds invested for more than a single period can be reinvested.

residual claim The type of claim represented by common stock, in which the owners of common stock are entitled to any assets of the firm left over after meeting all the firm's other financial obligations.

risk aversion A measure of one's willingness to pay to reduce one's exposure to risks.

risk exposure The degree to which an entity's welfare is affected by a source of risk.

risk management The process of formulating the benefit-cost trade-offs of risk reduction and deciding on the course of action to take.

risk-adjusted discount rate Also called *market capitalization rate.* The expected rate of return that investors require in order to be willing to invest in a project.

risk-management process A systematic attempt to analyze and deal with risk.

security market line In the capital asset pricing model, the relation showing that the risk premium on any asset is equal to its beta multiplied by the risk premium on the market portfolio.

self-financing investment strategy An investment strategy that requires only an initial cash outlay with no subsequent cash infusions.

sensitivity analysis A method of testing a project's worthiness even if some of the underlying variables turn out to be different from what was originally assumed.

share repurchase A method of cash distribution by a corporation to its shareholders in which the corporation pays cash to buy shares of its stock in the stock market, thereby reducing the number of shares outstanding.

short position In a financial contract, the term used to describe the position of the seller.

simple interest The interest rate times the original principal, not including interest on interest.

sole proprietorship A firm in which the assets and liabilities of the firm are the personal assets and liabilities of the proprietor.

speculators Investors who take positions that increase their exposure to risks in the hope of increasing their wealth.

spot price The price specified for immediate delivery of an item in a forward contract.

spot-futures price-parity relation The relation among the futures price, the spot price, and the riskless interest rate.

spread The difference between two asset prices or rates of return.

standard deviation The statistic that is most widely used to measure the volatility of a stock's probability distribution of returns. The larger the standard deviation, the greater the volatility of the stock.

strategy A plan that takes into account future decisions in making current decisions.

strike price The fixed price specified in an option contract. See also *exercise price.*

sustainable growth rate The rate of growth in a firm's owners' equity. A firm cannot grow any faster than its sustainable growth rate.

swap contract An agreement between two parties to exchange a series of cash flows at specified intervals over a specified period of time.

synergy The combination of two companies that results in the value of the operating assets of the combined firm exceeding those of the two companies taken separately.

time line A diagram used for analyzing the timing of cash flows.

time value (of an option) The difference between an option's price and its value if the current time were its expiration date.

time value of money The concept that a given amount of money in hand today is worth more than the claim to the same amount to be received in the future.

transaction costs Costs that accompany a sale, including the costs of shipping, handling, insuring, and broker fees.

triangular arbitrage An arbitrage transaction that involves three currencies.

unit of account The medium in which payments are denominated, usually a currency (e.g., dollars, francs, and yen), sometimes a commodity such as gold or silver or some standard basket of goods and services.

volatility A commonly used measure of an asset's riskiness, related to the range of possible rates of return and to their likelihood of occurring. In options trading, used synonymously with standard deviation, as in *implied volatility.*

weighted average cost of capital A method of calculating a project's net present value using a weighted average of the cost of equity capital and the after-tax cost of debt. The weights are the market values of equity and debt as a fraction of the present value of the investment.

working capital The difference between a firm's current assets and current liabilities.

yield curve A curve depicting the relation between the promised interest rates (yields) on fixed-income instruments of a given risk and the maturity of the instrument.

yield spread The difference in yields between two instruments.

yield-to-maturity The discount rate that makes the present value of a bond's stream of promised cash payments equal to its price; the internal rate of return of a bond.

Index

Page numbers followed by *n* refer to footnotes